The Historical Epic
and
Contemporary Hollywood

The Historical Epic
and
Contemporary Hollywood

From *Dances with Wolves*
to *Gladiator*

James Russell

continuum

NEW YORK • LONDON

2007

The Continuum International Publishing Group Inc
80 Maiden Lane, New York, NY 10038

The Continuum International Publishing Group Ltd
The Tower Building, 11 York Road, London SE1 7NX

www.continuumbooks.com

Printed in the United States of America

Library of Congress Cataloging-in-Publication Data

Russell, James, 1977–
  The historical epic and contemporary Hollywood : from Dances with
Wolves to Gladiator / James Russell.
     p. cm.
  Includes bibliographical references and index.
  ISBN-13: 978-0-8264-2798-4 (hardcover : alk. paper)
  ISBN-10: 0-8264-2798-7 (hardcover : alk. paper)
  ISBN-13: 978-0-8264-2799-1 (pbk. : alk. paper)
  ISBN-10: 0-8264-2799-5 (pbk. : alk. paper)
  1. Historical films—United States—History and criticism.
  2. Epic films—United States—History and criticism. I. Title.

PN1995.9.H5R87 2007
791.43'658—dc22

                                              2006036504

Contents

Acknowledgements vii

Notes on Sources viii

Introduction 1

   1. A Brief History of the Historical Epic 3
   2. The Historical Epic as a Genre 7
   3. Definitions of the Epic 9
     Conclusion 16

Chapter One: Big-Theme Films: Epics in the Roadshow Era 22

   1. The Economics of the Roadshow Epic 23
   2. Creative Conditions After World War II 30
   3. Epics and Audiences 41
   4. The Hollywood Epic in Decline 45
     Conclusion 46

Chapter Two: The Epic, the Western and
***Dances with Wolves* (1990)** 54

   1. Westerns and Epics, 1970 to 1990 56
   2. Constructing *Dances with Wolves* 59
   3. Narrative, Nostalgia and Film History 62
   4. Critical and Commercial Responses 67
     Conclusion 71

Chapter Three: Steven Spielberg, the Holocaust
and *Schindler's List* (1993) 77

   1. Spielberg, Hollywood and World War II 80
   2. Judaism and the Origins of *Schindler's List* 83
   3. The Holocaust in *Schindler's List* 88
   4. Virtue in *Schindler's List* 92
     Conclusion 100

Chapter Four: The Baby Boomers, Remembrance and
Saving Private Ryan **(1998)** 106

    1. Spielberg and the Baby Boom 108
    2. The Baby Boom and American Film Culture 111
    3. Generations in *Saving Private Ryan* 116
       Conclusion 125

Chapter Five: DreamWorks SKG and *The Prince of Egypt* **(1998)** . 131

    1. The Establishment of DreamWorks SKG. 133
    2. *The Prince of Egypt* and the Epic Tradition 139
    3. DreamWorks as Promised Land 144
       Conclusion 148

Chapter Six: *Gladiator* **(2000) and the Film Marketplace** 156

    1. The Epic at the Millennium 159
    2. *Gladiator* and Public Entertainment 165
    3. The Epic in the Film Marketplace 173
       Conclusion 181

Chapter Seven: Religion, Ritual and
The Passion of the Christ **(2004)** 187

    1. Presenting *The Passion* 190
    2. The Power of *The Passion* 198
       Conclusion 206

Conclusion: The Epic in the Age of Shock and Awe 215

Bibliography 223

Index 243

Acknowledgements

I would like to extend heartfelt thanks to all the people who made thoughtful contributions to the many earlier drafts of this book. They include Yvonne Tasker, Andrew Higson, Charles Barr, Justine Ashby, Sheldon Hall, Jon Stubbs and Harri Kilpi. Professors Steve Neale and Mark Jancovich made some particularly useful comments during a lively and enjoyable Ph.D. assessment panel, and my new colleagues at De Montfort University have also been extremely patient with me as I struggled to finish the final draft. I would also like to thank the Arts and Humanities Research Council for the provision of a full-time Ph.D. research award. However, greatest thanks must be reserved for Peter Krämer, whose insight is visible in almost every line I have written. This book would certainly not exist without Peter's endless guidance, enthusiasm and friendship.

Finally, I would like to thank my parents, Martin and Pat, and my wife, Hannah, for their love and support. Hannah, in particular, read (or listened to) many earlier drafts, and put up with my occasional periods of absence, poverty and indecision throughout the writing process with astonishing good grace. I could never have done it without her.

Notes on Sources

The following acronyms are used in the footnotes and bibliography to refer to archival collections:

AMPAS   Academy of Motion Picture Arts and Sciences, Margaret Herrick Library, Los Angeles

BFIL   British Film Institute Library, London

NYPL   New York Public Library, Performing Arts Collection, Lincoln Center, New York

UCLA   Arts Special Collections, University of California, Los Angeles

Introduction

Executives were trying to stay upbeat, but the word in the trade press was that James Cameron's *Titanic* (1997), a film depicting one of the greatest seafaring disasters of the twentieth century, might also prove a major disaster for Twentieth Century Fox. After one early screening, Tom Sherak, the Fox executive who commissioned the film, told *Newsday*, "What the screening said to us was that we had an epic that could do very well—the 1990s version, in our minds, of *Doctor Zhivago*, one of those love stories that could last forever."[1] However, the writers at *Variety* speculated that "Cameron's romantic epic . . . represents the biggest roll of the dice in film history."[2] *Titanic* had cost a reported $200 million to make, far more than any single production in the industry's history. Shortly before its release, the most respected and successful filmmaker in Hollywood, Steven Spielberg, told *Premiere* magazine, "I think we're at DEFCON three right now. It's not going to be too long before an average film, without marketing, is going to cost $55 million. Right now we're squeezing the middle class out of Hollywood and only allowing the $70 million plus films or the $10 million minus films. And that is going to spell doom for everyone."[3] Prime offender was Cameron's film, the most expensive blockbuster ever made.

To make matters worse, *Titanic* was a defiantly old-fashioned project, with few obvious links to other major hits of the 1990s. Cameron told *American Cinematographer*, "I think the film owes more stylistically to the Technicolor epics of the 1940s and especially the '50s, where they were moving the camera a lot more often and letting the actors play the frame, but still slamming in when there was a dramatic moment."[4] He also claimed, "I wanted to make an epic in the sense of *Doctor Zhivago*. I

1

decided to do it as Romeo and Juliet on the *Titanic*."[5] James Cameron was apparently attempting to reproduce the sort of extravagant, spectacular historical epic that had flourished in the 1950s and 1960s, but which had vanished from production schedules in the 1970s and 1980s. He was willing to risk his reputation, as well as a great deal of Fox's money, proving *Variety* wrong.

Of course, he turned out to be right. If grosses are not adjusted for inflation, *Titanic* made more money than any other movie had ever made before.[6] Reviews praised the old-fashioned, nostalgic nature of the project. In the *New York Times*, Janet Maslin wrote, "Just as David O. Selznick had Atlanta to burn, now James Cameron has a ship to sink, but he also has much more calamity to explore in this gloriously retrograde new epic. *Titanic* is the first spectacle in decades to invite comparison to *Gone with the Wind*."[7] In the *New Yorker*, Anthony Lane wrote, "For all its narrative dexterity and the formidable modernity of its methods, [*Titanic*] is an old-fashioned picture."[8] In general, Peter Krämer argued that, "Hollywood epics of the past provided writers, and also, presumably, audiences, with an important reference point for their understanding of, and response to, the film."[9] But why were audiences ready to embrace such a 'gloriously retrograde' project? For that matter, why would James Cameron, the man who had made *The Terminator* (1984), *Aliens* (1986) and *True Lies* (1994), suddenly want to make 'an epic in the sense of *Doctor Zhivago*'? And, perhaps most perplexing of all, why was Twentieth Century Fox willing to commit $200 million to a film that was generally perceived as a work of nostalgic hubris? These are just some of the questions that this book will answer.

Cameron's epic may have been perceived as both audacious and foolhardy, but he was only one of many filmmakers who had attempted to revisit and revive a long defunct tradition of epic Hollywood moviemaking during the 1990s. As we will see, historical epics had last been vital features of the American film industry's production strategies in the 1950s and 1960s, when films such as *The Ten Commandments* (1956), *Ben-Hur* (1959), *Spartacus* (1960) and *Lawrence of Arabia* (1962) dominated at the box office, and assumed 'classic' status for a generation of filmgoers and filmmakers, but spectacular epic films disappeared from production schedules in the early 1970s. For over two decades epic films appeared rarely, and generally failed to attract large audiences. Then, at the beginning of the 1990s, the marginal status of the historical epic underwent a period of revision. Kevin Costner's western epic *Dances with Wolves* (1990) was followed by Steven Spielberg's Holocaust epic *Schindler's List*

(1993), Mel Gibson's medieval epic *Braveheart* (1995), and then James Cameron's romantic epic *Titanic*.

This book asks why so many filmmakers felt compelled to produce epics over the last fifteen years, why it made sense for the Hollywood majors to facilitate their work, and, ultimately, how historical epics moved from the absolute periphery of Hollywood's production strategies to the apex of mainstream film production and popular interest. By 2003, a seachange had clearly occurred in Hollywood's attitudes toward historical epics. Peter Weir's *Master and Commander: The Far Side of the World* (2003) was followed by Anthony Minghella's *Cold Mountain* (2003), Ed Zwick's *The Last Samurai* (2003), Mel Gibson's *The Passion of the Christ* (2004), Wolfgang Petersen's *Troy* (2004), John Lee Hancock's *The Alamo* (2004), Antoine Fuqua's *King Arthur* (2004), Oliver Stone's *Alexander* (2004) and, in 2005, Ridley Scott's *Kingdom of Heaven*—since which point, epics have again diminished in volume. Consequently, these films can be studied as a discrete cycle with a beginning, a middle and, perhaps, an end.

Of course, the modern group of epics is the latest in a long line of grandiose historical films, whose history is outlined below. To place such films in context, the remainder of this introduction attempts to define the Hollywood historical epic as a genre and as a production category. The concluding section outlines the chapters that will follow.

1. A Brief History of the Historical Epic

Although the relative scarcity of academic writing on the subject suggests otherwise, the historical epic has been a central genre throughout the history of the American cinema. As Jon Solomon puts it, "[T]he young cinema immediately adopted antiquity as one of its initially favorite subjects [in response to] the popularity that antiquity displayed in the theatrical, literary and educational worlds at the turn of the century."[10] Grand historical subjects, and stories of nations in crisis, have been addressed again and again since the invention of cinema, often appearing repeatedly under identical titles. Early examples include Georges Méliès's 1899 version of *Cleopatra*, Pathé's *Samson and Delilah*, which appeared in 1903, and a British adaptation of the popular novel *Sign of the Cross* released in 1904. However, Solomon argues that "1908 saw the virtual birth of the epic cinema as we know it," when Italian filmmaker Arturo Ambrosio's hugely popular *Gli Ultimi Giorni di Pompeii (The Last*

Days of Pompeii) inspired hundreds of imitators, including other massive successes such as Enrico Guazzoni's *Quo Vadis?* in 1912 and Giovanni Pastrone's *Cabiria* in 1913.[11] The success of these, and other, early epic films in the expanding American market established a long-lasting domestic interest in epic historical subjects. The first known American version of the hit stage show and novel *Ben-Hur* was released in 1907, while versions of *Cleopatra* and *Jesus of Nazareth* appeared in 1912, along with many other similar releases.

In 1915, a clear sign of the epic film's ability to generate revenues far beyond the average came in the form of D. W. Griffith's *The Birth of a Nation*, which earned $10 million in rentals—$6.5 million more than any film released before 1931.[12] Griffith's Civil War epic was both a genuine advancement of cinematic technique and an "incendiary, hateful" call to racist violence, as Linda Williams has argued.[13] Griffith followed *The Birth of a Nation* with an even more expensive epic, *Intolerance* (1916), which was budgeted at $400,000 ($300,000 more than *The Birth of Nation*), but which failed to earn even one-tenth of the rentals generated by his previous film, thus becoming the first of many releases to demonstrate the inherent 'riskiness' of epic films as investments.[14] Nevertheless, highly budgeted historical epics such as the Great War-themed *The Four Horsemen of the Apocalypse* (1921) and *Ben-Hur* (1925) continued to be released and continued to attract large audiences throughout the silent period.[15] In particular, the historical films of director/producer Cecil B. DeMille proved consistently popular from the 1920s to the 1950s. DeMille should be seen as a central figure in American film history, both for establishing the conventions of the Hollywood historical epic and for forging continuities across thirty years of Hollywood history. DeMille's earlier epics included *The Ten Commandments* (1923), *The King of Kings* (1927), *The Sign of the Cross* (1932) and *Cleopatra* (1934). His most memorable films are historical stories that were simultaneously edifying and titillating. Writing retrospectively, the critic Vincent Canby has argued that DeMille had specialised in "heavy breathing costume epics that teach fearsome lessons about sin, and at the same time, give us ordinary folk a chance to see what first-class sin, committed on a grand scale, looks like."[16]

DeMille's films remained relatively popular throughout the 1930s, but the most successful epic of this period, and one of the most influential Hollywood films ever released, was producer David O. Selznick's *Gone with the Wind* (1939)—a high-budget epic, funded and distributed by MGM but produced independently by Selznick, which returned, albeit in slightly less controversial style, to the southern Civil War setting of *The*

Birth of a Nation. The film's combination of romance and war, its direct address to female viewers, its lavish spectacle and its uncommon production method helped *Gone with the Wind* to generate rentals of over $31 million ($23 million more than any other film released in the 1930s).[17] In fact, if box office statistics are adjusted for inflation, *Gone with the Wind* remains the highest grossing film release of all time, earning an estimated $300 million more, in contemporary terms, than its closest competitor, *Star Wars* (1977).[18] Although it was an exceptional release by any standards, *Gone with the Wind* (like DeMille's films) was part of a production trend that Tino Balio has described as the 'prestige picture.' As Balio puts it, "[T]he prestige picture is not a genre—rather the prestige picture is typically a big-budget special based on a pre-sold property, often as not a 'classic,' and tailored for top stars."[19] This prestige trend continued into the 1940s, but historical epics declined in production volume until DeMille revived his interest in historical subjects with *Samson and Delilah* in 1949.

From this point onwards, the Hollywood historical epic entered its golden age. *Samson and Delilah* was followed by outstanding hits such as *Quo Vadis* in 1951, *The Robe* in 1953, DeMille's remake of his own *The Ten Commandments* in 1956, *Ben-Hur* in 1959, *Spartacus* in 1960 and *Doctor Zhivago* in 1965, as well as many others. These can be counted as some of the most commercially successful Hollywood films ever released. Indeed, the films of this period played a vital role in defining the essence of a historical epic film. They have had a key influence on filmmakers ever since, including those behind the epics of the 1990s, as we will see throughout the remainder of this introduction and in the next chapter.

For twenty years, the epic remained a vital feature of the film landscape, but by the end of the 1960s, the epic film was diminishing both in visibility and presumed commercial viability. For reasons discussed in chapters 1 and 2, historical epics all but disappeared from Hollywood's production schedules in the early 1970s. Epic films remained popular when they were screened on television, and a cycle of historical epic TV miniseries reached large audiences throughout the 1970s and 1980s (including *Roots* in 1978 and *Shogun* in 1981). Nonetheless, cinematic epics appeared infrequently and generally failed to generate the kinds of excessive grosses that had characterised earlier cycles. Furthermore, the spectacular commercial failure of Michael Cimino's western epic *Heaven's Gate* in 1980 was "widely regarded by the industry as [a] test of the genre's viability and [its] fate was interpreted as evidence of an exhausted market," in the words of industry historian Stephen Prince.[20]

Distributor United Artists spent almost $40 million on *Heaven's Gate*, but Cimino's lengthy, inaccessible film failed to generate more than $2 million in box office grosses, and United Artists were forced to file for bankruptcy as a result.[21] Nevertheless, Peter Krämer has argued that the special effects-driven family films that became Hollywood's primary mainstream output after 1977 did incorporate 'epic' elements, albeit in a fantasy setting.[22] For instance, Krämer suggests that "the *Star Wars* trilogy is clearly epic and explicitly spiritual" in a manner that invoked veiled memories of earlier biblical epics.[23]

Some historical epics, usually produced with European funding, were released during the 1980s, such as *Gandhi* (1982), *Out of Africa* (1985) and *The Last Emperor* (1987). These were met with critical acclaim and at least one, *Out of Africa*, achieved some commercial success, but none inspired consistent imitation, presumably because American distributors had grown wary of funding epics in the wake of *Heaven's Gate*.[24] However, the presumption that epics (especially epics with a western setting) were commercially unworkable was proven erroneous following the success of Kevin Costner's *Dances with Wolves* in 1990. Although Costner's film was an independently produced 'vanity project', it generated worldwide revenues of $424.2 million, making it the fourth highest grossing international release of the year.[25] From this point onwards, the number of American historical epics in production, and on release, gradually increased. At first, Costner's success opened a space for other filmmakers, with a similar passion for supposedly unpopular epic films, to achieve limited funding for their essentially 'maverick' epic projects. These included Steven Spielberg, Mel Gibson and James Cameron—all respected stars and filmmakers with enough industry standing to merit a 'risky' investment on the part of distributors.

Many of the 'maverick epics' proved popular with audiences, and one, James Cameron's *Titanic*, defied industry sceptics to become one of the highest grossing films of all time. Following the equally unexpected success of Steven Spielberg's *Saving Private Ryan* (1998), the major Hollywood distributors began to design and green-light historical epics in a more routine fashion; this resulted in a number of related releases in the late 1990s and early 2000s, including *Gladiator* in 2000 and producer Jerry Bruckheimer's *Pearl Harbor* in 2001. In particular, Spielberg's studio/distributor, the newly formed DreamWorks SKG, focused on epic films in their early production schedules as a way of establishing a distinct 'brand identity' in the marketplace. As well as *Saving Private Ryan*, the first release from the studio's animation division was a musical remake of DeMille's *The Ten Commandments* entitled *The Prince of Egypt* (1998). In 2000, the studio achieved critical and commercial success with *Gladiator*—the most obvious attempt to revisit the thematic and narrational terrain of the 1950s/1960s epic yet produced, to the extent that the film bordered on extended pastiche.

Gladiator's success inspired another wave of epics, which drew directly on films such as *Ben-Hur* and *Spartacus*, discussed briefly above. However, it appears that *Troy, King Arthur, Kingdom of Heaven*, et al., did not generate high enough box office returns to encourage continued investment, and the future of the Hollywood historical epic now looks fairly uncertain. Nevertheless, the history of Hollywood suggests that the historical epic film will not disappear for long.

2. The Historical Epic as a Genre

The preceding account is dependent on certain assumptions, most obviously that the majority of viewers can easily identify a historical epic film. In reality, the generic labels 'epic' and 'historical epic' are notoriously difficult to define. Charlton Heston, whose presence in many epics of the 1950s and 1960s has made him a virtually integral feature of the genre, once said that "defining an epic is only slightly less complicated than making one . . . [it is] the easiest film to make badly."[26] Despite his unwillingness to provide a simple definition, Heston raises an interesting point—'epicness' is often dictated by production values as well as narrative content. However, before we can arrive at a stricter definition of the historical epic, we must first clarify what we mean when we say that the epic is a 'genre.'

Although film critics and academics have in the past sought to divide up the map of Hollywood's releases into discrete generic categories, recent work on genre has argued that the film industry actually uses generic labels in a far less systematic fashion than previously assumed. As Richard Maltby puts it:

> For producers, generic distinction offers a layered system of classification which they use in an opportunitistic way that does not assume that one generic category excludes others. These classifications are being constantly revised, so there is always more than one classification system in operation at any one time, and inevitably contradictions arise.[27]

Rick Altman and Steve Neale have both extended Maltby's work to argue that we should understand film production in terms of relatively limited, 'generically marked' cycles, rather than viewing Hollywood releases as part of a historical continuum of coexisting yet distinct genres.[28] Consequently, the history of the historical epic outlined above should be understood as the history of many related cycles, and connections are often only visible retrospectively. These cycles can be identified by the use of particular generic labels, but such labels are not exclusive or fixed, and they are subject to redefinition over time, because economic imperatives invariably take precedence over strict, critical acts of generic definition. Furthermore, definitions of particular genres tend to be fairly subjective.[29] One person's horror film is another's psychological thriller—thus any act of definition must be vague in order to accurately reflect loosely shared (yet ultimately subjective) conceptions of generic status. As Mark Jancovich has argued, "[G]enre definitions are produced more by the ways in which films are understood by those who produce, mediate and consume them, than they are by the internal properties of the films themselves."[30]

Nevertheless, generic terms remain worthy of study because such labels are invariably applied as a means of planning release schedules and marketing. Rick Altman therefore suggests that the widespread adoption of a particular generic term can be taken as evidence that a cycle or genre has achieved 'validity' as a production trend and as a feature in the public consciousness.[31] In support of Altman's point, we will see that popular use of the generic label 'epic' has become more commonplace during the 1990s, in concert with greater levels of investment in the cycle. However, it would be mistaken to focus entirely on the terms in use at a particular moment. Most scholars of American cinema now recognise that a confluence of individual creative agendas and obsessions, institutional considerations, economic imperatives, currents in social history and shifts in the political climate all contribute to the emergence of new cycles (and the development of existing cycles). This book takes a comparative approach to the recent historical epic cycle. I identify pivotal 'epic' releases by looking at the terms used by filmmakers, marketing departments and critics.[32] The films are examined through an ever-broadening interpretive lens, and over the next seven chapters, I use empirical, archive-based historical research methods to identify individual agendas, which are then explored in relation to social history, industrial concerns and economic logic.

3. Definitions of the Epic

So how can we define the 'shared-yet-subjective' features of the epic genre? The term *epic* is clearly derived from ancient poetical traditions, and in terms of extended length and thematic richness, the Hollywood historical epic does bear resemblance to the narrative poems of Homer, Virgil, Milton, et al. According to Derek Elley, "The chief feature of the historical epic film is not imitation but reinterpretation [of the literary epic]. Spectacle is the cinema's own transformation of the literary epic's taste for the grandiose, realised on sufficient scale to impress modern audiences."[33] Furthermore, these literary precursors have been repeatedly plundered by Hollywood filmmakers for story material, most recently in the case of Wolfgang Petersen's *Troy*. For a sizable proportion of viewers, the literary epic offers a clear reference point to interpret the epic film. However, many more viewers are liable to define the epic in accordance with their memories of earlier filmic epic cycles. Certainly most of the filmmakers and reviewers discussed in this book looked back to the epics of the 1950s and 1960s when they described their own historical epics.

Indeed, Steve Neale has argued that any attempt to categorise the Hollywood epic must look back to this earlier cycle. He writes:

> Epic is essentially a 1950s and 1960s term. It was used to identify, and to sell two overlapping contemporary trends: Films with historical, especially ancient world settings; and large scale films of all kinds which used new technologies, high production values and special modes of distribution and exhibition to differentiate themselves from both routine productions and from alternative forms of contemporary entertainment, especially television.[34]

The specifically *historical* epic cycle existed at the point where the two trends overlapped. Neale observes that these particular films were marked by "a dramatic and thematic concern with political and military power, political and military rule, and political and military struggle [which] found articulation on national, international and sometimes global and cosmic scales."[35]

However, Bruce Babington and Peter William Evans have provided perhaps the best thematic definition of the epic in their book *Biblical Epics*. They write:

The cinematic Epic takes as its subject world historical events, the distant myths or more recent turning points of the culture. These must be treated 'epically', that is with resources of cinematic style approximating the effects of the epic in literature, great events given the largest scale of treatment; *great* as in *massive*, but also connoting grandeur and overwhelming cultural significance.[36]

Most viewers would likely agree that an 'epic film' is defined by a grandeur of thematic focus and production. A historical epic is always centred on a particularly memorable, cataclysmic or decisive historical event in history, a 'turning point of the culture,' as Babington and Evans put it, which is usually depicted on the screen, in a manner that stresses its cultural magnitude. As Melani McAlister has written, "Like the Holy Land images of the nineteenth century, epic films promised historical and religious knowledge, combined with the promise of 'views' and spectacle."[37] In the *historical* epic, the spectacular events will have really occurred (even if considerable liberties are taken with the details of the historical record). Historical epics can feature all manner of conflicts, political shifts and even defining spiritual or religious events (when they are deemed crucial to contemporary society and treated as having 'really occurred' by adherents). By contrast, *fantasy* or *science fiction* epics concern themselves with essentially fictitious, yet equally apocalyptic, occurrences. The label 'epic' is likely to be accepted by viewers and filmmakers to describe any film in which issues of international or 'civilisational' importance constitute the central focus of the narrative. In every case, as Babington and Evans observe, the spectacular (and therefore expensive) nature of such depictions invariably serves to emphasise the seriousness, integrity and commitment of the film itself. Or, as Vivian Sobchack has argued, in the historical epic film "a correlation is clearly established between the present events of a film's production and the past events it is intended to represent."[38] Usually, this takes the form of elaborate, expensive spectacle.

In the 1950s, several historically specific production and exhibition tactics helped to emphasise the spectacle and prestige of the historical epic film. Epics were hugely expensive, often shooting on location with a massive cast and crew, and filmed with new widescreen (and 'big-screen') processes such as Cinerama and CinemaScope. They were then exhibited in a similar fashion to theatrical productions at prestigious city centre theatres adapted to the new exhibition technologies, on extended runs that could last for several years (a practice known as 'roadshowing').[39] In this way, viewing an epic became an exceptional experience, where historical subjects and cinematic spectacle connected in a unique fashion. In fact, it has frequently been claimed that historical films only moved to prominence at this time in order to showcase new technologies that apparently allowed Hollywood to 'compete' with the supposedly rival medium of television.[40] Chapter 1 will argue that this assumption does not take the real creative and economic conditions of 1950s Hollywood into account.

As well as higher budgets, and a larger cinematic frame, the epics of the 1950s were characterised by extended running times, sometimes in excess of three hours (*The Ten Commandments* ran for 219 minutes, *Ben-Hur* for 217 minutes, *Lawrence of Arabia* [1962] for 221 minutes). In order to fill this enlarged narrative space, most epics would feature bigger casts than more routine productions, include a greater number of subplots, and, as a result, work according to a more episodic structure than one might expect to find in mainstream Hollywood releases. In this way, epic films could be said to challenge the conventions of the tightly drawn 'Classical Hollywood Narrative' identified by Bordwell, Staiger and Thompson.[41] The temporal excess of such films was often mirrored in the narratives themselves, which took place over months, years, decades, or even, in the case of John Huston's *The Bible: In the Beginning* (1966), millennia.

Stylistically, epic films were defined by a sense of scale that exceeded the Hollywood norm. The wide screen allowed for expansive long shots of landscapes, lavishly constructed sets and the thousands of extras facilitated by the vastly increased production budgets. An exemplary epic scene involves the positioning of the individual subject within massive landscapes, huge crowds, or in the forefront of sizable and opulent sets. The use of widescreen composition, expanded running time, a lengthy cast of characters, thousands of extras and sweeping vistas of the past meant that the epic of the 1950s was usually *bigger* than other releases in almost every way. These opulent production techniques helped to stress the cultural importance of the events being depicted and the narrational 'stakes' at play, but they have also traditionally served to stress the importance, seriousness and industrial clout of the filmmakers responsible for such depictions.

For example, the most memorable sequence of DeMille's 1956 version of *The Ten Commandments* sees Moses, played by Charlton Heston, step up to the edge of the Red Sea and declare in a deep, booming voice, "The Lord of Hosts will do battle for us. Behold His mighty hands!" He stretches out his arms, and the ocean parts then before him in one of the great trick shots in cinema history. In a wide, sweeping shot, which takes in the spectacle of hundreds of Hebrew extras as well as the parting seas, the will of God is enacted on the screen, and a founding moment of Judeo-Christian history is recreated. The awed responses of the Hebrews confronted by this wondrous spectacle seem to provide audiences with an eminently fitting model to emulate, although Charlton Heston, who is perhaps accustomed to such things, remains entirely composed. In this scene, it is useful to think of Moses as an allegorical surrogate for the epic filmmaker. Traditionally, the historical epic has itself been presented as a spectacular intervention in public affairs. The epic filmmaker seeks to make a statement, the scale and importance of which is reflected in the size of the production. As Michael Wood argues:

> The ancient world of the epics was a huge, many-faceted meta-phor for Hollywood itself. . . . [T]hese movies are always about the creation of such a world in a movie. The hero of *The Ten Commandments* is not Moses, but DeMille himself, who set up the whole show, the voice of God and the burning bush and the miracles of Egypt included.[42]

DeMille himself emphasised the contemporary resonance of his film in an introduction, where he appeared at a lectern to deliver a short lecture explaining that "the theme of this picture is whether men are to be ruled by God's law or by the whims of a dictator," thus linking *The Ten Commandments* to the ongoing events of the Cold War.

In the epic, then, the narrational focus on pivotal and therefore 'important' historical events, as well as the highly visible nature of the production technique, have served to emphasise the presence, and prestige, of the filmmakers. Most epics seek to edify and entertain audiences in equal measure, which is one reason why the genre has been treated as innately prestigious by filmmakers and, to a lesser extent, by audiences. Academically inclined critics, accustomed to searching for more oblique forms of meaning, have tended to treat the epic as somewhat crass and obvious (as Mark Jancovich has observed).[43] Furthermore, in dealing with historical events, epic films place filmmakers in a position of some cultural standing. Much of the critical discourse surrounding Steven Spielberg's *Schindler's List* was concerned with whether or not scholars should accept Spielberg as a historian of sorts.[44] In a similar fashion, James Cameron's first, unfilmed draft of the script for *Titanic* attempted to explain the wider historical significance of the sinking of the ocean liner. In this draft, Rose begins her story by saying, "Understand this. When the ship went down it seemed that the world was suddenly on warning, and that God may not be in His heaven after all. It was the first great tragedy in a century of tragedies. World war and Holocaust and famine and assassination. The loss of that ship was their first stirring."[45] This desire to comment on the past was as visible in the epics of the 1950s as in those of the 1990s. Throughout this book we will see that filmmakers have used the power to depict the past both to stress their own cultural standing and to make politically and socially resonant statements about the past and the present.

Although I do not look in any particular detail at the historical accuracy of the films discussed in this book, I will explore what filmmakers have sought to achieve in their attempts to recreate the past. As David Eldridge has observed, in producing a depiction of the past, "[T]he filmmaker has interacted with professional historiography, public attitudes, political utilisation of history and the conventions of the historical film genre to craft a narrative and style that convey a perspective on the past through cinematic means."[46] Viewers are by no means obliged to accept a filmmaker's interpretation of the past. As Natalie Zemon Davies notes, "[S]pectators may delight in a historical film, be interested in it or repelled by it . . . but they do not believe automatically what they see in a historical film: rather, they ask about it, argue about it, and write letters of protest about it."[47] Nevertheless, most spectators are likely to have their understanding of the past affected in some way by watching a historical film. Furthermore, the epic's focus on supposedly 'important' events lends itself to overt forms of allegory. In the 1950s and 1960s, epics often told stories of ancient conflict, which resonated with contemporary concerns such as the Cold War, Zionism, the Suez Crisis, the aftermath of World War II and internal political division, as we will see in chapter 1. Subsequent chapters explore how similar issues have been incorporated into the modern cycle by filmmakers eager to use their status for edifying, and thus prestigious, purposes.

A reliable indicator of resulting popular (but not academic) prestige is the performance of epics at the Academy Awards, described by Gillian Roberts as the film industry's "legitimate classifier and taste-making body."[48] Oscar historian Emanuel Levy observes that "historical epics have featured prominently in the Oscar competition. . . . [W]hile not many epics are produced, those that do get made receive disproportionate attention from the Academy and stand a good chance to be nominated."[49] Until *Titanic* drew level, the film with the highest number of Oscar wins (eleven) was William Wyler's *Ben-Hur* in 1959, and Levy notes that, as of 1999, sixteen of the seventy-two Best Picture winners (almost one quarter) were, by his estimation, historical epics.[50] Perhaps surprisingly, the decade that saw the greatest number of historical epics achieve this honour was not the 1950s or 1960s but the 1990s. Kevin Costner's *Dances with Wolves* won in 1990, Steven Spielberg's *Schindler's List* in 1993, Robert Zemeckis's *Forrest Gump* in 1994, Mel Gibson's *Braveheart* in 1995, Anthony Minghella's *The English Patient* in 1996 and Cameron's *Titanic* in 1997. One could add *Gladiator's* 2000 win to Levy's list, and many of the nominees and winners in other categories were also epics. For example, Spielberg won the Best Director award for *Saving Private Ryan* in 1998, a year which also saw Terrence Malick's World War II epic *The Thin Red Line* and Shekhar Kapur's *Elizabeth* nominated in multiple categories.

Although the 1950s and 1990s epic cycles have functioned in a very similar fashion, there are some key differences. In the 1950s, epic films invoked a sense of 'special-ness' partly through innovative exhibition technologies and practices. By contrast, the cycle of historical epic films released in the 1990s was usually exhibited in an identical fashion to any other contemporary release. In purely experiential terms, one might say that it was no more special an experience to watch *The Last Samurai* (2003) than it was to watch the musical comedy *School of Rock* (2003), which was released at the same time, and which could be playing on an identical screen in the next multiplex auditorium. How, then, has the modern cycle of historical epics sought to convey the sense of cultural magnitude essential to the epic as a conceptual category?

At a narrational level most 1990s epics retain a focus on 'great events given the largest scale of treatment'—however, Geoff King has proposed that the forms of spectacle associated with the Hollywood epic have undergone a profound transformation in the modern era. King argues that in *Gladiator,* "the dominant aesthetic of [the] Roman epic [is] reduced at times to little more than a blur of hyperkinetic montage, whip-pans and other camera movements," which effectively replace "the large-scale vista."[51] Certainly, closely filmed and rapidly cut action sequences feature in many epics, but they usually occur alongside the sort of expensively realised vistas that defined the genre during the 1950s. *Gladiator* is no exception, with its lingering shots of ranged armies in Germania, a packed Coliseum from above and the riotous streets of Rome. Again, such sequences serve to demonstrate the expense lavished on a particular production, but in this case, the filmmaker's power is closely tied to the processing power of the expensive computers used to realise such spectacles rather than the actual assemblage of extras and construction of elaborate sets. Curiously, any focus on computer-generated imagery (CGI) in the marketing of modern epics tends to closely resemble a focus on production resources, which was equally visible in the marketing of most 1950s epics. In both cases, expense and technological innovation has been equated with cultural significance.

Like their precursors, most modern epics are also very long. *Dances with Wolves* lasted 180 minutes, *Schindler's List* 195 minutes, *Braveheart* 177 minutes, *Titanic* 194 minutes and *Gladiator* 154 minutes; as a result, discussion of these films in the trade press often centred on how unwieldy and unhelpful such excessive length was for current exhibition strategies. When it was pointed out to James Cameron that "at three hours, you won't get as many screenings a day," he responded:

> It's an additional thing Fox was thinking about. No sequel poten-
> tial, no merchandising, no theme park rides, and, by the way, it's a
> three-hour picture that will have fewer shows per day. There's [a]
> definite economic hit taken when you've got a long film. But you've
> also had very successful long films. There's a need on the part of
> the audience for something of substance occasionally. A *Godfather*
> [1972], a *Dances with Wolves*, a *Gone With the Wind*.[52]

Similar trade discussion surrounded the release of *Pearl Harbor* in 2001. Reporting on the opening weekend, *Variety* noted that "*Pearl* can expect only three show-times a day, compared with the usual four, five or even six daily showings for most shorter pics. . . . Disney concedes that a 183-minute running time likely held its opening in check."[53] Extreme length is an important defining characteristic of the 1990s cycle because so many other features of the 1950s and 1960s epics are no longer pertinent. It is one of the few features that marks a contemporary epic as different from other productions at the level of exhibition. The fact that filmmakers, and the major studios, have been willing to produce such apparently overlong movies is also a sign of the intense fervour with which contemporary filmmakers sought to revive the historical epic, in defiance of perceived economic logic. Epics in the 1990s were so long that they risked losing money, but they still got made. A sense of cultural and artistic significance, which transcended purely economic logic, is therefore still firmly attached to the epic film.

Conclusion

Each of the following chapters is a case study that relates the production history of a recent epic film to a range of related contextual concerns. Although it is focused on a very recent period in Hollywood's history, this book is very much a work of film history, which attempts to explain a recent cycle through as comprehensive an investigation of as many relevant factors as possible. In the words of Kristin Thompson and David Bordwell, "A study of film genres [must] involve both aesthetic and cultural factors, and a person's life cannot easily be separated from his or her working conditions within a film industry or from the contemporary political context."[54] To this end, an early focus on individual agendas gradually gives way to a broader exploration of the social, economic and political factors that inspired the increased production of epic films during the 1990s and into the 2000s. The only exception is chapter 1, which offers a broader overview of the historical epic cycle that predominated during the 1950s and 1960s, variously taking individual agency, policy and industrial developments into account. In part, chapter 1 lays out the historical backdrop against which the modern cycle can be understood. However, it is also intended to redress a relative paucity of writing on the 1950s epic cycle. I argue that the epics produced at this time had their roots in changes to Hollywood's mandate initiated by various policy institutions during the Second World War. Furthermore, the altered moviemaking climate of the 1950s allowed a number of relatively independent, highly motivated filmmakers to produce essentially 'personal' projects with unprecedented production resources. We will see, too, that many 1950s epics were targeted at families and younger viewers in a manner that stressed their implicit educational worth. The chapter concludes by arguing that this preoccupation with education and moral edification ensured that future generations of filmmakers would come to regard historical epics in a similar fashion.

Chapter 2 traces the decline of the historical epic throughout the 1970s and 1980s, before shifting to examine the impact of Kevin Costner's *Dances with Wolves* in 1990. Arguably, the film's elegiac narrative, filled with nostalgic longing for the lost life of the Sioux Indians, mirrors Costner's apparently foolhardy and nostalgic attempt to revive epic and western genres. Chapter 2's close focus on Costner is an attempt to explain the revival of epics "in light of the attitudes or behaviour of individuals," to quote Thompson and Bordwell.[55] We also will see how the varied use of the terms *epic* and *western* in the marketing of *Dances with Wolves*, and its critical reception, had a lasting impact on subsequent production cycles.

Like chapter 2, chapter 3 focuses again on the ways that an individual's beliefs, feelings and creative agenda impacted upon production trends, this time by exploring Steven Spielberg's Holocaust epic *Schindler's List*. An examination of Spielberg's long-standing fascination with World War II, along with his cultural and ethnic connection to the events of the Holocaust, is followed by a close analysis of *Schindler's List*; here I argue that the film was an attempt to combine educational elements with a broader emotional experience that allowed modern audiences to make 'sense' of the Holocaust on an immediate, personal level. Chapter 3 concludes by arguing that the thematic and narrational strategies employed to generate feelings of commemoration and comprehension in viewers would quickly become key formal features of the 1990s epic cycle. Furthermore, Spielberg's attempt to position himself as a serious participant in historical debates further cultivated the assumed cultural 'prestige' of the historical epic film amongst both audiences and filmmakers.

Chapter 4 retains a focus on Spielberg but attempts to position him within a larger generation of filmmakers who all set out to revisit the historical epic film, for essentially personal reasons, at roughly the same time. The chapter addresses one of the dominant 'group causes' for the revival of the historical epic by looking at the experiences and attitudes of the "baby boom" generation (those born between 1946 and 1964 in the USA), to which Spielberg, Costner, Cameron, Gibson, et al., belong. The baby boomers' early moviegoing experiences, their impact as filmmakers and as audiences, and their cultural preoccupations are all explored. The chapter then argues that Spielberg's *Saving Private Ryan* can be understood as a key 'baby boomer epic' precisely because its wartime narrative combines a veneration for the epic film that seems to unite so many baby boomer filmmakers with a close focus on the debts of responsibility and memory that bind different generations together.

Chapter 5 looks at a very different 'group cause' for the revival of the epic by examining the activities of the newly founded studio, DreamWorks SKG, during the mid-1990s. DreamWorks SKG's early release strategies helped to construct a coherent 'brand identity' for the studio—an image partially founded on the preexisting reputations of the three founders, Spielberg, ex-Disney producer Jeffrey Katzenberg, and music industry mogul David Geffen. Chapter 5 argues that the DreamWorks founders focused production resources on a series of historical epic films, partly to exploit emergent trends, and partly to suggest an aura of permanence and cultural integrity. The studio's early releases are initially discussed, and the chapter then moves on to examine DreamWorks SKG's first animated release—*The Prince of Egypt*. Ultimately, *The Prince of Egypt* is presented as an attempt, on the part of animation boss Jeffrey Katzenberg, to revisit the foundation of DreamWorks SKG as a mythic allegory with parallels to the Moses story—making the film an epic *about* epics. The details of this allegory are unpicked in the final section of chapter 5.

Chapter 6 shifts focus again to explore the broader economic logic of the epic cycle in the late 1990s and early 2000s. At the turn of the millennium, all of the major studios designed and released hugely expensive historical epic productions, initially on a fairly experimental basis and then, following the success of DreamWorks SKG's *Gladiator* in 2000, as a matter of routine. At this moment 'commonsense' assumptions about the economic viability of the historical epic genre were effectively undone by a number of shifts that had occurred in Hollywood's economic operation since the late 1960s. Chapter 6 discusses the various epic cycles of the late 1990s and early 2000s, focusing specifically on DreamWorks SKG's *Gladiator*. The film's narrational preoccupation with the politics of popular entertainment is discussed, and then the chapter moves on to examine market conditions in more detail. The chapter concludes by arguing that the growth of the DVD market, and increasing significance of international audiences, had a lasting effect on the revenues generated by epic films, which in turn ensured the ongoing visibility of the historical epic into the mid-2000s.

With the revival of the historical epic established, chapter 7 looks in more detail at audience responses to one extremely unusual entry in the cycle, Mel Gibson's *The Passion of the Christ* (2004). Gibson's film returns to a key subject for the epics of the 1950s and 1960s (the life and death of Christ), but in direct contrast to earlier biblical epics, his film generated an enormous degree of controversy, both for its potential anti-Semitism and for its extreme violence. Nevertheless, it proved hugely successful with American audiences, and the final chapter seeks to understand how Gibson's film spoke to contemporary American cinemagoers. The film's address to a politically and religiously divided audience is discussed alongside a broader investigation of the film's spiritual resonances. Thus, this book finishes by attempting to understand just how the past can be used to speak to a complex, sometimes divided modern audience.

In similar fashion, the conclusion provides a brief overview of my findings, and it also assesses the political resonances that seemed to inform so many epics released after 9/11. As we have seen, the epic has traditionally offered filmmakers a means to talk about the present in the form of historical allegory. This book concludes by looking at the allegories used to discuss both U.S. intervention in the Middle East and the broader climate of international tension that has developed as George W. Bush's 'war on terror' rolls on. Throughout the book we will see repeatedly that the historical epic film may not be the most subtle or sophisticated form of political or social commentary available to filmmakers, but its 'obviousness' is also its great strength. When filmmakers have wanted to make relevant, meaningful statements, the epic has provided them with the tools. As chapter 1 will show, this was as true of the 1950s as it has been of the 1990s.

Notes

1. Quoted in Colin Covert, "Secret Voyage of the *Titanic*," *Newsday* 11 Nov. 1997, B8.

2. Todd McCarthy, "Spectacular *Titanic* a night to remember," *Variety* 3 Nov. 1997, 7.

3. Quoted in Tom Shone, *Blockbuster, or, How I Learned to Stop Worrying and Love the Summer* (London: Simon and Schuster, 2004), 250–251.

4. Quoted in David E. Williams, "Captain of His Ship," *American Cinematographer* Dec. 1997, 52.

5. Quoted in Maximilian Potter, "Cameron Boards *Titanic*," *Premiere* Aug. 1996, 42.

6. Even if figures are adjusted for inflation, it is interesting to note that *Titanic* is one of many historical epics in the top twenty highest grossing movies of all time. The full chart is available from Box Office Mojo, http://www.boxofficemojo.com/alltime/adjusted.htm.

7. Janet Maslin, "A Spectacle as Sweeping as the Sea," *New York Times* 19 Aug. 1997, E1.

8. Anthony Lane, "The Shipping News," *New Yorker* 15 Dec. 1997, 159.

9. Peter Krämer, "'Far Across the Distance': Historical Films, Film History and *Titanic*," in Tim Bergfelder and Sarah Street, eds., *The Titanic in Myth and Memory: Representations in Visual and Literary Culture* (New York: I.B. Tauris, 2004), 167.

10. Jon Solomon, *The Ancient World in the Cinema* (New York: A.S. Barnes, 1978), 16.

11. Solomon, 16.

12. Figures from Joel W. Finler, *The Hollywood Story* 3rd ed. (London: Wallflower, 2003), 356.

13. Linda Williams, "Race, Melodrama and *The Birth of a Nation* (1915)" in Lee Grieveson and Peter Krämer, eds., *The Silent Cinema Reader* (London: Routledge, 2004), 251.

14. Finler, 41.

15. See Finler, 41.

16. Vincent Canby, "For DeMille, Moses' Egypt Really Was America," *New York Times* 25 Mar. 1984, 19.

17. Finler, 356.

18. For an inflation-adjusted chart, see Box Office Mojo, http://www.boxofficemojo.com/alltime/adjusted.htm.

19. Tino Balio, *Grand Designs: Hollywood as a Modern Business Enterprise, 1930–1939* (New York: Scribner's, 1993), 179.

20. Stephen Prince, *A New Pot of Gold: Hollywood Under the Electronic Rainbow, 1980–1989* (Berkeley: University of California Press, 2000), 309.

21. See Steven Bach, *Final Cut: Dreams and Disaster in the Making of* Heaven's Gate (New York: Morrow, 1985).

22. Peter Krämer, *The New Hollywood: From* Bonnie and Clyde *to* Star Wars (London: Wallflower, 2005), 97–98.

23. Krämer (2005), 98.

24. *Out of Africa* earned $43.4 million in domestic grosses (Finler, 361).

25. Financial data obtained from Box Office Mojo, http://www.boxofficemojo.com/yearly/chart/?view2=worldwide&yr=1990&p=.htm.

26. Quoted in Derek Elley, *The Epic Film: Myth and History* (London: Routledge and Kegan Paul, 1984), 13.

27. Richard Maltby, *Hollywood Cinema* 2nd ed. (Oxford: Blackwell, 2003), 79.

28. See Rick Altman, *Film/Genre* (London: BFI, 1999) and Steve Neale, *Genre and Hollywood* (London: Routledge, 2000).

29. David Bordwell argues that "no strict definition of a single genre has won widespread acceptance," in David Bordwell, *Making Meaning* (Cambridge, MA: Harvard University Press, 1989), 147.

30. Mark Jancovich, "Genre and the Audience: Genre Classifications and Cultural Distinctions in the Mediation of *The Silence of the Lambs*," in Melvin Stokes and Richard Maltby, eds., *Hollywood Spectatorship: Changing Perceptions of Cinema Audiences* (London: BFI, 2001), 33.

31. See Altman, 66.

32. Film reviewers are treated as particularly important because their writing provides a glossary of terms that viewers and film producers can use to define individual [films]. Reviews tell us not "what to think, so much as what to think about." See Robert C. Allen and Douglas Gomery, *Film History: Theory and Practice* (New York: McGraw-Hill, 1985), 154.

33. Elley, 1.

34. Neale, 85.

35. Ibid.

36. Bruce Babington and Peter William Evans, *Biblical Epics: Sacred Narrative in the Hollywood Cinema* (Manchester: Manchester University Press, 1993), 4.

37. Melani McAlister, *Epic Encounters: Culture, Media and U.S. Interests in the Middle East* (Berkeley: University of California Press, 2001), 56.

38. Vivian Sobchack, "'Surge and Splendor': A Phenomenology of the Hollywood Historical Epic," in Barry Keith Grant, ed., *Film Genre Reader* 2nd ed. (Austin: University of Texas Press, 1995), 288.

39. A comprehensive account of the history of roadshowing can be found in Sheldon Hall, *Hard Ticket Giants: Widescreen Blockbusters in the Roadshow Era* (Ph.D. Thesis, University of East Anglia, 2000).

40. For an otherwise excellent account that nevertheless favours a slightly 'technologically determinist' reading, see John Belton, *Widescreen Cinema* (Cambridge, MA: Harvard University Press, 1992). For a historical account that emphasises the 'rivalry' between the film and TV industries, see James Chapman, *Cinemas of the World* (London: Reaktion, 2003), 128.

41. See David Bordwell, Janet Staiger and Kristin Thompson, *The Classical Hollywood Cinema: Film Style and Mode of Production to 1960* (London: Routledge, 1985), 1–84.

42. Michael Wood, *America in the Movies, or, 'Santa Maria, It Had Slipped My Mind!'* (London: Secker and Warburg, 1975), 173.

43. Mark Jancovich, "Dwight MacDonald and the Historical Epic," in Yvonne Tasker, ed., *Action and Adventure Cinema* (London: Routledge, 2004), 85.

44. Yosefa Loshitzky, ed., *Spielberg's Holocaust: Critical Perspectives on* Schindler's List (Bloomington: Indiana University Press, 1997).

45. James Cameron, *Titanic* Screenplay—Working Copy (Undated), Paramount Script Collection, AMPAS, 20.

46. David Eldridge, *Hollywood's History Films* (London: I.B. Tauris, 2006), 3.

47. Natalie Zemon Davies, *Slaves on Screen: Film and Historical Vision* (Cambridge, MA: Harvard University Press, 2000), 15.

48. Gillian Roberts, "Circulations of Taste: *Titanic*, the Oscars, and the middlebrow," in Julian Stringer, ed., *Movie Blockbusters* (London: Routledge, 2003), 155.

49. Emanuel Levy, *Oscar Fever: The History and Politics of the Academy Awards* (New York: Continuum, 2001), 151.

50. Levy, 151. Subsequent data on the Oscars is taken from this source unless otherwise specified.

51. Geoff King, "Spectacle and Narrative in the Contemporary Blockbuster," in Linda Ruth Williams and Michael Hammond, eds., *Contemporary American Cinema* (London: McGraw-Hill, 2006), 340.

52. James Cameron, quoted in Michael Fleming, "Fantastic Voyage," *Movieline* Dec. 1997, 69.

53. Dade Hayes, "Super-Size *Pearl* pushes time limit," *Variety* 4 Jun. 2001, 42–49.

54. Kristen Thompson and David Bordwell, *Film History: An Introduction* 2nd ed. (New York: McGraw-Hill, 1997), 5.

55. Thompson and Bordwell, 5.

～1～

Big-Theme Films:
Epics in the Roadshow Era

I n an interview that ran under the heading '*Braveheart* resurrects the epic', Mel Gibson told *Variety* that "I saw all the epics as a kid. . . . All the 'Ben-Hurs' and all the 'Spartaci.'"[1] Gibson went on to present *Braveheart* as a natural successor to the epics of the 1950s, and in the process he suggested a correlation between his boyhood viewing experiences and his adult career as an actor/director. Such claims recur again and again in the marketing of almost all of the epic films released in the 1990s. When discussing *Dances with Wolves,* Kevin Costner recalled that, as a boy, "I'd lose myself in the movies. . . . I had a very active fantasy life. I can remember as a ten-year-old watching *How the West Was Won* and certain moments made me tingle with the magic of it."[2] Alternatively, Steven Spielberg remembered that "after the experience of seeing *Lawrence of Arabia,* I never wanted to do anything else with my life but make films."[3] According to biographer Joseph McBride, Spielberg was also deeply affected by the experience of watching William Wyler's *Ben-Hur.*[4] Jerry Bruckheimer, the producer of *Pearl Harbor* and *King Arthur,* identified Sam Spiegel as a role model and expressed great admiration for the independent producer's *Bridge on the River Kwai* (1957) and *Lawrence of Arabia.*[5] In a similar vein, Martin Scorsese, who directed *The Last Temptation of Christ* (1988), *Kundun* (1997), *Gangs of New York* (2002) and *The Aviator* (2004), has said, "I still remember one of the great experiences I had in my film-going, back in 1953. I was ten or eleven years old. It was at the Roxy Theatre, the curtain began to open, and continued to open, until it revealed the biggest screen I'd ever seen. On it was the first CinemaScope picture, *The Robe* (1953)."[6] Scorsese also wrote that "DeMille's later epics made an indelible impression on me, particularly *Samson and Delilah*

[1949] and his own remake of *The Ten Commandments,* which I have seen countless times. DeMille presented such a sumptuous fantasy that if you saw his movies as a child, they stuck with you for life."[7]

The memory of lavish spectacles and grand historical stories, played out on the largest of screens, in the most opulent possible environment, was clearly an experience that profoundly affected some viewers. As a result, it is perhaps unsurprising that so many modern filmmakers have sought to recreate the kinds of movies that wowed them as children. In their own words, the epics of the 1950s had been key formative influences, and although it took some time for a more recent generation of filmmakers to seriously engage with the legacy of the historical epic, they were eventually drawn back to the genre. But just what were these filmmakers seeking to recapture? And why had epic films dominated so absolutely throughout their formative years?

This chapter explains how economic, artistic and logistical factors contributed to the increased production of the epics in the 1950s and 1960s. Section 1 outlines the economic logic behind the growing dominance of the historical epic film in production trends in the two decades after World War II. Section 2 explores broader transformations in the socially agreed scope, function and political meaning of cinematic entertainment after World War II, by examining shifts in policy and the creative agendas of individual filmmakers. Section 3 then looks at the marketing of several key historical epics, paying particular attention to the ways that epics were presented as educational experiences to younger audience members. Section 4 outlines the decline of the historical epic in production schedules, and the conclusion examines the more long-lasting impact of the 1950s epic cycle on film trends, by exploring Spielberg's memories of *Ben-Hur* in more detail. As well as providing some important background information, this chapter offers a new account of the role that epics have played in film culture. Rather than viewing the epic film as a means to showcase technological advances, as many scholars have implicitly suggested, I argue that the epics of the 1950s and 1960s must be understood as serious films made by impassioned filmmakers, much like the epics of the 1990s.

1. The Economics of the Roadshow Epic

After 1950, historical films of all types assumed a sudden and unprecedented prominence in Hollywood production schedules. As David

Eldridge has observed, "40 percent of all films made in the fifties were set in the past."[8] Epics could be distinguished from a broader continuum of swashbucklers, period romances and westerns by their exceptional production values and highly prestigious forms of exhibition. Furthermore, the highly budgeted epic trend gradually became the most commercially successful cycle of historical films on release during the decade. So how did the economic conditions of the film industry shift to favour the epic film over other releases?

Perhaps the most significant change ever to occur in Hollywood's market conditions was the sudden decline of audience attendance levels in the late 1940s. Between 1930 and 1946, the average number of movie tickets sold per week in the United States had never dropped below 50 million.[9] Often sales far exceeded this, and between 1943 and 1946, over 80 million tickets were sold on average every week. In 1940, the U.S. Census Bureau recorded the population of the United States as being 132.2 million.[10] Even taking into account the fact that many attended the movies several times a week, moviegoing was a habit for a huge percentage of Americans at this time. In 1943, over one-quarter of the average American's recreational expenditure went toward going to the movies.[11] However, when World War II ended, cinemagoing patterns changed in an unprecedented fashion. Average weekly attendance dropped from 82 million in 1946 to 42 million by 1953. This pattern continued into the 1960s; by1961, average weekly attendance was 30 million, and it dropped continually until it reached a nadir of 16 million in 1971.[12] Put simply, going to the movies became a marginal part of American cultural and commercial life.[13] Although many audiences had stopped going to cinemas entirely, many more had simply stopped going with any degree of regularity. To further complicate matters, at exactly the same time as the effects of the shift were beginning to be felt, the majors were forced to substantially alter their operating practices by the U.S. government's successful prosecution of Paramount Pictures in a landmark antitrust suit.

The 'Paramount Decrees,' as they are sometimes known, were designed to open up the film market to independent competitors. After 1948, the vertically integrated majors were instructed to separate their exhibition interests from their other activities, either by a process of divestiture (selling these divisions to independent companies) or divorcement (entirely dividing their corporate structure, thus rendering one wing independent from the others). Furthermore, all of the majors, including Columbia, United Artists and Universal, were required to adopt new methods of licensing movies for exhibition in theatres. Tactics for negotiating with exhibitors that were perceived as unfair were outlawed.[14] The new rules forced the majors to change their operations at a time when revenues from movie exhibition in America were becoming uncertain. Ironically, the changes that were forced on the industry ultimately served to benefit the majors in the long run, because they shifted responsibility for coping with declining audiences onto the newly minted exhibition sector. The new modes of operation and production strategies that appeared in the 1950s and 1960s were therefore calculated to maintain the preeminence of the major studios and stimulate demand for their product in ways that limited the power of theatre chains.

The main strategy employed in the 1950s was a reduction in the number of films produced for cinemas by the majors. In 1941, the majors had released a total of 379 movies.[15] In 1963, the majors released 142 movies.[16] The logic was that reducing supply helped stimulate demand amongst theatre owners who needed product. The majors were then able to negotiate more favourable rental fees from an increasingly desperate exhibition sector.[17] Furthermore, the outstanding hits of the mid-to-late 1940s suggested that a tighter concentration of resources on fewer, larger productions might work in the changed marketplace. Two prestigious 1946 films, *Duel in the Sun* and *The Best Years of Our Lives*, produced independently but distributed by the Selznick Releasing Organization and UA respectively, had each grossed around $10 million—far more than any single release since *Gone with the Wind* (as we have already seen, itself another highly budgeted independent production).[18] In 1949, Cecil B. DeMille's *Samson and Delilah*, earning over $9 million for MGM in a year when no other release exceeded $5 million in revenues, sparked the full-fledged initiation of the 1950s epic.[19]

These exclusive releases were all 'roadshow' releases—they were initially exhibited at a handful of extremely prestigious city centre theatres, with substantially increased ticket prices and other trappings of the legitimate theatre such as bookable seats, intermissions and overtures.[20] Although such movies would eventually appear on first- and second-run theatre circuits, the roadshow release could still run for years in the same theatre, attracting large audiences on the basis of increased prestige. This made economic sense because the majors usually received a greater percentage of the ticket price in roadshow theatres than in subsequent-run circuits, and the spectacle and exclusivity of the roadshow setting could continue to attract audiences even after a film appeared on lower-run circuits.[21] Roadshowing had been employed occasionally for decades, as Sheldon Hall has shown, but in the 1950s, the majors devoted a significantly increased volume of production resources to expensive roadshows, which cost more than ordinary productions, but which were also capable of generating far higher returns.[22] With the release of *This Is Cinerama* in 1952 and *The Robe* in 1953, the roadshow phenomenon became inextricably linked to innovative widescreen and big-screen technologies such as Cinerama, CinemaScope and Todd-AO.[23]

Furthermore, while the majors were reducing the number of movies they released, they were also penetrating the television market. In 1948, when two-thirds of the American population went to movie theatres on a weekly basis, there were roughly 1.5 million television sets in use in the United States.[24] By 1960, this had risen to over 45 million sets, and by 1962, over 90 percent of American homes owned at least one television.[25] The rise of television is generally seen as the major cause of declining theatrical attendance, but the roadshows that predominated in the 1950s and 1960s were not really attempts to compete with television, as is sometimes claimed. As Christopher Anderson's extensive research has shown, the Hollywood majors became the dominant providers of television product by the mid-1950s, and the roadshow epic trend was primarily an attempt to differentiate between different lines of product rather than a combative gesture.[26]

Just as the size of the movie screen increased, so did the potential revenue that any one movie could generate. Throughout the 1950s and 1960s, historical epics and prestige musicals consistently earned rentals that were virtually unheard of in the studio era. As Richard Maltby has observed, "[B]efore 1960 only twenty movies had grossed over $10 million in the domestic market; by 1970, more than 80 had."[27] *The Ten Commandments* earned $34.2 million in the United States, *Around the World in 80 Days* (1956) $22 million, *Ben-Hur* $36.7 million, *Doctor Zhivago* $43 million and *The Sound of Music* (1965) $77 million.[28] Furthermore, a significant proportion of the highest grossing films in the twenty-four-year period between 1946 and 1970 were straight historical epics or (to a lesser extent) musicals of epic scope with a historical setting. Many were international in terms of their appeal and their production. As budgets had risen, overseas production had begun to make sense.[29] Not only was it cheaper to film in Europe, or even the Middle East, than in Los Angeles, but international productions were more easily marketable to an international audience, which was growing considerably in the aftermath of WWII, at exactly the same time as the American audience diminished. As Tino Balio has observed, "[I]n 1949, 19 American-interest features were made abroad; in 1969, 183."[30]

For a variety of reasons, then, the majors increasingly focused their movie production budgets on a handful of prestigious epics. Cecil B. DeMille's *Samson and Delilah*, released by Paramount, established a formula that reappeared in various films throughout the next two decades. In his history of Hollywood in the 1940s, Thomas Schatz describes it as "more a film of the 1950s than the 1940s. Although it recalled DeMille's earlier Biblical Epics [it] was actually quite radical. The film was a lavish spectacular with global appeal designed to exploit Paramount's strengths as a producer-distributor."[31] However, it was the success of MGM's *Quo Vadis* in 1951 that cemented the emergence of an epic cycle.[32] DeMille's film had grossed $9 million in rentals, while *Quo Vadis* grossed $10.5 million.[33] *Samson and Delilah* could have been interpreted as a one-off hit, but the subsequent success of Mervyn LeRoy's film indicated that spectacular biblical movies could consistently generate unusually high returns.

The other majors took note, and in 1953 *Variety* ran an article entitled "Biblical Film Cycle Hits New High; 12 Upcoming," which listed the majors' forthcoming biblical roadshows, including Fox's *The Robe* (Henry Koster, 1953).[34] Like *Quo Vadis*, *The Robe* was based on a bestselling novel that dramatised the death of Christ and the emergence of Christianity at the height of the Roman Empire.[35] It was used by Fox to showcase the widescreen CinemaScope format. Widescreen processes had proved a box office phenomenon after the success of *This Is Cinerama* in 1952. Essentially a novelty production with travelogue elements, *This Is Cinerama* was designed to demonstrate the potential of the Cinerama exhibition technology, which used three 35mm cameras and projectors to create an ultra-wide image on a curved screen. Even though the film could only be shown in the handful of theatres that had installed the expensive Cinerama technology, it ultimately brought in rentals of $12.5 million.[36] Fox's CinemaScope system was also expensive to install, but only required one camera and one projector, thus making it cheaper to shoot with and more suited to conventional narrative films. In *The Robe* an emergent cycle of biblical epics collided with technological innovations that broadened the cinematic frame, thus adding potential for larger scale spectacles. The result was remarkably successful, with rentals of $17.5 million.[37] In the process the historical epic became indelibly linked to widescreen spectacle, and the roadshow epic moved towards industrial dominance.

Of the twelve biblical films listed by *Variety*, only *The Robe* went on to become a genuine success (most of these early epics, like MGM's 1955 release *The Prodigal*, failed commercially). Nevertheless, the success of *The Robe* inspired all of the majors to increase investment in epics. These films, more than any others, seemed to appeal to broad sections of the audience at a time when attendance was falling dramatically. Again not all subsequent epics were major hits, and Warner Bros.' epics *The Silver Chalice* (1954), *Land of the Pharaohs* (1955) and *Helen of Troy* (1956) fared particularly poorly. However, as the 1950s continued, a series of standout hits emerged, most notably Paramount's *The Ten Commandments* in 1956, as well as MGM's *Ben-Hur* in 1959 and UA's *Around the World in 80 Days* in 1956.

Sheldon Hall has argued that roadshow releases in the 1950s and 1960s went through several different stages.[38] Initially, the success of *Quo Vadis* and *The Robe* inspired widespread imitation, and then the standout success of subsequent roadshow epics in the latter part of the decade encouraged even greater levels of production. Throughout this time, an enormous number of epics were released. Biblical extravaganzas included *Demetrius and the Gladiators* (Fox's 1954 sequel to *The Robe*), Fox's *David and Bathsheba* (1951), UA's *Solomon and Sheba* (1959) and Columbia's *Barabbas* (1962); alternatively, Universal's *Spartacus* (1960) was a Roman epic that replaced biblical trappings with a broader anti-slavery message; UA's *The Vikings* (1958) was a Dark Ages epic; MGM's *How the West Was Won* (1962) was a western epic filmed in Cinerama; Fox's *The Longest Day* (1962) a WWII epic; *Lawrence of Arabia* a WWI epic; *Exodus* (1960) a post-WWII Zionist epic; and UA's *Khartoum* (1966) and Paramount's *55 Days at Peking* (1963) were epics of nineteenth-century imperialism. Although these films differed wildly in terms of setting, they were united by lengthy, sincere historical narratives, by forms of spectacle and scenic construction associated with wide- and large-screen processes, by roadshowing, and by a thematic preoccupation with significant events in world history, which, of course, distinguishes them as epics.

The disappointing performance of Fox's *Cleopatra* (1963) briefly suggested that the roadshow trend might be in decline. However, the success of two epics in 1965, MGM's *Doctor Zhivago* and Fox's *The Sound of Music*, encouraged even higher levels of investment in roadshows, many of which failed catastrophically at the box office in the late 1960s. Production had virtually ceased by 1970, marking the end of the cycle.[39] Further investment in the cycle was discouraged after hugely expensive epics, including *The Fall of the Roman Empire* (a Paramount/Samuel Bronston co-production) in 1964, *The Greatest Story Ever Told* (produced by UA) in 1965 and *The Bible: In the Beginning* (a Fox/de

Laurentiis co-production) in 1966, failed to recoup their production costs. However, despite their gradual disappearance, roadshow epics had been the dominant Hollywood production trend for almost twenty years for several keys reasons.

Peter Krämer has argued that roadshow epics were attempts to address audiences who visited the cinema infrequently.[40] Such films successfully attracted occasional viewers, often families and older people, who had abandoned cinemagoing as a regular activity but might be drawn back to theatres by something spectacular, edifying and prestigious—the 'must-see' movie of the year. Although smaller productions remained a constituent part of the studios' output, scale and spectacle began to predominate. With the rise of roadshow epics, the blockbuster approach that characterises cinema today took shape. The films themselves were not a new phenomenon—large-scale hits had occasionally appeared in Hollywood's past, but just as epic blockbusters began to predominate, so did the independent production methods that had previously been associated with them.

As we have seen, some of Hollywood's biggest hits in the 1930s had been produced by visionary independents who relied on the majors for funding and distribution, but who organised and oversaw their own productions. A good example is David O. Selznick, who produced *Gone with the Wind* for MGM. Selznick had previously worked as a production chief at RKO and MGM, but when he went independent he was able to transcend the mass-production ethos of the studios and focus all of his attentions on occasional prestige releases. Selznick produced a string of megahits, such as *A Star Is Born* (1937) and *The Prisoner of Zenda* (1937), which ensured that the major studios were invariably willing to distribute his productions. When such investments paid off, they did so in unprecedented fashion.[41] Other successful independent producers operating in the studio era included Walter Wanger, Samuel Goldwyn and Darryl F. Zanuck (at least until his independent '20th Century' productions merged with Fox Studios in 1935). Goldwyn and other independents such as Walt Disney, Selznick and the British mogul Alexander Korda had found a home at United Artists, the studio founded as a distributor of independent movies.

Throughout the 1950s and 1960s, this model of independent production became the norm. As Tino Balio has observed, UA offered a template for survival in a post-antitrust industry.[42] Rather than maintaining the assembly-line structure of the studio era, the majors recognised that movie production could be more profitable if staff, resources and capital were assembled as they were needed for individual productions, a model Janet Staiger has called the 'package unit system.'[43] It was no longer necessary to produce movies for theatrical release at a pre-1948 level, and so movies were increasingly packaged as one-off events, and production resources were rented on an ad-hoc basis. In this climate, the power of individual stars, producers and directors increased to the point where such people had a vastly increased share of control over their own productions. As we will see, this may be one reason why historical epics came to predominate. The look and length of epics was clearly influenced by shifting economic circumstances and changes in exhibition formats. However, the grandiose historical stories that these films told cannot be accounted for in these terms. More often than not, the producers of the outstanding epics of the era were some of the most highly regarded and powerful figures in the film industry, including multiple-Oscar winners like William Wyler, Joseph L. Mankiewitz and George Stevens. Virtually all of the key creative personnel behind the epic trend of the 1950s and 1960s had reached positions of great influence. Changes in the industry opened up a space for these filmmakers to work with the largest budgets and speak to the largest audiences, but the shift to independent production also helped to ensure that what they said was ultimately up to them. Furthermore, the legacy of World War II seems to have had a profound influence both on the regulation of the American film industry and on the ambitions of the 'creative community,' which further encouraged commercial and creative investment in epic films.

2. Creative Conditions After World War II

Although the new economic order did both facilitate and encourage the adoption of higher budgets and larger screens, it would be naïve to assume that the historical epic achieved industrial dominance purely in response to economic and technological shifts. The rapid emergence and development of the cycle clearly depended on a degree of independent creative agency, which is to say that some filmmakers were clearly attracted to the historical epic before the commercial viability of the genre was proven. As David Eldridge explains, "Economic circumstances enabled certain types of historical films to get made, but how filmmakers then depicted or used the past was an issue that was influenced by very different attitudes and expectations."[44] In particular, it seems that the broad geopolitical resonances of the epic film allowed filmmakers to make "imaginative use of historical settings to achieve political statements. . . . [They] found that history could provide them with some very 'usable' pasts."[45] Although critics with a background in 'high' culture have tended to dismiss epics as essentially 'irrelevant' entertainments, it seems that many working in the film industry saw the epic film as an eminently appropriate vehicle for political allegory. An investigation into the production histories of some key releases shows us just how such allegories were integrated and deployed.

In a memo intended for MGM's French press office, entitled 'Why Ben-Hur?' the director William Wyler wrote, "Admittedly I had misgivings about directing Ben-Hur when first approached by Metro-Goldwyn-Mayer some years ago. But beneath the spectacle and grandeur there lay a particularly pertinent theme—though not new—that of freedom versus tyranny. So I undertook to do Ben-Hur in spite of the spectacle, not because of it."[46] He went on to note that "it was particularly important that the spectacular aspects should not submerge the characterisations." Wyler apparently viewed Ben-Hur as more than a simplistic, audience-wowing spectacle. He saw in the story the potential to make a political statement, and in a subsequent interview he told Ronald Davies, "It had an angle to it. It showed the Jews of Judea, as it was called then, threatened by the Romans. The same situation as it exists still today, except it's not the Romans, it's the Arabs. The Romans had taken over their land and they were trying to fight for their freedom and their country."[47] In Wyler's hands, Ben-Hur became a tale of Zionism and Israel as much as it was 'A Tale of the Christ,' and it is possible to trace how this view was incorporated into the narrative of the film by tracing changes in the script as the production process gained momentum.

Some confusion exists over who wrote the 1959 version of Ben-Hur. Karl Tunberg received the sole screenplay credit, much to the chagrin of William Wyler, who thought that it should have gone to the English poet Christopher Fry. Fry had carried out extensive rewrites on the script and had been on set throughout shooting, making changes and adding scenes on a day-to-day basis. The novelist and critic Gore Vidal also performed a rewrite and has famously been credited with suggesting that the initial meeting between the Jewish nobleman Ben-Hur and his Roman childhood friend Messala should be played as if the pair had once been homosexual lovers.[48] However, the various versions of the film's script held in archival collections indicate that Vidal's input was not comparable to Fry's or Tunberg's (indeed, star Charlton Heston has claimed that Vidal worked on Ben-Hur for a paltry three days).[49] In particular, Christopher

Fry rewrote many of the scenes prior to the chariot race and was solely responsible for the second half of the film. He worked closely with Wyler as these rewrites were carried out, and the changes wrought on Tunberg's original script show quite clearly how the themes that Wyler wished to invoke were incorporated into the story. In particular, the depiction of Christ's final hours at the end of the film changed radically, and, in the process, the meaning of *Ben-Hur* as a whole also changed.

An early script, written by Karl Tunberg and dated 20 July 1954, has Christ play an active role in the narrative. Ben-Hur listens to the Sermon on the Mount and afterwards talks to Christ. He offers to defend the Messiah against his enemies, but Christ tells him, "I must die so that men may live. When I am gone they will go on trying to kill me, over and over again. Then I will need your services."[50] Christ then heals Ben-Hur's mother and sister of leprosy before his imprisonment, and Ben-Hur goes to the court of Pilate to act as an advocate for Christ during his trial. Nevertheless, Caiaphas, the head Jewish priest, convinces Pilate to crucify Christ, against his better judgement. Throughout, Ben-Hur is presented as a putative Christian, and at the moment of the crucifixion he is converted. This had all changed in the finished film. Between them, Christopher Fry and William Wyler produced a very different ending, in which Christ and Ben-Hur never meet, and the crucifixion takes on a different meaning. There are no scenes with Caiaphas (although we do see Pilate silently washing his hands in tableau at the trial), and Ben-Hur is not converted to Christianity at the climax, as he is in the original novel and all other stage and screen versions of the story. Instead, Wyler's Ben-Hur remains a Jew, but he is inspired by Christ's torment to forget his hatred of Rome, and need for violent revenge, in favour of forgiveness and peace. The blood of Christ then heals his mother and sister.[51] In part, the minimisation of Christ's role as an active participant in the narrative may well be linked to the concerns of the Production Code Administration (PCA), which advised producer Sam Zimbalist in October 1954 that "it would be unacceptable to quote Christ in any way other than directly from the Bible."[52] Although these logistical constraints certainly affected *Ben-Hur*, we can nevertheless assume that the broader narrative transformation wrought by Wyler was clearly intended to support a Zionist agenda.

Ultimately, *Ben-Hur* works as a defence of Zionism by stressing repeatedly that the Hebrews are the rightful occupants of the Holy Land, and by presenting Ben-Hur as a freedom fighter engaged in the process of liberating his homeland. Furthermore, the film was in production at the time of the 1956 Suez Crisis and was certainly also intended to comment allegorically on the related geopolitical events of the day. Israel's invasive attempt to secure control of the Suez Canal, encouraged and supported by British and France colonial interests, marked a key moment of transition in colonial politics. America averted an extended military misadventure by blocking British and French military support for Israel, and in the process the U.S. tested its close relationship with a putative Jewish state. Melani McAlister has argued that *Ben-Hur* interrogates America's relationship with the Middle East, stressing the unity of Israeli and Arabic neighbours (embodied by the character of Sheik Ilderim, played by Hugh Griffith), stoic resistance of ancient colonial powers (Romans with strong British accents) and acceptance of America's "benevolent supremacy"— in a direct response to the Suez Crisis.[53]

However, Wyler's stated attempt to produce a specifically Zionist allegory complicates McAlister's reading. As we have seen, Wyler, the guiding creative force behind the film, suggested that the Romans be understood as surrogates for contemporary Arabic aggressors. Although McAlister argues that the film was an example of America talking to the world about the Middle East, it would be more in keeping with Wyler's goals to read *Ben-Hur* as the work of an American Jew with firm Zionist convictions addressing his fellow countrymen, and the world, on the subject of Israel. Wyler sought to produce a film that preached stoic Israeli resistance of Arabic *and* English antagonists and which also stressed the historical permanence of an Israeli state in the face of assault and occupation. To this end, he altered the narrative of *Ben-Hur* to argue for an Israeli and American unity informed by an acceptance of religious, national and ethnic difference. Thus, Ben-Hur is not converted to Christianity at the end of Wyler's film. Rather he, and his people, are reaffirmed as the rightful rulers of the Holy Land and are shown to tolerate the foundation of Christianity (in some respects a founding moment of American identity) without partaking in the associated beliefs.

Of course, the film's story resonates across many political currents, taking in the legacy of World War II, the escalation of the Cold War and a range of other contemporary concerns, as McAlister, as well as Maria Wyke and Martin M. Winkler, have all demonstrated.[54] Different members of the cast and crew brought other agendas, which can also be used to account for *Ben-Hur*'s shifting relevance and popularity. Furthermore, Richard Maltby has observed that political meaning in Hollywood films is always left vague to encourage diverse readings and include a broad cross-section of audience views.[55] Nevertheless, Wyler's chief intention was clearly to produce a pro-Israeli historical epic, and providing an oblique commentary on Israel was a constituent feature of many other epics. According to Maria Wyke, Kirk Douglas was motivated by similar impulses when he chose to produce and star in Stanley Kubrick's *Spartacus*. She writes, "[I]t was Douglas's Zionist convictions that above all caused an ideological rift between the narrative drive of [Howard] Fast's novel and that of the Hollywood film, for the Zionist Spartacus appears on screen as a leader of a mass migration of slaves back to their homelands rather than as a revolutionary aiming to overthrow the oppressive Roman state."[56] Zionism was also the subject of Otto Preminger's 1960 roadshow epic, *Exodus*.[57]

In a similar vein, Alan Nadel argues that Cecil B. DeMille's epic *The Ten Commandments* "can be read as a product of cold war ideology, that highlights and localises the foci of America's political, theological and economic conflicts."[58] By appearing on screen at the beginning of the film to discuss the contemporary resonances of an age-old narrative of slavery and liberation, DeMille actively encouraged such readings. However, he was also keen to present his films as serious spiritual experiences, and in 1957, he told legendary Hollywood journalist Hedda Hopper:

> In the three pictures I have made—*The Ten Commandments* is the giving of the law—*King of Kings* is the interpretation of the law—and *Sign of the Cross* is the preservation of the law. They are a triumvirate that go together. *Samson and Delilah* is the power of prayer and faith—But no matter how deep our troubles there is a solution if one will turn back again to prayer and truly believe.[59]

The King of Kings was a 1927 Jesus biopic that had enjoyed continued popularity at church screenings well into the 1950s.[60] *The Sign of the Cross* (1932) was based on the Wilson Barrett play of the same name that dramatised the trials of early Christians under the emperor Nero (the same story as *Quo Vadis*). It had been re-released in 1943 with a new prologue, which linked the ancient Roman story to events of WWII (and Mussolini's Rome), proving fairly successful at the box office in the process. Before 1949, DeMille had concentrated on what Jon Solomon has called "the ancient moralising film" of the 1920s and 1930s—a related cycle discussed in the introduction.[61] Despite the occasionally uneasy tone of these films, DeMille had nevertheless taken his work seriously, and when his historical films took on increasingly epic dimensions in the 1950s, so did his ambitions.

DeMille's comments to Hopper indicate that he viewed his biblical films as part of an ongoing creative project with strong spiritual dimensions. Again, the remake of *The Ten Commandments* may have partially resulted from an increased industrial will to bankroll such productions, but it was also a personal project. Of all Hollywood directors in the 1950s, DeMille enjoyed perhaps the greatest share of creative license. His lengthy relationship with Paramount and proven box office success allowed him to develop his own projects, and the model of semi-independent production that was becoming prevalent across the industry had long been associated with DeMille.[62] So although it was likely that DeMille would produce another biblical film at this time, it is not unreasonable to assume that remaking *The Ten Commandments* was also an attempt to clarify and extend his existing filmmaking agenda.

Of the films that DeMille discussed with Hedda Hopper, only the original *Ten Commandments*, with its contemporary setting, was an uncomfortable fit. In 1956, DeMille took the opportunity to revise his story of 'the giving of the law.' The original script for the film began with the creation of the universe and hastily ran through the garden of Eden and the killing of Abel before it arrived at the Hebrews in Egypt.[63] These inclusions indicate a desire to produce a definitive, all-encompassing Bible movie, which would unify DeMille's self-styled 'triumvirate.' His strongly felt anticommunist beliefs therefore chimed with his religious sentiments in a manner that, Alan Nadel has suggested, perfectly captured the tenor of a popular debate in the 1950s that equated religious identity and political belief.[64] *The Ten Commandments* was therefore intended as both a spiritual and political tract. However much DeMille employed spectacle and titillation, he saw his film as a valuable forum to enlighten viewers as much as to entertain.

Although the production of epics fell off towards the end of the 1960s, examples of the genre still appeared, and we can see more evidence of similar convictions at play in a late roadshow epic, *Tora! Tora! Tora!* (1970). Shortly before its release, Fox head Darryl F. Zanuck gave the film a very public 'spin' by taking out full-page advertisements in the *New York Times*, *Los Angeles Times* and other national newspapers. Here Zanuck claimed, "The basic reason for producing the film, which is the second most expensive in history, was to arouse the public to the necessity for preparedness in this acute missile age where a sneak attack could occur at any moment."[65] The studio head was responding to controversy surrounding the assistance offered to filmmakers by the U.S. Navy, which was the subject of a disparaging report on television's *60 Minutes* in May

1969.[66] Zanuck had known that the report was going to air for some time, as a telegram from Zanuck to the film's producer, Elmo Williams, in March 1969 indicates. In this note, marked 'Confidential', Zanuck wrote:

> As I recall most of your Washington trips were for the purpose of verifying authenticity as well as requesting normal cooperation that has always been extended to any film that the government considers historical or of benefit to the armed services and certainly our retaliation after Pearl Harbor was a great achievement in American history.[67]

In private, Zanuck, it seems, viewed the production of *Tora! Tora! Tora!* as a necessary illustration of 'a great achievement in American history' was well as a valuable social lesson. Furthermore, Zanuck had a long-standing preoccupation with 'preparedness' that linked back to his experiences as a filmmaker during the Second World War.

Not every roadshow epic stemmed from personal creative agendas to quite this degree. Once the formal qualities of the cycle became established, studios were keen to develop and initiate similar projects, but making an epic film continued to mean making a serious statement about the past. David Eldridge attributes this desire to the 'politicisation' of the film industry during the notorious anticommunist 'witchhunts' carried out by the House Un-American Activities Committee (HUAC) in the early 1950s.[68] From 1947 onwards, HUAC sought to expose a supposed Communist influence in the film industry, leading initially to the 'blacklisting'—i.e., rendering certain individuals unemployable—of ten screenwriters and other personnel. In the early 1950s, the blacklist was extended to include well over 100 Hollywood personnel, including highly respected figures such as Charlie Chaplin. Certainly, the investigation into Hollywood's affairs encouraged those in the film industry to see themselves as political beings, engaged in a sometimes bitter ideological struggle that spilled over into the movies. However, the roots of a political consciousness in mainstream Hollywood entertainment can be traced back considerably further than the HUAC hearings.

In 1915, concern over the potential propagandising power of the cinema led the Supreme Court of the United States to rule that the burgeoning movie industry had "to produce demonstrably harmless entertainment that needed no further, externally imposed censorship," in Richard Maltby's words.[69] In part the ruling benefited the film industry because it created broad guidelines that staved off regional censorship, thus ensuring the continued 'openness' of the domestic market. However, the decision also made it a matter of government policy that movies could only function as 'harmless entertainment,' and the industry was regulated by the PCA, which enforced strict political and moral prohibitions. Overt attempts at political commentary were discouraged, and the court ruled that the movies would not be protected as free speech by the First Amendment of the Constitution. Although politically resonant comment was never entirely eliminated from Hollywood's product, the American cinema favoured vague, uncontroversial depictions and allegories throughout the years of studio stability. Crucially, the movies were generally categorised by distributors as blank documents, onto which viewers could project their own interpretations, rather than as defiantly and specifically meaningful texts. Furthermore, the political agendas of individual filmmakers were frequently downplayed in marketing efforts.

The status quo changed substantially in the years immediately preceding America's entry into World War II. Richard Maltby has noted that "Hollywood became a significant centre of progressive political activity in the late 1930s," and as the war in Europe escalated, the broader societal debate over potential American intervention began to be felt on cinema screens.[70] A number of powerful figures within Hollywood actively encouraged the production of veiled pro-interventionist allegories and stories dealing with war themes in the context of the European conflict. In 1940, Warner Bros. enjoyed considerable commercial success with *The Fighting 69th*, a World War I narrative that acted as a loosely veiled allegory, while UA had hits with the Walter Wanger and Alfred Hitchcock production *Foreign Correspondent* and Charlie Chaplin's *The Great Dictator*. The latter two films in particular were examples of relatively autonomous producers with clear political goals, fashioning obvious commentaries on the European crisis. Of course, far more overt images of the European war also dominated newsreel features. Unsurprisingly, perhaps, a number of concerned isolationists took action in September 1941 at a series of prosecutorial hearings where they demanded that the Interstate Commerce Committee investigate Hollywood's "warmongering propaganda," in the words of Senator Gerald P. Nye.[71] The committee hearings identified a growing and sometimes unapologetic will to address contemporary geopolitical events. Harry Warner told the committee, "You may charge me with being anti-Nazi. But no one can charge me with being anti-American."[72] Similar sentiments were expressed by other studio executives and filmmakers, including Daryl F. Zanuck, who declared, "If you accuse us of being anti-Nazi you are right, and if you accuse us of producing films in the interests of preparedness and national defence you are also right."[73] In fact, Zanuck had already taken a post as the chair of a Hollywood-based reserve unit of the Army Signal Corps, devoted to the production of training and information films.

While the committee hearings and the PCA struggled to restrain the production of increasingly overt pro-interventionist narratives, the war rumbled on. Eventually, the committee was rendered irrelevant by the bombing of the Pearl Harbor naval base by the Japanese in December 1941, after which point President Roosevelt mandated that Hollywood should play a clear role in mustering and maintaining support for the American war effort. To facilitate this new role, Roosevelt established the Office of War Information (OWI) in June 1942, and Hollywood's voluntary support for the war was formalised within a matter of months. The OWI was based in Hollywood and worked, much like the PCA (with which it often clashed), to ensure that Hollywood products met federally dictated requirements in the political commentary they offered. What once had been forbidden suddenly became the *sine qua non* of the industry. In the process, filmmakers were forced to rethink their understanding of Hollywood's social role and their place within it.

Perhaps unsurprisingly, war-related fiction films came to dominate production schedules in the early 1940s, as Hollywood sought to meet Roosevelt's requirements. The OWI never proved a particularly adept regulator of narrative content, but in many ways the creative impulse to design movies with a propagandising element had predated its establishment, and most Hollywood moguls required little encouragement to produce films that, in their eyes, combined national interests, high moral imperatives and decent financial returns.[74] In concert with several other bodies, including Zanuck's branch of the Army Signal Corps, the OWI was more effective in encouraging production of documentaries and information films.[75] Across genres, Guy Westwell argues that "the OWI required Hollywood to develop a new breed of heroism premised on the abnegation of self and an appreciation of the value of cooperative enterprise."[76] Numerous filmmakers were willingly co-opted into this project and were forced to reassess the nature of their work in the process.

Having defended Hollywood's right to produce socially resonant war movies, Daryl F. Zanuck was made a lieutenant colonel in the Army Signal Corps and charged with recording the Allied invasion of North Africa for a documentary propaganda movie, a task which took him to areas of heavy fighting. As the war drew to a close, Zanuck returned to Hollywood with a keen sense that the American audience would continue to expect new, more resonant forms of entertainment when the fighting finally ceased. He called a meeting of key personnel on the Fox back lot in 1943 and told them:

> The war is not yet over, but it soon will be. And when the boys come home from the battlefields overseas, you will find they have changed. They have learned things in Europe and the Far East. How other people live, for instance. How politics can change lives and start wars. How something happening in Yugoslavia or China or Singapore can affect the lives of a farmer and his family in Iowa or Nebraska. The war has made Americans think, and they aren't going to be interested in trivial, trashy movies any more. . . . They're coming back to us with new thoughts, new ideas and new hungers. It's up to us to satisfy them with our movies. They'll want to know more about our world, and this is where I think we at Fox have got to plan to measure up to their new maturity. We've got to start making movies that entertain but at the same time match the new climate of the times. Vital, thinking men's blockbusters. Big theme films.[77]

David Eldridge notes that "the characteristic Zanuck picture[s] of the 1930s had been . . . period films depicting small-town Americana."[78] The war had clearly broadened Zanuck's perceptions, and one can interpret the subsequent rise of the historical epic in Fox's schedules in the context of Zanuck's newfound commitment to 'big theme films.' Although the studio's releases didn't immediately fall into line with his vision, Fox found success in the 1950s with *The Robe*. Other roadshow epics such as *The Egyptian* (1954) and *Prince Valiant* (1954) followed, as well as the Hemingway adaptation *The Snows of Kilimanjaro* (1952) and the musical *The King and I* (1956), all prestigious films set in exotic locales. This trend continued well into the 1960s, when Zanuck seemed even more willing to engage directly with memories of World War II, in *The Longest Day*, *Tora! Tora! Tora!* and, in a different way, *The Sound of Music*. The two former films were characterised as pleas for 'preparedness' in a manner that closely resembled Zanuck's defence of Fox in 1941. Clearly, Zanuck's personal experiences of war had altered his understanding of Hollywood's social role, and Fox's epics were the result.

As a Jewish émigré from Germany, William Wyler had been involved with antifascist organisations well before the war started, and his convictions were readily apparent in his work.[79] Wyler's 1942 film *Mrs. Miniver* was a clear piece of pro-interventionist propaganda, and in the same year Wyler became a major in the Army Air Force, charged, like Zanuck, with making documentaries. He saw combat and produced the acclaimed *Memphis Belle* (1944). Then, when the war finished, Wyler's next fictional film was *The Best Year of Our Lives*, which dramatised the plight of combat veterans re-integrating into postwar American society. It won seven Oscars, including Best Picture and Best Director, and it was the highest grossing film of the decade, with domestic rentals of $10.4 million. Martin Winkler has also suggested that *Ben-Hur* speaks on Nazism and the Holocaust in a subtly related fashion.[80]

Alternatively, at sixty, Cecil B. DeMille was considered too old to fight when the war broke out. Instead, he contributed by making patriotic fictional films like *The Story of Dr. Wassell* (1944). Although DeMille was not calling on personal experiences of war for his later work, the 1956 version of *The Ten Commandments* is clearly a more politically meaningful and internationally inclusive take on the story than that featured in the 1923 version. The creative climate had changed in the intervening years, and *The Ten Commandments* had become a story of nations in conflict rather than a specifically American moral allegory.

In the words of Richard Maltby, "[E]ven in the reactionary climate of the Cold War the ground gained by liberals during World War II would not be surrendered."[81] The war effectively handed filmmakers a license to produce more socially meaningful films, which was formalised during the 1948 antitrust hearings, which in turn led to the movies being brought under First Amendment protection (finalised in 1953). By categorising cinema as *free* speech, the federal government effectively mandated that filmmaking was a *form of speech*—a public expression of individual ideas. The conscious social significance and allegorical resonance of the historical epic film embodied a newly 'politicised' understanding of filmmakers and filmmaking loosely shared by government, industry and audiences. The grandiose statements about history, religion, politics and society informing the epics of DeMille, Wyler and Zanuck were not necessarily new. What had changed was that such films could be presented *to audiences* as politically meaningful statements. Certainly, the delegates sitting on the HUAC in the late 1940s and early 1950s assumed without question that movies were forms of individual political expression. HUAC attempted to combat what it perceived as a pernicious Communist influence, but the committee never directly suggested that the presence of politically 'subversive' content was merely a regulatory failure on the part of the PCA. Even as it attempted to silence the expression of a leftist political view, HUAC implicitly treated the movies as a form of individual expression. Another sign of the close links between the political climate and the historical epic film came as the Hollywood blacklist was finally discarded. The writer Dalton Trumbo, an original member of the so-called 'Hollywood Ten' identified in 1947, had been working in Hollywood under pseudonyms throughout the 1950s. However, his pariah status was effectively revoked in 1960, when director Otto Preminger and star/producer Kirk Douglas ensured that Trumbo received credits for his work on *Exodus* and *Spartacus* respectively. It was no coincidence that Trumbo's politically charged return to respectability occurred in association with the epic film. Following World War II, forthright claims to relevance and significance were no longer taboo, and, as we shall see, viewers of all ages in the 1950s and 1960s were actively encouraged to interpret Hollywood's films (especially historical epics) as amalgamations of entertainment, commentary and educational content.

3. Epics and Audiences

In his review of *The Ten Commandments* for the *New York Times*, Bosley Crowther wrote:

> Against the raw news of the conflict between Egypt and Israel—a conflict that has its preamble in the Book of Exodus—Cecil B. DeMille's *The Ten Commandments* was given its world premiere last night at the Criterion Theatre, and the coincidence was profound. For Mr DeMille's latest tells an arresting story of Moses, the ancient Israelite who was a slave with his people in Egypt and who struggled to set them free.[82]

Crowther's immediate attempt to relate *The Ten Commandments* to the ongoing Suez crisis is a sign that, by 1956, critics and audiences were willingly looking to the mainstream Hollywood epic for meaningful commentary on contemporary events. That DeMille's film had not been conceived of as a response to the Suez crisis was of little concern. Rather, Crowther's review suggested that *The Ten Commandments* could aid viewers in their understanding of the history behind current events— that the film was an essentially meaningful and educative cinematic experience. Of course, DeMille had encouraged this kind of interpretation via his onscreen prologue, but Crowther's response helps us to see that some audiences, having come from watching the daily news or reading his review, would presumably have interpreted the film within the terms established by DeMille. As Crowther put it, "This is unquestionably a picture to which one must bring something more than a mere wish for entertainment in order to get a full effect from it. But for those to whom its fundamentalism will be entirely credible, it should be altogether thrilling and perhaps even spiritually profound."[83]

A more overt use of political allegory and social comment was only one consequence of the increased license that World War II and First Amendment protection conferred upon mainstream Hollywood productions. In a climate where filmmakers were more likely to view mainstream cinema as inherently resonant, filmmakers also became more likely to perceive their movies as equivalent in some respects to the work of academic historians. David Eldridge argues, "[T]he 1950s witnessed a growing awareness in Hollywood that the work of professional historians also involved fictional construction and imagination. Naïve as the insight might have been, it further encouraged filmmakers to pose as 'public historians,' who could displace 'dry and dusty' academics."[84] Although the 'Hollywood version' of historical events might deviate wildly from accepted academic accounts (usually for reasons of entertainment value), some filmmakers nevertheless came to see their role as equivalent to educators. To make films about the past, especially films as self-consciously 'important' as historical epics was, in essence, to tell audiences about the past—to make sense of history in a meaningful yet creative fashion.

Educative significance was also attached to epics by the employment of academic consultants during the production process. One such was Henry Noerdlinger, who worked closely with DeMille on *Samson and Delilah* and *The Ten Commandments*. Noerdlinger's research for the latter film was published as *Moses and Egypt: The Documentation to the Motion Picture* The Ten Commandments—a book which was supposed to function as an equivalent to the list of sources and citations that one might expect from an academic work. Alan Nadel has argued that *Moses and Egypt* is ultimately very weak academia, but for DeMille the publication aided the popular perception of his meaning as an educative experience amongst key audience demographics—"the educated clergy, Sunday school teachers, newspapers and magazine editors."[85]

Noerdlinger's private correspondence with DeMille and other studio executives also reveals just how the historian and the filmmakers understood their work. Writing to his employers about a rare negative review in *Time* magazine, which described *The Ten Commandments* as 'the most vulgar movie ever made,' Noerdliner quoted the *OED* definition of vulgar as "of or pertaining to the people." Therefore, he argued, "'The most vulgar movie ever made' means a film made for the widest possible dissemination, to be understood by all the peoples of the world who have seen it or will see it. In that sense, *The Ten Commandments* is vulgar."[86] Effectively, Noerdlinger suggested that DeMille was engaged in a mainstream historical project that sought to educate, but not alienate, audiences across the world. So how was this project reflected in the publicity materials that mediated between filmmakers and their audiences?

According to the press kit that accompanied the release of *Ben-Hur*:

> Since the opening of *Ben-Hur* special student performances throughout the country have proved a lucrative source of additional revenue. Today, more than ever before, educators, religious leaders and parents are seeking entertainment of a high moral and educational nature for the young people they are guiding. *Ben-Hur* is that kind of entertainment, and for this reason your welcome at various schools and youth organizations will be a hearty one.[87]

The pamphlet went on to suggest various ways that exhibitors might attract the interests of Scout groups, Girl Guides, church youth groups and schools of all sorts. Included were sample letters addressed to school heads and advertisements for a study guide that accompanied the film's release. This study guide was written by a Dr. Joseph Mersaud and was described by MGM as "one of the most complete pamphlets of its kind ever prepared."[88] The press notes unashamedly declared that "it will lend itself to full and interesting classroom discussions of the film."[89]

Similar materials accompanied the release of most roadshow epics. As well as *Moses and Egypt*, *The Ten Commandments* was promoted by another all-important study guide and a book entitled *The Ten Commandments for Children*, which "features the figure of Charlton Heston as Moses on its cover, together with picture credits prominently displayed. In addition, inside front cover carries a quotation from Cecil B. DeMille," according to the press notes.[90] Children were also appealed to with a colouring pencil set and book, "manufactured in three denominations—Catholic, Protestant and Jewish."[91] Promotional material provided by the studios also usually included a colouring contest, which, the press kit for *Samson and Delilah* claimed, "should certainly appeal to children and head them towards your theatre to see the film."[92] A line drawing of a Japanese pilot presiding over a row of bombed aircraft carriers was used to promote *Tora! Tora! Tora!* "As well as attracting the all-family audience, the painting block illustrates the fantastic action sequences of the film," ran the descriptive spiel.[93]

Maria Wyke has shown that study guides and other promotional material accompanying the release of DeMille's 1934 *Cleopatra* made overt the film's underlying concern about women's roles in 1930s America.[94] Additionally, Richard Maltby has argued that 1930s study guides "encouraged the bourgeois audience to recognise Hollywood's cultural respectability."[95] The material used to promote many of the roadshow epics in the 1950s performed a similar function. Much of it was directed at schoolchildren and reinforced claims that these films were educative, religious and historical experiences. In this way, the act of visiting the cinema and watching *Ben-Hur* or *The Ten Commandments* was framed as something more than entertainment. Press kits, study guides, games and outfits, promotions aimed at school groups and children's books all targeted young moviegoers and are clear evidence that the studios considered children an essential, and valuable, segment of the audience. These materials also provided the context in which the films were supposed to be experienced. Even before they arrived at the cinema, MGM hoped that children would have become aware of *Ben-Hur* either at school or at church.

In the 1950s, children probably made up a sizable segment of the audience. It is difficult to find reliable surveys for the period, but Garth Jowett has compiled an overview of audiences in 1957, when *The Ten Commandments* was still being roadshown, and one can assume that his findings are fairly representative of general cinemagoing habits in America across the mid-to-late 1950s. The survey suggests that moviegoers under the age of nineteen accounted for 52 percent of weekly cinema admissions.[96] Peter Krämer has analysed the revenues generated by *Ben-Hur*, which made up 7.6 percent of the industry's takings in a year when 534 films were released.[97] Wyler's film was far and away the breakaway hit of the year, which was highly likely to have been viewed by most, if not all, of the young viewers who continued to go to the cinema regularly throughout the 1950s and 1960s. As we saw earlier in this chapter, epics were designed to attract family groups and infrequent cinema attendees. The educative elements associated with these films served to encourage such groups, which could easily justify an expensive trip to the movies as a valuable educative experience for old and young alike. Within this diverse audience were children like Mel Gibson and Steven Spielberg, members of a group targeted by the studios who may have seen the film in a school party if they hadn't gone with their families.[98] Young viewers were also made aware, through marketing and through a general climate of public debate, some of which was filtered back to them by study guides and studio-sanctioned classroom discussion, that these films were important, and that they were educational as much as they were exciting.

There is, then, compelling evidence that roadshow epics were frequently received in the same sort of spirit that they were made, as serious social, educative and spiritual comments, and that marketing efforts played a key role in fostering this perception. As we will see throughout this book, promotional efforts geared towards children also had one unexpected side effect—by watching epics in the 1950s, a future generation of filmmakers were learning that making movies—specifically large-scale historical movies—could be a valuable social activity.

4. The Hollywood Epic in Decline

By the end of the 1960s, the epic film's status as a dominant trend was coming to an end. At an industrial level the cycle was compromised by overproduction, as both Sheldon Hall and Peter Krämer have demonstrated.[99] Because epics were so massively expensive, they needed a massive market share in order to break even (something approaching the 7.6 percent of total takings received by *Ben-Hur*). In the mid-1960s, too many epics were produced in the hope of capitalising on the success of two key roadshows, *Doctor Zhivago* and *The Sound of Music*.[100] In the meantime, the overall market declined, which meant that there was a smaller audience for a larger number of hugely expensive films.[101] Even if one film broke away from the rest, the studios had too much money tied up in too many epics for the entire exercise to be financially viable. Famous 'flops' like *Cleopatra* and *Tora! Tora! Tora!* were actually successful at the box office but had been so costly to produce that it was difficult for them to make a profit.[102]

Furthermore, American films in the 1970s were becoming more focused on specifically American subjects, and budgets were diminishing.[103] The economic crises of the late 1960s and a broader relaxation of censorship codes opened up a space for more 'edgy' subject material, addressing a youthful cine-literate audience—a period sometimes known as the "Hollywood Renaissance." The younger generation of filmmakers associated with this movement exhibited little interest in the kinds of epics that had defined the 1950s and 1960s, and the genre quickly came to be seen by some as an example of an older, patrician industry, out of keeping with more liberal times. The practice of roadshowing was also in decline, as city centre theatres became increasingly shabby, dangerous spaces, and in the multiplexes that arose to replace roadshow theatres, 'specialness' was a far more difficult quality to realise. [104] Such spaces were also considerably less appealing for the families that had previously made up the epic film's core audience. The epic film quickly declined in production volume and popularity, although three related cycles remained significant after 1970, which can retrospectively be labelled 'military procedural epics', 'revisionist epics' and 'fantasy epics'. Military procedural epics documented key events of World War II in a manner that resembled *The Longest Day* (1962) and *Tora! Tora! Tora!*. The cycle included *Midway* (1976) and *A Bridge Too Far* (1977). Such films appeared very occasionally throughout the 1970s, but none achieved particularly high revenues, and a lasting cycle was not established. Alternatively, 'revisionist epics' employed the historical setting and resonant thematic structure of the historical epic to produce dark, violent and pessimistic visions of the past. They included *The Godfather* (1972), *The Deer Hunter* (1978), *Apocalypse Now* (1979) and the western epic *Heaven's Gate* (Michael Cimino, 1980). Coppola's and Cimino's first films were resounding commercial successes, but, again, revisionist epics failed to consistently appeal to audiences.[105] Finally, a series of science fiction and fantasy films retained a focus on important events, expensively realised, which can retrospectively be seen as epic. However, none were labelled as epics on release, and although *Star Wars* (1977) and *Close Encounters of the Third Kind* (1977) proved enormously popular and influential, they failed to spark any obviously epic cycles. None of these films were conceived of, or received, in the same manner as the roadshow epics, despite extended running times. Epics of all sorts became highly exceptional and unprofitable features in production schedules over the course of the 1970s, and the commercial failure of *Heaven's Gate* in 1980 effectively marked the end of any related cycles for almost a decade.

Conclusion

The next chapter will begin to detail the emergence of an epic cycle in the early 1990s, by looking in more detail at Kevin Costner's *Dances with Wolves*. However, a particularly telling illustration of the connection between the epics of the 1950s and those of the 1990s came on 17 January 1994, during the release of Steven Spielberg's Holocaust epic,

Schindler's List. At a screening of the film organised by Castlemont High School in Oakland, California, a number of students were ejected from the auditorium by the theatre owner after they reportedly laughed during one of the many scenes of Holocaust violence. Over the next few days, Castlemont became the centre of national media interest, and stories about the incident appeared in newspapers across the USA. The film's director was apparently paying attention, and on April twelfth of that year, Spielberg went to Castlemont High School and told the students, "I was thrown out of *Ben-Hur* when I was a kid for talking. I think we have to put this one under 'privileges of youth.'"[106] Despite his conciliatory tone, Spielberg was accompanied by the then governor of California, Pete Wilson. The pair used their visit to announce "the creation of an educational program that will combine teaching about the Holocaust with the showing of Mr. Spielberg's movie to high school students, called the *Schindler's List* Project."[107] It was also reported that twenty-five other states had expressed interest in the project, which involved several hours of study in the classroom followed by a visit to see *Schindler's List* at a private cinema screening. Sixteen thousand high school students participated in the program in California alone.

It is certainly interesting that Spielberg chose to compare the laughter during *Schindler's List* with his own experience of talking during *Ben-Hur*.[108] In essence, the director suggested that his sombre epic and Wyler's widescreen spectacle offered similar experiences—both were, in his mind, solemn, culturally valuable historical films, which required 'appropriate' forms of audience response.[109] More significantly, the '*Schindler's List* Project' worked to position Spielberg's film in an educational context, just as the study guides attached to earlier epics had done. As with the epics of the 1950s and 1960s, providing an educational frame was not just extremely efficacious marketing—it was also a sincere expression of Spielberg's creative agenda. *Schindler's List* sought to edify and educate audiences, and the very fact that Spielberg went out of his way to visit Castlemont High School demonstrated the extent to which he did not want his work treated as routine entertainment. By effectively 'forgiving' the offending students, Spielberg was assuming the role of historical commentator in a manner that closely paralleled earlier efforts by DeMille, Wyler, Zanuck, et al. To watch *Schindler's List*, Spielberg obliquely stated, was to learn something.[110] The cinema owner was one of many who bought into Spielberg's project, and he immediately perceived the students' laughter as an inappropriate form of cultural transgression. They had so transcended preferred reactions to *Schindler's List* that they were excluded from the screening, and the media interest that swirled briefly around the controversy spoke of a broader public consensus that regarded *Schindler's List* as a serious work of popular history (discussed further in chapter 3). More than anything, the furore surrounding the Castlemont incident can be taken as a clear sign that, by 1994, historical epics were being taken seriously by viewers and filmmakers once more.

Spielberg's attempt to link his own memories of watching *Ben-Hur* as a child to the experiences of contemporary children watching *Schindler's List* today brings to light the connections between past and present cycles of historical epics. Clearly, Spielberg's perception of mainstream cinema, and the potentialities of filmmaking, had been shaped by a broader confluence of economic, creative and logistical factors that favoured epics in the 1950s and 1960s. Furthermore, when Spielberg achieved a position of power in the film industry equivalent to, if not greater than, that occupied by Wyler, DeMille and Zanuck, he set about producing films that at times closely resembled those of Wyler et al. Similar sentiments motivated a diverse group of other filmmakers. Perhaps the most overt example of a filmmaker returning to his youth, literally recreating a defunct cinematic world, can be seen in the film that effectively sparked the 1990s revival. In *Dances with Wolves*, Kevin Costner starred in an epic game of 'cowboys and Indians,' and a second sustained cycle of epics was initiated.

Notes

1. John Brodie, "*Braveheart* resurrects the epic," *Variety* 26 Mar. 1996, 75.

2. Todd Keith, *Kevin Costner: The Unauthorised Biography* (London: Ikonprint, 1991), 19.

3. Quoted in Steven S. Caton, *Lawrence of Arabia: A Film's Anthropology* (Berkeley: University of California Press, 1999), 3.

4. Joseph McBride, *Steven Spielberg: A Biography* (London: Faber and Faber, 1997), 81.

5. The *New York Times* has noted of Bruckheimer and Spiegel, "Asked if he stands in that narrative tradition, Mr. Bruckheimer demurred: 'You'd have to say that. I hope someday I'd achieve that, yeah. To be able to tell those big stories.'" See Todd S. Purdum, "Jerry Bruckheimer, A Showman Turns to War to Knock 'em Dead," *New York Times* 20 May 2001, 4.

6. Martin Scorsese and Michael Henry Wilson, *A Personal Journey with Martin Scorsese through American Movies* (London: Faber and Faber, 1997), 87.

7. Scorsese and Wilson, 75.

8. David Eldridge, *Hollywood's History Films* (London: I.B. Tauris, 2006), 1.

9. All figures relating to attendance in this paragraph, unless otherwise stated, are taken from Joel W. Finler. *The Hollywood Story* 3rd ed. (London: Wallflower, 2003), 378.

10. U.S. Census Bureau, *Statistical Abstract of the United States 2003*, obtained via download from http://www.census.gov.

11. Finler, 376.

12. Ibid., 379.

13. See Robert Sklar, "'The Lost Audience': 1950s Spectatorship and Historical Reception Studies," in Melvyn Stokes and Richard Maltby, eds., *Identifying Hollywood's Audiences: Cultural Identity and the Movies* (London: BFI, 1999).

14. For a full list of the requirements of the consent decrees, see Michael Conant, *Antitrust in the Motion Picture Industry* (New York: Arno, 1978), 98–99.

15. Finler, 364–365.

16. Ibid., 366–367.

17. Rentals are the percentage of the box office gross that goes back to the distributor (usually around 50 percent of the total box office gross). Unless otherwise stated, all figures in this chapter refer to rentals.

18. For financial data, see Finler 357. The attempt to distribute *Duel in the Sun* independently was a stark demonstration of why the majors remained major. Despite the film's massive rentals, the cost of distributing one film alone ruined Selznick. See David Thomson, *Showman: The Life and Times of David O. Selznick* (New York: Knopf, 1992).

19. Finler, 357.

20. For more details on the history of roadshowing, see Sheldon Hall, "Tall Revenue Features: The Genealogy of the Modern Blockbuster," in Steve Neale, ed., *Genre and Contemporary Hollywood* (London: BFI, 2002), 12–15.

21. Sheldon Hall estimates that on occasions the distributor could demand rentals of up to 90 percent after the theatre's operating costs were deducted. See Hall (2002), 14.

22. See Sheldon Hall, *Hard Ticket Giants: Hollywood Blockbusters in the Widescreen Era*, PhD Dissertation, University of East Anglia, 2000.

23. See John Belton, *Widescreen Cinema* (Cambridge, MA: Harvard University Press, 1992).

24. Figures from William D. Romanowski, *Pop Culture Wars: Religion and the Role of Entertainment in American Life* (Downer's Grove, IL: Intervarsity, 1996), 188.

25. Romanowski, 188.

26. See Christopher Anderson, *Hollywood TV: The Studio System in the Fifties* (Austin: University of Texas Press, 1994).

27. Richard Maltby, "'Nobody Knows Everything': Post-classical histriographies and consolidated entertainment," in Steve Neale and Murray Smith, eds., *Contemporary Hollywood Cinema* (London: BFI, 1998), 31.

28. Finler, 358.

29. Paul Monaco, *The Sixties: 1960-1969* (New York: Scribner's, 2001), 11–15.

30. Tino Balio, "Retrenchment, Reappraisal and Reorganisation, 1948–" in Tino Balio, ed., *The American Movie Industry* rev. ed. (Madison: University of Wisconsin Press, 1985), 408.

31. Thomas Schatz, *Boom and Bust: The American Cinema in the 1940s* (New York: Scribner's, 1997), 393–394.

32. Schatz (1997), 394.

33. Finler, 357–358.

34. "Biblical Film Cycle Hits New High; 12 Upcoming," unpaginated clipping without author details, *Variety*, 17 June 1953, obtained from the 'Religious Films' file, AMPAS.

35. For an interesting analysis of these early biblical epics, see Thoms H. Pauly, "The Way to Salvation: The Hollywood Blockbuster of the 1950s," *Prospects: An Annual of American Cultural Studies* 5 (1980), 467–487.

36. Finler, 358.

37. Ibid., 358.

38. See Hall (2000), 8–13.

39. See ibid., 249–250.

40. Peter Krämer, *The New Hollywood: From* Bonnie and Clyde *to* Star Wars (London: Wallflower, 2005), 23.

41. The full inflation-adjusted chart is available at Box Office Mojo, http://www.boxofficemojo.com/alltime/adjusted.htm.

42. Tino Balio, *United Artists: The Company Built by the Stars* (Madison: University of Wisconsin Press, 1976).

43. See David Bordwell, Janet Staiger and Kristen Thompson, *The Classical Hollywood Cinema: Film Style and Mode of Production to 1960* (London: Routledge, 1985), 330.

44. Eldridge, 55.

45. Ibid., 78.

46. Memo from William Wyler, dated 30 Mar. 1960, the William Wyler Collection (53), Box 20, File 8, UCLA. Subsequent quotes from the same source.

47. Transcribed interview with William Wyler, Ronald L. Davies Oral History Collection File 175, AMPAS, 6–7.

48. See comments made by Gore Vidal in the *Ben-Hur: The Making of an Epic* documentary accompanying the 2001 DVD release of *Ben-Hur*. For a discussion of homosexuality in the film, which uses Vidal's comments as a starting point, see Leon Hunt, "What Are Big Boys made of? *Spartacus, El Cid* and the Male Epic," in Pat Kirkham and Janet Thumin, eds., *You Tarzan: Masculinity, Movies and Men* (London: Lawrence and Wishart, 1993).

49. Transcribed interview with Charlton Heston, Ronald L. Davis Oral History Collection, File 464, AMPAS, 53.

50. Karl Tunberg, 'Original' Screenplay for *Ben-Hur*, dated 20 July 1954, Turner-MGM Script Collection, AMPAS, 170.

51. Blood is very important throughout the film. Ben-Hur describes the corruption of Messala as an affliction of the blood, and the influence of Rome is repeatedly figured in similar terms. This emphasised an underlying preoccupation with race in the film that has yet to be explored in any detail by scholars.

52. Memo to Sam Zimbalist from 'EGD' dated 11 Oct. 1954: 'MPAA' File Collection, AMPAS.

53. Melani McAlister, *Epic Encounters: Culture, Media and U.S. Interests in the Middle East* (Berkeley: University of California Press, 2001), 78.

54. See also Maria Wyke, *Projecting the Past: Ancient Rome, Cinema and History* (London: Routledge, 1997), and Martin M. Winkler, "The Roman Empire in American Cinema after 1945," in Sandra T. Joshel, Margaret Malamud and Donald T. McGuire Jr., eds., *Imperial Projections: Ancient Rome in Modern Popular Culture* (Baltimore, MD: Johns Hopkins University Press, 2001), 65–76.

55. Richard Maltby, *Hollywood Cinema* 2nd ed. (Oxford: Blackwell, 2003), 305.

56. Wyke, 70.

57. See Yosefa Loshitzky, "National Rebirth as a Movie: Otto Preminger's *Exodus,*" *National Identities* 4, no. 2 (2002), 119–131.

58. Alan Nadel, "God's Law and the Wide Screen: *The Ten Commandments* as Cold War 'Epic,'" *PMLA* 108, no. 10 (1993), 416.

59. Unpublished interview notes by Hedda Hopper, dated 10 Dec. 1957, 'Cecil B. DeMille' File, The Hedda Hopper Collection, AMPAS.

60. Anon., "DeMille Remake Recalls Silent Era; UA New Policy Set," *Los Angeles Times* 1 June 1952, Screen, 4.

61. Jon Solomon, *The Ancient World in the Cinema* 2nd ed. (New Haven and London: Yale University Press, 2001), 13.

62. For more on the relative independence of DeMille see Finler, 58.

63. See "*The Ten Commandments*: A Tentative Script for LIMITED DISTRIBUTION" dated 1 May 1954, the Paramount Script Collection, AMPAS.

64. Nadel, 416.

65. Darryl F. Zanuck, advertisement entitled "Why *Tora! Tora! Tora!?*" *New York Times* 16 June 1969, 10.

66. See Lawrence H. Suid, *Guts and Glory: The Making of the American Military Image in Film* rev. ed. (Lexington: University Press of Kentucky, 2002), 293.

67. Darryl F. Zanuck, Telegram to Elmo Williams dated 24 Mar. 1969, The Elmo Williams Collection, file 157, AMPAS.

68. Eldridge, 78–101.

69. Maltby (2003), 273.

70. Ibid., (2003), 280.

71. Quoted in Thomas Schatz, "World War II and the War Film," in Nick Browne, ed., *Refiguring American Film Genres: History and Theory* (Berkeley: University of California Press, 1998), 99–100.

72. Quoted in Maltby (2003), 281.

73. Ibid.

74. Schatz (1998), 107.

75. For a detailed account of the OWI's documentary traditions, see Ian Scott, "From Toscanini to Tennessee: Robert Risking, the OWI and the Construction of American Propaganda in World War II," *Journal of American Studies* 40, no. 2 (2006), 347–366.

76. Guy Westwell, *War Cinema: Hollywood on the Front Line* (London: Wallflower, 2006), 31.

77. Quoted in Leonard Mosley, *Zanuck: The Rise and Fall of Hollywood's Last Tycoon* (London: Granada, 1984), 289–290.

78. Eldridge, 50.

79. Martin Winkler notes that Wyler's wife had described him as "a premature anti-fascist" in the 1930s, that Wyler had a relative in the Dachau concentration camp during the war, and that he altered the script of *Mrs. Miniver* (1942) to play up this angle. See Winkler, 66.

80. See Winkler, 65–76.

81. Maltby (2003), 285.

82. Bosley Crowther, rev. of *The Ten Commandments*, *New York Times* 9 Nov. 1956, 35.

83. Ibid., 35.

84. Eldridge, 8.

85. Quotes are from Eldridge, 148.

86. Henry Noerdlinger, Letter to Art Arthur, dated 8 Nov. 1956, The Henry S. Noerdlinger Collection, Folder 6, AMPAS.

87. MGM Pictures, *Ben-Hur* press kit, BFIL, 35.

88. Ibid., 34.

89. Ibid.

90. Paramount Pictures, *The Ten Commandments* press kit, BFIL, 8.

91. Ibid.

92. *Samson and Delilah* press kit, 4.

93. Twentieth Century Fox Pictures, *Tora! Tora! Tora!* press kit, BFIL, unpaginated.

94. Wyke, 92.

95. Richard Maltby, "Sticks, Hicks and Flaps: Classical Hollywood's Generic Conception of Its Audience," in Melvyn Stokes and Richard Maltby, eds., *Identifying Hollywood's Audiences: Cultural Identity and the Movies* (London: BFI, 1999), 38.

96. According to Jowett's sources, 16 percent of total admissions were under nine years of age, 15 percent were between ten and fourteen, and 21 percent were aged fifteen to nineteen. See Garth Jowett, *Film: The Democratic Art* (Boston: Little Brown, 1976), 478.

97. Figures taken from Finler, 358, 364 and 377.

98. Viewers' memories of watching *The Ten Commandments* compiled in Tom Stempel's interviews with ordinary American moviegoers reinforce this view, and several refer to viewing the film as a family experience. Tom Stempel, *American Audiences on Movies and Moviegoing* (Lexington: University of Kentucky Press, 2001), 24–28.

99. See Hall (2000) and Krämer (2005).

100. For further details see James Russell, "Debts, Disasters and Mega-Musicals: The Decline of the Studio System," in Linda Ruth Williams and Michael Hammond, eds., *Contemporary American Cinema* (London: McGraw-Hill, 2006), 41–61.

101. Average weekly attendance continued to decline throughout the 1960s, dropping from 27 million in 1961 to 16 million in 1972. See Finler, 378–379.

102. *Cleopatra* ultimately took $26 million and was the highest grossing film of 1963, and *Tora! Tora! Tora!* took $13.7 million, making it the seventh highest grossing film of 1970. See Finler, 359.

103. Krämer (2005), 40–47.

104. See Douglas Gomery, "Motion Picture Exhibition in 1970s America," in David O. Cook, *Lost Illusions: American Cinema in the Shadow of Watergate and Vietnam 1970–1979* (Berkeley: University of California Press, 2000), 397–398.

105. See Michael Hammond, "Some Smothering Dreams: The Combat Film in Contemporary Hollywood," in Neale (2002), 64–65.

106. Susan Spann, "Laughter at Film Brings Spielberg Visit," *New York Times* 13 April 1994, B11.

107. Spann, B11.

108. Joseph McBride reports that Spielberg liked *Ben-Hur*, and makes no mention of him being ejected from the cinema. See McBride, 81.

109. There are also deeper parallels: The strong pro-Zionist elements of *Ben-Hur* also find expression in *Schindler's List*.

110. Further evidence of Spielberg's attempts to influence public reaction to *Schindler's List* appeared in a *Los Angeles Times* article, which reported that marketing efforts had "carefully position[ed] it in the marketplace as an important 'experience' rather than a movie." Claudia Eller, "Will *List* Speak for Itself?" *Los Angeles Times* 22 Nov. 1993, F1. See also chapter 3 of this book.

~2~

The Epic, the Western and
Dances with Wolves (1990)

I t is difficult to pinpoint the exact moment when a film cycle begins. Usually, the coexistence and interaction of different cycles means that, at the moment of its release, a film may not be presented in the same way that it is subsequently classified. For instance, Edwin S. Porter's silent short *The Great Train Robbery* (1903) is often described as the 'first' western movie, the moment when a fledgling American movie industry first adopted the conventions of western novels and stage plays. However, Charles Musser has shown that the film was conceived of and marketed as a mixture of railway travel movie and violent crime movie, both popular cycles at the time.[1] As Rick Altman notes, "[I]t wasn't until much later in the decade that the western took on the self-conscious trappings of an accepted genre."[2] When we look back, we can see that *The Great Train Robbery* brought together elements in a way that are now recognisably intrinsic to the western movie, but the film was not conceived of in this way at the time of its release. The same is also true of the historical epic in the 1990s. The epic did not spring back into life immediately, with all of its narrational conventions in place. Instead a series of related releases sparked the epic's revival. It was a slow process, with many false starts and dead ends, but it began with the release of *Dances with Wolves* in 1990.

Dances with Wolves opened on 9 November 1990 and went on to gross $184.2 million at the domestic box office, and a further $240 million overseas, on an $18 million budget.[3] It won seven Academy Awards, including Best Picture and Best Director.[4] This critical and commercial success proved pivotal for the revival of the Hollywood historical epic. Since the early 1970s, recognisably epic films had all but vanished from Hollywood's theatrical production schedules. Although *Dances with*

Wolves was an American film, with a major star attached, it had originated outside the mainstream production complex. The high box office
returns generated by the film across the world provided the first indication that a nostalgic epic, constructed to resemble the films that director
Kevin Costner had loved as a child, could prove a substantial success
with audiences. As a result, the film inspired a series of imitations and
helped foster a climate where individual filmmakers with an interest in
the epic were able to find funding for similar projects from the major studios. Although more limited in scale, the situation was not entirely dissimilar from the climate of the late 1940s and early 1950s, when Zanuck,
Wyler, DeMille and others had slowly gained the power to realise their
most grandiose cinematic visions. *Dances with Wolves* occupies a related
position, when the commercial prospects of epics appeared to shift.
Furthermore, Costner's attempt to produce an 'old-fashioned' western
epic provides a fitting illustration of the nostalgia for the breakthrough
hits of the roadshow era, which fuelled the production of epics in the
early 1990s. Kevin Costner's desire to revisit his own memories of 1950s
film culture was mirrored in a narrative that seemed to duplicate his nostalgia at the level of allegory.

As well as exploring Costner's agenda, this chapter assesses the pivotal
role that *Dances with Wolves* played in broader production trends. The
first section examines the fortunes of epic and western films over the
course of the 1970s and 1980s. As well as looking at the declining theatrical presence of such releases, the section explores the growing profile of
epics on television throughout the period. A second section looks at the
origins of *Dances with Wolves*, and a third analyses the links between
Costner's nostalgic filmmaking project and the nostalgic story of the
film itself. A fourth section then looks at the generic terminology used
in the marketing and reception of the film and moves to examine the
various cycles that sprung up in the wake of *Dances with Wolves*. In these
later sections I focus on critical uses of generic terminology because they
provide an insight into the ways that Costner's film was interpreted by
viewers and by other filmmakers, thus defining the generic qualities of
films produced in imitation, in accordance with Rick Altman's producer's
game. Altman has argued that shifts in the uses of generic terminology
are important moments in the establishment of production cycles.[5] On
its release, *Dances with Wolves*' generic status was up for grabs. Rapidly,
the marketing campaign and movie critics began to favour the label 'epic'
over 'western'. To understand why this occurred, one must know the
industrial associations attached to both of these terms. Before the impact

of Costner's film can be assessed, the fortunes of the epic and western films in the aftermath of the roadshow era must be examined.

1. Westerns and Epics, 1970 to 1990

The thousands of films set on the American frontier after 1860, which together effectively constitute the 'western,' arguably form the most long-lived of Hollywood genres. Cycles of western-themed movies occupied a particularly privileged position in Hollywood's repertoire of genres throughout the 1930s, 1940s and 1950s, when mainstream western pictures coexisted with a vast mass of 'B' westerns—shorter, cheaper productions, designed to run alongside a more prestigious 'A' picture. However, the attempts of writers such as John Cawelti, Will Wright and others to treat the western as one century-long storytelling tradition, with thematic ebbs and tides that reflect broader social and cultural shifts, invariably fail to acknowledge the diverse range of subtly different western cycles that have coexisted throughout Hollywood's history.[6] Like the epic, the western is a steadily evolving conceptual category, embodied by a mass of coexisting cycles that have been designed to capitalise on presumed audience preference. Of these cycles, Sheldon Hall has noted that "epic westerns are generally the most conscious of the genre's basis in an actual, as opposed to mythic, past," but, with the exception of *How the West Was Won* (1962), very few "westerns of authentically epic scale and ambition" have ever been released.[7] Significantly, Kevin Costner repeatedly cited *How the West Was Won* as the key influence on *Dances with Wolves*.

Westerns remained relatively popular during the 1950s and 1960s—partly because the studios maintained the visibility of the genre by selling many of their old 'B' westerns for television exhibition and initiated production of television serials such as *Wagon Train* (1957–1965). However, the number of western movies in production declined steadily throughout the 1970s—although not with the same degree of rapidity that marked the demise of the 1950s and 1960s epic.[8] Initially, the western genre proved attractive to a new generation of filmmakers, many of whom tried to update the traditional western by altering and subverting its constituent elements. David A. Cook identifies four different western cycles that emerged as a result. Aside from the 'Traditional Western,' the 1970s also saw the emergence of 'Vietnam Westerns,' 'Modernist or Anti-Westerns' and 'Comic or Parodic Westerns.'[9] As the labels suggest, these films often attempted to revise the history of the West featured in many earlier cycles of the western movie.[10] A case in point is Arthur Penn's *Little Big Man* (1970), which Margo Kasdan and Susan Tavernetti claim "inverts the common mythologies of the American frontier usually presented in the western film genre" by presenting the Indians as "victims of malevolent treatment by the United States Army."[11] In *Little Big Man*, the Indians are heroes and the Americans are murderous invaders, a theme that resonates in *Dances with Wolves*. However, as Kasdan and Tavernetti note, Penn's film is more "comic and ironic" in tone than Costner's stately, tasteful and more recognisably epic approach.[12]

Such productions remained a part of the Hollywood firmament until 1980, when the fortunes of the genre were tainted by the failure of Michael Cimino's *Heaven's Gate*. Stephen Prince has written, in his study of 1980s Hollywood, that this film was "widely regarded by the industry as [a] test of the genre's viability and [its] fate was interpreted as evidence of an exhausted market."[13] *Heaven's Gate* mixed epic and western elements in the story of a clash between landowners and cattle ranchers in 1890s Wyoming. It cost $35 million to make and $6 million to market, but it received disastrous reviews, and by 1983 it had only returned $1.5 million.[14] As we have seen, the loss effectively destroyed United Artists as a film distributor, and it entirely discouraged other studios from bankrolling expensive epics or westerns.[15] Twenty years later, *Heaven's Gate* remains an anecdotal yardstick for the financial ruin that epics can represent for their investors, as chapter 6 will demonstrate.

The more marginal, relatively low-budget, overseas-funded historical epics released subsequently in the 1980s did not compare, in terms of theme or spectacle, to the extravagance of the 1950s cycle and seemed to confirm industry assumptions that the epic had become a marginal generic format. Production of western movies reached an almost total standstill, with only a handful of productions appearing in theatres throughout the decade—and none achieving any real success. In the words of Stephen Prince, "[T]he western was the most miserably performing genre of the decade."[16] In the mid-to-late 1970s, the industry had discovered a new formula for box office success, and by the 1980s, a large proportion of production resources had been given over to tongue-in-cheek action films and entertaining family movies in the tradition of Spielberg's and Lucas's earlier work, as both Thomas Schatz and Peter Krämer have argued.[17] This marked a re-engagement with the family audience that was such a constituent factor in the roadshow epic's appeal, but the cinematic epic itself remained marginal. However, epics did not completely disappear from widespread public view. Across the world, large audiences were still watching historical epics, but not at the cinema.

According to data compiled by Cobbet Steinberg, the highest rated Hollywood movie ever screened on American television was *Gone with the Wind* (1939) when it was shown in two parts on 7–8 November 1976.[18] It was not, however, the highest rated TV film of all time. That accolade goes to the equally epic final episode of the miniseries *Roots* (1977). In fact, the historical epic retained its popularity and visibility throughout the 1970s and 1980s on television, through broadcasts of popular roadshows and in the form of miniseries like *Roots*, *Holocaust* (1978) and *Shogun* (1981). These were expensive, prestigious televisual events, scheduled to run on consecutive nights, thus demanding that the viewer stay in and make a concerted effort to watch (in the process aping the exclusivity of the event in a manner akin to roadshowing). The series themselves dramatised significant events in global history and, like the epic films that preceded them, sought to both educate and entertain. The most successful of these was *Roots*, based on the best-selling novel of the same name by Alex Haley.[19]

Over twelve hours, *Roots* told the story of African slaves struggling to survive in nineteenth-century America and was focused on one of Haley's ancestors, Kunta Kinte (played by LeVar Burton, among others, on television). In her review, Pauline Kael saw the series as a challenge to the movie industry and wrote that "great filmmakers have been grandiose dreamers for attempting considerably less than a 12-hour black epic."[20] *Holocaust*, another big hit with audiences, followed the Jewish Weiss family through the Second World War and, in a famous sequence, actually into the gas chambers at Auschwitz-Birkenau. *Shogun* followed in 1981. Over twelve hours, this series, which was based on a novel by James Clavell, followed the exploits of a fictional seventeenth-century English sailor shipwrecked in Japan. In many ways its story of captivity and eventual integration into an alien but noble ancient culture clearly had some influence on *Dances with Wolves* and, more recently, *The Last Samurai* (2003).

Epic miniseries were produced throughout the 1980s, and other key examples included *The Winds of War* (1983), *North and South* (1985) and, most expensive and ambitious of all, *War and Remembrance*, screened by ABC in 1988.[21] This star-studded, thirty-hour, $104-million series attempted to dramatise almost every significant event of World War II, by focusing on the friends and family of a naval officer played by Robert Mitchum. It was, however, a major failure with audiences. *War and Remembrance* was screened in two blocks, eighteen hours in late 1988, and the remaining twelve hours in May 1989. After the first block had been shown, the *New York Times* reported that its calamitous ratings figures effectively marked the end of the epic historical miniseries, at least so far as ABC vice president Alan Wurtzel was concerned.[22] However, before the second block was shown, rival network CBS had a major hit in the form of the epic western miniseries *Lonesome Dove*, shown in February 1989. This highly acclaimed and popular show provided an early sign that western and epic subjects might prove more popular with audiences than the film industry had assumed.

Lonesome Dove was based on a Pulitzer Prize–winning novel by Larry McMurtry, which followed a pair of retired Texas Rangers, played by Robert Duvall and Tommy Lee Jones, on one last cattle drive across the American West.[23] It was eight hours long, cost $20 million to make (more than *Dances with Wolves*) and received excellent reviews.[24] Steve Neale has argued that the show stemmed from the same impulse that motivated production of Clint Eastwood's *Pale Rider* and Lawrence Kasdan's *Silverado* in 1985—to *revive* the western but not necessarily *revise* it.[25] Both of these films are an example of the majors providing limited financing to established successful filmmakers as an experimental venture, to see if there was any life left in the western as a cinematic tradition. Their poor box office performance seemed to confirm that there was not. However, critical interest in the epic remained strong, even if investment was not forthcoming. In March 1990, several months before the release of Costner's film, an article appeared in the *Los Angeles Times* bemoaning "the demise of the epics," which noted that "the epic survives in its purest form not on the big screen but on the small, as miniseries . . . [but now it is] high time to revive the romance at the movies."[26] Kevin Costner was also seeking to revive the western film and to revisit the great epics that he had enjoyed as a child. By the time that *Lonesome Dove* reached the small screen, Costner was filming *Dances with Wolves*, but it had not been easy to get the project off the ground.

2. Constructing *Dances with Wolves*

Kevin Costner's fondness for western movies stretched back to his childhood and has defined his career as a Hollywood star and as a director. As noted in the previous chapter, Costner claimed that, as a child, "[he could]remember as a ten-year-old watching *How the West Was Won* and certain moments made [him] tingle with the magic of it."[27] On the set of

Silverado, in which he played the character of Jake, Costner apparently spent his days reenacting scenes from the westerns he had watched in his youth, and while publicising that film he told the press, "I waited my whole life to be in a western." He dedicated his performance to "everyone who ever dreamed of being in a western."[28] David Thomson has described Costner's later career as "the most blatant example in screen history of an actor following his own fantasies—at enormous cost sometimes, but doggedly, like some lone scout mapping the far northwest."[29] Reviews of *Dances with Wolves* emphasised and sometimes mocked Costner's commitment to the western. For instance, J. Hoberman wrote in the *Village Voice*, "Who even admits liking westerns, let alone raising $18 million to make one? More garrulous than the old Gary Cooper ever was, Costner has let it be known that the 1962 roadshow *How the West Was Won*, the *Ben-Hur* of the horse opera, is among his favorites."[30] Recently, Costner's profile may have diminished, but he has continued to star in, and direct, westerns, from taking the title role in Lawrence Kasdan's unsuccessful *Wyatt Earp* (1994), through to his directorial effort, *Open Range* (2003). In the introduction to the 'making of' book that accompanied *Dances with Wolves'* release, Costner wrote, "There is little doubt I will make other movies, but if I could not *Dances with Wolves* would complete the picture I have had of myself since I was a little boy. It will forever be my love letter to the past."[31] Costner's comments exhibit a deep attachment to westerns and, to a lesser extent, epics, which closely parallels the experiences of many other modern filmmakers—as we saw in the introduction to chapter 1. Consequently, *Dances with Wolves* can easily be understood as the fulfilment of a childhood dream—a return to a preferred genre that seems to have been, in Costner's mind, inextricably linked to the presumed 'innocence' of youth. In keeping with this 'rose-tinted' view of the past, Costner rarely distinguished between different western cycles, and his nostalgia seems to erase or elide the more pessimistic, revisionist westerns of the 1970s. In fact, *Dances with Wolves* presents essentially revisionist sentiments (which critique the expansion of whites into 'Indian territory') as part of a 'classic' western narrative, suggesting that Costner's highly nostalgic conception of the Hollywood western differs radically from critical accounts. Thus a highly subjective nostalgia informed both the film's production and its narrative.

The origins of *Dances with Wolves* can be traced back to the early 1980s. In 1981, Kevin Costner starred in a low-budget gambling drama called *Stacy's Knights* (released in 1983), which was directed by Jim Wilson and written by Michael Blake. Wilson, Blake and Costner became friends, and at some point Costner suggested that Blake turn one of his movie ideas, about a cavalry officer on the American frontier, into a novel.[32] Blake, a radical journalist turned screenwriter, obliged. The novel was completed in 1986, and the trio immediately set about reconstructing it as a movie. Later, Costner would claim that "Michael managed to forge all the elements most attractive to me—simplicity, dignity, humour and poignancy" into both the story and the character of John Dunbar.[33] At this point Costner's career was starting to take off with roles in Kevin Reynolds's *Fandango* (1985), Lawrence Kasdan's *Silverado* and the lead in Brian De Palma's *The Untouchables* (1987). Paying him out of his own funds, Costner insisted that Blake rewrite the project six times, until he was absolutely satisfied.[34] The novel, meanwhile, was published in 1987.

Even with a script completed, the major studios were reluctant to green-light *Dances with Wolves* at a time when westerns and epics were considered box office anathema. The legacy of *Heaven's Gate* effectively ensured that the project would remain in 'development hell' until Costner, hot off the success of *Field of Dreams* (1989), decided to raise funding for the project on his own. Costner and Jim Wilson set up their own company, Tig Productions, and, after a series of failed deals, brought in renowned deal maker Jake Eberts, who raised enough capital to commence preproduction by selling overseas distribution rights.[35] Later, the autonomy offered by this strategy provided Costner with a bargaining chip when the film was eventually sold to an American distributor. The U.S. rights were sold on the understanding that Costner retained final cut. Two weeks before production was due to start, Costner, Wilson and Ebert convinced the mini-major Orion Pictures to put up the $9 million they needed, in return for domestic distribution rights. The budget was estimated at $15 million, and Kevin Costner would co-produce, direct and star.[36]

According to co-founder Mike Medavoy, Orion Pictures had been conceived of as a studio "where filmmakers could realize their visions without interference from executives."[37] The company had been formed by departing United Artists executives in 1978, who envisaged a studio devoted to interesting, relatively highbrow product—an equivalent to the failing UA dream. Throughout the 1980s, Orion enjoyed critical and commercial success with Oscar-oriented films such as *Amadeus* (1984) and *Platoon* (1986) as well as exploitation-type productions like *Bull Durham* (1988) and *RoboCop* (1987).[38] The studio was one of many independent financier-distributors to emerge in the 1980s, as video increased demand for product and opened up opportunities for studios other than the established majors to prosper.[39] However, by the end of the decade, Orion was mired in financial difficulties, and although two of the films initiated at this time—*Dances with Wolves* and *The Silence of the Lambs* (1991)—went on to become massive hits, the studio filed for bankruptcy in 1991.

Despite its 'hands off' mandate, Costner clashed with Orion executives several times during filming, and at least one of their decisions may have exacerbated their financial difficulties in the long run. When Costner started to go over budget Orion insisted that he forfeit his salary in favour of a share of the gross. Costner duly agreed, and $3 million was channelled away from the star and back into the film. The movie eventually came in at $18 million, a scant 5 percent over its projected costs. Although Orion executives were apparently unhappy with Costner's three-hour cut, the deal that Costner had arranged meant that they had to release his version of the film.[40] At the time, many in the industry were dismissive of the project, which seemed to contradict a great deal of received wisdom regarding successful box office trends.[41] Therefore, the film can be read as Costner's highly personal attempt to revisit the epic western tradition, in defiance of commercial wisdom or interference, and Costner must be understood as the guiding creative hand behind the movie.[42] The film certainly was not part of a calculated attempt by studio executives to exploit potential audiences. Furthermore, the scenes of sacrifice and suicidal moral commitment within the film seem to reflect the daring, nostalgic nature of *Dances with Wolves*.

3. Narrative, Nostalgia and Film History

The title, *Dances with Wolves*, is intentionally multifaceted. It is the name that John Dunbar adopts at the moment when he becomes accepted as a Lakota Sioux warrior; it is a key point of transition in the narrative, when Dunbar is spotted by the Indians performing a war dance in the company of his pet wolf; and finally, it is an allegory for the film itself. Dunbar finds himself alone on the frontier, surrounded by people he has been trained to think of as violent savages—wolves of a sort. He chooses not to fight these 'wolves' but to enter into a more friendly, ultimately benevolent relationship. He 'dances,' with all the implications of submission and sensuality that the term suggests. This dance leads him to an ancient and, the film implies, spiritually purifying existence. Through his encounters with the Sioux, the Union soldier Dunbar is redeemed. However, the civilisation of life that he encounters is dying, and the film is riddled with nostalgia for a better, older, way of life. Arguably, this nostalgia echoes Kevin Costner's attempt to revisit, and revive, the epic western.

The film begins with an injured and dispirited Dunbar attempting to commit suicide on a Tennessee battlefield in 1863. His attempt to end his life by charging Confederate lines inadvertently allows his Union compatriots to mount a surprise attack and rout the enemy. Dunbar is declared a hero and is offered the posting of his choice as a reward. He elects to head out to the western frontier, away from the fighting, but also away from the modern world. His first stop is Fort Hays, the last functioning Union outpost before the frontier. There Dunbar is given his orders by an obviously insane Major Fambrough, who tells him, "I am sending you on a knight's errand, you will report to Captain Cargill at the furthermost outpost of the realm, Fort Sedgewick." After Dunbar departs, Fambrough cries out, "To your journey and to my journey!" and shoots himself in the head. Dunbar is guided by Timmons (described by Fambrough as a 'peasant'), a lewd, dirty man about whom Dunbar writes in his diary (a device that initially justifies the voice-over), "Were it not for the company, I would be having the time of my life." Despite the presence of Timmons, at this point the film begins to focus on the beauty of the landscape. Wide, epic shots introduce the unspoilt West. Dunbar then arrives at Fort Sedgewick to find it abandoned and polluted by its previous occupants, but he decides to stay nonetheless.

All the Anglo-American characters in this opening section, except Dunbar, are shown to be dirty, destructive and demented. The fighting in Tennessee is chaotic and lacks any stated ideological purpose, while Fort Hays has driven Fambrough to mental collapse. In both places, a central character attempts suicide as a means of escape. Timmons exhibits little appreciation for the beauty that surrounds him as he travels west, and he is killed by an Indian raiding party as he heads home. An extended cut of the film, released in Europe a year after the film's theatrical release and subsequently screened on American television, shows the original occupants of Fort Sedgewick driven to despair and eventually fleeing east. However, when Dunbar crosses the frontier, he moves back in time, away from the corrupt, violent present of 1863 towards an ancient and, the film suggests, ennobling form of existence. As a result of his suicide attempt, Dunbar is able to literally escape into the distant past, prompting Native American critic Edward D. Castillo to suggest that the bulk of the film should be read as a posthumous fantasy, a 'dream quest' in which Dunbar dies and then uncovers his true identity.[43]

At Fort Sedgewick, Dunbar cleans the camp and maintains routine patrols. As time passes, he finds himself drawn to the local Sioux. In direct contrast to the Anglo-American characters in the film, the Sioux Indians inhabit an enviable world of familial harmony and contentment. We see them discussing what to do about the white man, and they decide, in eminently democratic fashion, that Dunbar is a man with whom treaties can be arranged. Gradually, Dunbar comes into closer contact with the Sioux. He saves a white Sioux adoptee, Stands With A Fist (Mary McDonnell), from committing suicide (the third suicide attempt in the film) and brings the anxious Sioux news of an approaching buffalo herd. In time, he learns the Sioux language, Lakota, becomes close friends with Kicking Bird (Graham Greene) and falls in love with Stands With A Fist. In the process, Dunbar is transformed into Dances with Wolves. However, when Dunbar returns to Fort Sedgewick to collect his journal, he is captured by Union soldiers. Dunbar refuses to speak to his captors in English or acknowledge the person he had been, and as a result, he is tortured. Eventually, the Sioux are able to rescue him, but Dunbar returns knowing that the Sioux are doomed, and that westward expansion of white civilisation cannot be stopped. He tells Kicking Bird, "You always ask me about the white people. You always want to know how many more are coming. There will be a lot, my friend. More than can be counted, like the stars. It makes me afraid for all the Sioux." Now a fugitive, Dunbar and his wife decide that they must go back to Anglo civilisation and defend the Indian nations. A postscript informs us that, "Thirteen years later, their homes destroyed, their buffalo gone, the last band of free Sioux submitted to white authority. The great horse culture of the plains was gone, and the American frontier was soon to pass into history."

Throughout the film, the equality and moral integrity of the Sioux stands in stark contrast to the depiction of Anglo characters. In part this depiction was closely allied to a burgeoning 'New Age' movement, which brought together Indian cultural trappings such as buckskin, dream catchers, sweat lodges, homeopathic healing and communal living, with ecological concerns and an eastern spirituality emphasising self-enlightenment.[44] As cultural historian Philip J. Deloria has observed, these simplistic conceptions of the Native American lifestyle and culture were offered as remedies to the social ills of suburban, corporate America.[45] Popular writing such as Ed McGaa's *Rainbow Tribe: Ordinary People Journeying the Red Road*, the work of Lynne Andrew, and James Redfield's *The Celestine Prophecies: An Adventure* presented the Native Northern and Central Americans as ecologically and spiritually harmonious figures with much to teach the contemporary United States.[46] *Dances with Wolves* can certainly be understood in this context. Indeed, the press kit used self-consciously 'spiritual' terms to sell the film, describing it as "the extraordinary journey of one hero's search for humanity in the ultimate frontier—himself."[47] However, by valorising the distant past over the present, the film also reflected a very different tradition of debate about the role of the media in contemporary American society.

Shortly after its release, *Dances with Wolves* won Best Film at the Independent Spirit Awards, an event designed to honour independently produced movies. In his acceptance speech, Costner lambasted the 'typical Hollywood movie' as "an incomplete, half-thought-out piece of shit."[48] He was by no means alone in his belief that there was something wrong with mainstream contemporary filmmaking. In 1992, Michael Medved published the best-selling *Hollywood vs. America: Popular Culture and the War on Traditional Values* in which he argued that Hollywood had become "an all-powerful enemy, an alien force that assaults our most cherished values and corrupts our children."[49] Medved claimed to speak for the 'silent majority' of Americans and quoted surveys which suggested that over 80 percent of Americans believed there was too much violence and profanity in the movies and that the situation was getting worse.[50] Medved's criticisms resulted from an ongoing conflict between conservatives (often those with evangelical religious agendas) and more liberal forces, which has informed American social and political life since the 1960s and is sometimes known as the 'culture wars.'[51] Medved's dismissal of Hollywood movies, for their violence and profanity, was very similar to Costner's dismissal of Hollywood movies at the Independent Spirit Awards.[52] In different ways Costner and Medved were both arguing that the quality and moral integrity of Hollywood filmmaking had diminished during the 1970s and 1980s and were appealing for a return to the more overtly edifying productions of their youth. Indeed, Jim Collins has argued that the 'old-fashioned' nature of Costner's film is an attempt to escape the challenges and uncertainties of a postmodern media environment.[53] Although Costner would likely have described his project differently, it is certainly the case that *Dances with Wolves* was an act of nostalgic recuperation, and Dunbar's journey can be read as a useful allegory of Costner's intentions.

Like the film's title, the significance of Dunbar's voyage into the past can be interpreted in several ways. Certainly for Kevin Costner, and perhaps for older viewers with fond memories of westerns and epics, *Dances with Wolves* offered an opportunity to regress to boyhood. When he arrives at the frontier Dunbar finds himself relying on the sorts of survival tactics familiar to Boy Scouts across the world. At times, Dunbar's life at the fort resembles nothing less than the sort of wholesome, outdoorsy fun usually found at the summer camps (often with 'Indian' names) that remain popular with American children today. When the Sioux appear, Dunbar becomes part of an adult game of 'cowboys and Indians', albeit one where the main participant decides to change sides halfway through. The comments made by Costner during the marketing of this film, which stressed his memories of watching westerns and epics, suggest that Costner was realising a boyhood fantasy not just to direct a western but also to participate in one. Just as Dunbar was able to escape a troubling present, so Costner had sought to escape a filmmaking climate where epics and westerns had virtually vanished, by returning to the cinematic terrain of his youth. This journey was closely associated with symbolic images of death and suicide, which abound in the film and which may suggest a keen awareness of the risk attached to a project like *Dances with Wolves*. However, by repeatedly stressing that the past is somehow more enriching and edifying than the present, *Dances with Wolves* arguably sought to champion the two defunct forms that were being reconstructed, the epic film and the western.

When Dunbar (and Costner) cross the frontier, the style of the film undergoes a subtle change. The tight close-ups and medium-distance shots of the opening section are replaced by a series of long shots, which take in the expansive landscape of the American West. As they leave Fort Sedgewick behind, Dunbar is increasingly dwarfed by these monumental, panoramic vistas, particularly in a later section when Dunbar and the Sioux hunt a vast buffalo herd across the grasslands. In these scenes, Costner introduces a self-consciously 'epic' visual style, which echoes the vistas of *How the West Was Won* and John Ford's *The Searchers* (1956), and is designed to contrast with the more claustrophobic scenes that open the film.[54] In effect, the journey into the past becomes a stylistic journey towards 'epicness'. One could even argue that this stylistic shift is an attempt to reclaim the cinematic roots of the epic. The early part of the film utilises techniques associated with television and then abandons them in favour of a more obviously 'cinematic' style. Consciously or not, Costner's film bridges the epic miniseries and an emergent cinematic epic revival in stylistic terms. *Dances with Wolves* also evoked *How the West Was Won* at a narrational level. In that film, James Stewart appeared as a mountain man, a tracker of unexplored regions, who is eventually tamed when a conventional eastern family arrive in his territory, and he falls in love with their daughter. In a later section, Stewart has become an all-American hero and dies fighting as a Union soldier. *Dances with Wolves* inverted this narrative, using the same elements to tell a story of escape from a corrupting Anglo society.

Furthermore, the chaos and violence of the East could easily be taken as a metaphor for film culture at the end of the 1980s. Although in reality family films predominated at the box office throughout this time, violence was a key concern of commentators such as Medved, who perceived an "addiction to graphic . . . and sadistic violence" in many Hollywood films.[55] Medved identified films from the late 1980s and early 1990s such as *Lethal Weapon 2* (1989), *Batman* (1989) and *Total Recall* (1990) as examples of a growing predilection for amoral violence. Such claims were not limited to conservative figures. Even *Variety* lamented *Total Recall's* "heedless contribution to the accelerating brutality of its time."[56] In fact, Costner's previous film, *Revenge* (1990), had been heavily criticised for its extreme violence and brutality. Consequently, the redemption that Dunbar finds amongst the Sioux could well be understood as equivalent to the sort of redemption that Costner was seeking by producing the film. As a star and a filmmaker, he was moving away from his perceived misdeeds in a violent present, exactly like Dunbar. Costner's agenda would come to be shared by other epic filmmakers as the cycle wore on, particularly by Mel Gibson, who self-consciously framed *The Passion of the Christ* (2004) in similar terms, despite the extraordinary violence of the film, as chapter 7 will demonstrate.

The hopeless voyage that Dunbar makes back into Anglo-American society can therefore be read as a metaphor for Costner's journey as a filmmaker. Dunbar took a suicidal risk in fighting for the Sioux, in order to bring about a greater understanding of and tolerance for the dying inhabitants of the American past. By making *Dances with Wolves*, Costner was offering the epic western as a cure for the ills of the modern age and, effectively, fighting for its survival (perhaps 'suicidally' sacrificing his popularity in the process). However, Orion's marketing department and movie critics presented the film in a slightly different light, and, as a result, its impact on film culture was not quite what Costner had hoped for.

4. Critical and Commercial Responses

During one promotional interview, Kevin Costner claimed of *Dances with Wolves*:

> I never saw it as a political film about the plight of the Indians. I'm aware that it has a political feeling and that there are other, harder stories to tell, but I was attracted to its humanity and to the sense of humour I felt I could bring to it. Also, I like its epic quality: *Silverado*, *The Untouchables* and *Field of Dreams* had that too. I like big movies. I like it when there's a lot at stake. I like big casts. I think the longer a movie is the better.[57]

The writer Michael Blake has said that he had always envisaged *Dances with Wolves* as "an epic movie. . . . I felt that the only way we could present the book in movie form was as an epic, something larger than life."[58] Although Costner was clearly motivated by an obsession with westerns, the film he produced was epic in scope. The fact that Costner was so keen to link *Dances with Wolves* and *How the West Was Won* is particularly telling in this regard.[59] As Sheldon Hall has observed, in the epic western, as in the historical epic, the depiction of pivotal moments in history is a primary thematic concern, and Costner's film was ultimately concerned with the end of Native American civilisation rather than with the more mythic terrain of the conventional western.[60] Through Dunbar, the audience experiences what historian Hugh Brogan has called "the white conquest of the continent" from the position of the conquered.[61] As a result, the marketing and critical reception of Costner's film played a pivotal role in reestablishing the cultural (and financial) capital of the term *epic*. Rick Altman and Steve Neale both assert that the use of generic terms plays an important role in establishing new cycles. By examining the use of key terms, it is therefore possible to trace *Dances with Wolves'* impact on production trends.

Although Orion had not been able to exert a great deal of influence on Costner during production, the studio was able to assume control of the film's marketing. Fearful of having its already dubious box office appeal further tarnished by association with the apparently unfashionable western, Orion chose to market the film as an epic.[62] *Dances with Wolves* was a prestigious historical film set in the American West, but, Orion attempted to assure audiences, it was not a western. Considerable linguistic somersaults were employed to describe the film in the accompanying press kit. Here it was presented as "an epic set in America's most historic period of change—the 1860s."[63] Note that mention of the West or the western is steadfastly avoided. Meanwhile, the 'making of' book that accompanied the film's release was entitled *Dances with Wolves: The Illustrated Story of the Epic Film*.[64] Again, the term *western* was never used. Orion's marketing department appeared to believe that epics were saleable but westerns were not. Therefore, Orion's marketing campaign seemed to contradict Costner's earlier agenda—to revisit and revive the epic Hollywood western.

Nevertheless, on release, many critics were quick to label *Dances with Wolves* a western. Roger Ebert described it as "one of the best Westerns I've ever seen," and the *New York Post* went so far as to claim that "Kevin Costner has single-handedly brought back the Western."[65] The film also won the National Cowboy Hall of Fame's Western Heritage Award.[66] However, other reviewers clearly interpreted the film as an epic. The *Los Angeles Times* claimed that "it's impossible to call it anything but epic" and compared it favourably with *Lawrence of Arabia* (1962).[67] Reviews in *New York Magazine*, the *Christian Science Monitor* and *Newsweek* used similar terminology.[68] This sort of reception was also visible in the United Kingdom, where one reviewer wrote, "Long devalued by being thrown at anything longish with a big budget, the word 'epic' is rescued by Kevin Costner's sweeping, moving and engrossing study of the American frontier."[69] When *Dances with Wolves* became a critical and commercial hit, these reviews offered those in the film industry a vital means of interpreting the film's appeal. Repeatedly reviewers expressed admiration for Costner's daring attempt to mine Hollywood's generic heritage. The film's exceptional box office performance suggested that this act of nostalgic recuperation had resonated with audiences across the world. As a result, *Dances with Wolves* inspired a diverse range of related productions, which all incorporated and emphasised different aspects of Costner's movie in accordance with the rules of what Rick Altman describes as the 'producer's game'.[70] According to Altman, the production of generically marked movies can be described by a simple set of rules, which expose how production schedules are designed to exploit the generic characteristics of prior hits:

1. From box office information, identify a successful film.
2. Analyse that film in order to discover what made it successful.
3. Make another film stressing the assumed formula for success.
4. Check box office information on the new film and reassess the success formula accordingly.
5. Use the revised formula as the basis for another film.
6. Continue the process indefinitely.[71]

To understand the effect of *Dances with Wolves* on Hollywood, one must play the producer's game and search for releases clearly designed to capitalise on its success.

Steve Neale has identified forty-one western movies, television series and documentaries that appeared between 1990 and 1995, including *Dances with Wolves*.[72] He argues that this cycle was related to a broader revitalisation of "'New Western' culture," with distant links to the 'New Age' movement but also to a burgeoning country music industry that was becoming increasingly popular with mainstream listeners. However, we can safely assume that it usually takes somewhere between two and three years for a film to go from the earliest stages of conception through to final release. Therefore, the noticeable increase in the production of westerns in 1992 and 1993 must be attributed to the success of *Dances with Wolves*. Clint Eastwood's *Unforgiven* was released in 1992 to widespread critical acclaim. Eastwood's film won four Academy Awards, including Best Picture. Although critics have hailed *Unforgiven* as a masterpiece, the film was nowhere near as commercially successful as *Dances with Wolves*. *Unforgiven* made $101.2 million in domestic receipts, and $58 million overseas, almost one-third of *Dances with Wolves'* takings.[73] The success of *Dances with Wolves* had made Eastwood's western seem like a viable financial investment. Unfortunately, audiences did not respond so well to later releases. Box office returns steadily diminished until the disappointing performance of *Tombstone* (1993) and *Wyatt Earp*, which grossed $56 million and $25 million respectively in the North American market, brought the limited cycle of westerns to an end.[74] The western has since reassumed the marginal position it occupied during the 1980s. Occasional forays into the genre do continue to be released but are usually personal projects produced at the margins of the industry, as in the case of *Open Range*. Despite Costner's best efforts, the cycle of western movies he sought to initiate stalled and died within a period of fewer than five years.

The early 1990s also saw a very limited cycle of what might be termed 'Native American' movies. These included the historical accounts *Geronimo: An American Legend* (1993) and *Black Robe* (1991), as well as *Thunderheart* (1992), a contemporary thriller set on an Indian reservation. On television, Ted Turner, another western aficionado, produced a series of TV movies under the 'Native Americans' banner for his TNT network. These were historical biopics such as *Squanto: A Warrior's Tale* (1994). Meanwhile, Costner himself hosted a documentary series about American Indian history called *500 Nations* (1995). None achieved particular success at the box office or in the ratings, and this cycle also quickly died out.

Several more obviously epic films also appeared in the wake of *Dances with Wolves*. Michael Mann's *The Last of the Mohicans* was released by Warner in 1992. It combined elements of the swashbuckler, romance and epic in a story about Indian trappers fighting in the Franco-Indian War. The emphasis on Native American customs and the story of whites learning the ways of Indians clearly resembled Costner's film. By revisiting the classic novel by James Fenimore Cooper and a 1936 film directed by

George B. Seitz, Mann, like Costner, was looking to reinvigorate a popular story from Hollywood's past. Although the film wasn't a flop, it only performed adequately at the box office. Budgeted at $40 million, it made $75.5 domestically.[75] The same was true of Ron Howard's *Far and Away* (1992) and Ronald F. Maxwell's *Gettysburg* (1993). Howard's film was a romantic tale of Irish settlers in the American West, budgeted at $60 million and released by Universal. It grossed $58.9 million domestically and $78.9 million overseas.[76] Maxwell's was a star-studded re-enactment of a famous Civil War battle, which had originally been intended for television (on Ted Turner's TNT network), but which had grown in scale during production and eventually received a limited release with the independent distributor New Line.[77] Other independently minded filmmakers, often with overt political agendas, were also able to find funding for epic projects of their own. Spike Lee made *Malcolm X* in 1992, while Oliver Stone directed *JFK* in 1991 and *Nixon* in 1995. Although none of these films were substantial box office successes, they nevertheless generated huge volumes of media comment, thus creating a climate where big-budget historical films with political significance could be considered increasingly commonplace. The existence of these productions was evidence that the studios were increasingly willing to green-light epics in the wake of *Dances with Wolves*, but most were not big enough hits to invite imitation and thus sustain the cycle. This changed with the release of Steven Spielberg's *Schindler's List* (1993), discussed in the next chapter, and Mel Gibson's *Braveheart* (1995).

Conclusion

Like *Dances with Wolves*, Spielberg's and Gibson's films were personal projects that the directors viewed as extremely unlikely commercial successes.[78] *Variety* described *Braveheart* as "a huge, bloody and sprawling epic . . . exactly the sort of massive vanity piece that it would be easy to disparage if it didn't essentially deliver."[79] In the 'making of' documentary that accompanied *Braveheart* on DVD, Gibson explained that "it was the epic films I liked in the sixties, when I was growing up, that really inspired me to do *Braveheart*."[80] He had originally been sent the script to star in but quickly set about convincing Paramount that he could direct. Like *Dances with Wolves*, *Braveheart* and *Schindler's List* had originated with powerful, maverick figures, famous for pursuing their own agendas, who were operating outside the production schemes of the majors by attempting to produce self-conscious assertions of artistic or educational resonance in the form of nostalgic epics. Like Kevin Costner, Gibson had to defer his fee when the budget ran over. [81] Unlike Costner's film, *Braveheart* was funded and distributed by Paramount and Fox and had been budgeted at a genuinely epic $72 million (domestic grosses were $75.8 million, with a further $134.8 million coming from overseas). [82] The film went on to win five Academy Awards, including Best Picture.

Braveheart's high budget was indicative of the epic film's growing revitalisation in the early part of the 1990s. Before 1990, it was virtually unthinkable that any of the major studios would budget a historical epic at over twice the annual average negative cost of a movie release. [83] By 1995, such productions had become an occasional feature of production schedules, as an increasing number of highly motivated maverick filmmakers were able to work within the form. In this way, *Dances with Wolves* initiated a small but significant shift in the majors' production strategies, which paved the way for the most successful epic of the modern era, James Cameron's *Titanic* (1997), at which point the longer term viability of the cycle was assured. However, until *Titanic*, one filmmaker more than any other assured the reemergence of the epic. The next two chapters examine the World War II epics of Steven Spielberg.

Notes

1. Charles Musser, "The Travel Genre in 1903–1904: Moving Towards a Fictional Narrative," in Thomas Elsaesser, ed., *Early Cinema: Space, Frame, Narrative* (London: BFI, 1990), 130.

2. Rick Altman, *Film/Genre* (London: BFI, 1999), 35.

3. Financial data from Box Office Mojo, http://www.boxofficemojo.com/?movies?id= dances withwolves.htm.

4. Emanuel Levy, *Oscar Fever: The History and Politics of the Academy Awards* (New York: Continuum, 2001), 358.

5. Altman, 49–68.

6. John Cawelti, *The Six Gun Mystique* (Bowling Green, OH: Bowling Green University Press, 1970); Will Wright, *Sixguns and Society: A Structural Study of the Western* (Berkeley: University of California, 1975). For a critique of these studies, see Richard Maltby, *Hollywood Cinema* 2nd ed. (Oxford: Blackwell, 2003), 85.

7. Sheldon Hall, "*How the West Was Won*: History, Spectacle and the American Mountains," in Ian Cameron and Douglas Pye, eds., *The Book of Westerns* (New York: Continuum, 1996), 255.

8. David O. Cook writes, "Domestic production of Westerns declined dramatically and proportionally year by year in the wake of . . . Vietnam and Watergate." See Cook, 182.

9. Cook, 173–182.

10. Of course, the western genre was made up of a series of smaller cycles identified in Michael Coyne, *The Crowded Prairie: American National Identity in the Hollywood Western* (London: I.B. Tauris, 1997).

11. Margo Kasdan and Susan Tavernetti, "Native Americans in a Revisionist Western," in Peter C. Rollins and John E. O'Connor, eds., *Hollywood's Indian: The Portrayal of the Native American in Film* (Lexington: University Press of Kentucky, 1998), 121.

12. Kasdan and Tavernetti, 122.

13. Stephen Prince, *A New Pot of Gold: Hollywood Under the Electronic Rainbow, 1980-1989* (Berkeley: University of California Press, 2000), 309.

14. Prince, 37. See also Steven Bach, *Final Cut: Dreams and Disaster in the Making of Heaven's Gate* (New York: Morrow, 1985).

15. In 1981, Paramount released Warren Beatty's *Reds*, a film about the Russian Revolution, which went on to earn Beatty the Best Director Oscar. *Reds* was already in production when *Heaven's Gate* was released, and although it was certainly an epic of sorts, its merely adequate box office performance failed to save the epic from obscurity.

16. Prince, 314.

17. Peter Krämer has argued that Hollywood has always been at its most successful when it appeals to this market. See Peter Krämer, "'The Best Disney Film Disney Never Made': Children's Films and the Family Audience in American Cinema since the 1960s," in Neale (2002), 185–200.

18. See Cobbet Steinberg, *Film Facts* (New York: Facts on File, 1980), 25–77 and 32–36. Subsequent data also from this source.

19. Alex Haley, *Roots* (London: Hutchinson, 1977).

20. Pauline Kael, "What's wrong with filmmakers," *Chicago Sun-Times* 13 March 1977: unpaginated clipping, *Roots* file, NYPL.

21. A comprehensive examination of the TV historical epic miniseries of the 1950s and 1960s can be found in Glen Creeber, *Serial Television: Big Drama on the Small Screen* (London: BFI, 2004), 19–44.

22. The paper reported that ABC, which financed and screened the series, "expected to lose $30–40 million" and described it as a "financial calamity." Bill Carter, "A Mini-Series Teaches ABC Hard Lessons," *New York Times* 8 May 1989, D1.

23. It may be a good indication of Kevin Costner's fondness for *Lonesome Dove* that he cast Robert Duvall in a very similar role in his own *Open Range*.

24. See, for example, Martha Bayles, rev. in *Wall Street Journal* 6 Feb. 1989, A9; and Anon., rev. in *Daily Variety* 15 Feb. 1989, 94.

25. Steve Neale, "Westerns and Gangster Films Since the 1970s," in Neale (2002), 31.

26. Peter Rainer, "The Epic, an Endangered Species," *Los Angeles Times* 11 Mar. 1990, Calendar, 30.

27. Todd Keith, *Kevin Costner: The Unauthorised Biography* (London: Ikonprint, 1991), 19.

28. Quoted in Keith, 63.

29. David Thomson, *The New Biographical Dictionary of Film* 4th ed. (London: Little Brown, 2002), 181.

30. J. Hoberman, rev. of *Dances with Wolves, Village Voice* 20 Nov. 1990, 69.

31. Kevin Costner, "Introduction," in Kevin Costner, Michael Blake and Jim Wilson, *Dances with Wolves: The Illustrated Story of the Epic Film* (New York: Newmarket, 1990).

32. See Keith 130, Orion Pictures, *Dances with Wolves* press kit, BFIL, 3, and Costner et al., viii.

33. Costner et al., vii.

34. Kelvin Caddies, *Kevin Costner: Prince of Hollywood* rev. ed. (London: Plexus, 1995), 77.

35. Mike Medavoy and Josh Young, *You're Only as Good as Your Next One: 100 Great Films, 100 Good Films and 100 for Which I Should Be Shot* (New York: Atria, 2002), 159.

36. Medavoy and Young, 95.

37. Ibid.

38. For more on the history of Orion see Yannis Tzioumakis, "Major Status, Independent Spirit," *New Review of Television Studies* 2, no. 1 (May 2004), 87–135.

39. See Justin Wyatt, "The Formation of the Major Independent: Miramax, New Line and the New Hollywood," in Neale and Smiths (1998), 75, and Justin Wyatt, "Independents, Packaging, and Inflationary Pressure in 1980s Hollywood," in Prince, 142–159.

40. For details of Costner's relationship with Orion, see Keith, 136 and Medavoy and Young, 163.

41. See Medavoy and Young, 160.

42. Because he controlled so many aspects of the production process, Costner can be understood as a "vertically integrated auteur," in the manner outlined in Warren Buckland, *Directed by Steven Spielberg: Poetics of the Contemporary Hollywood Blockbuster* (New York: Continuum, 2006), 15.

43. Edward D. Castillo, "Dances with Wolves," *Film Quarterly* 44 (1991), 16.

44. See Shari M. Huhndorf, *Going Native: Indians in the American Cultural Imagination* (Ithaca, NY: Cornell University Press, 2001), 162–198.

45. Philip J. Deloria, *Playing Indian* (New Haven, CT: Yale University Press, 1998), 183.

46. Ed McGaa, *Rainbow Tribe: Ordinary People Journeying the Red Road* (San Francisco, CA: HarperCollins, 1992); Lynn Andrews, *Medicine Woman* (New York: Harper and Row, 1981); James Redfield, *The Celestine Prophecies: An Adventure* (New York: Warner 1993). For more information on this trend see Dirk Johnson 'Spiritual Seekers Borrow Indian Ways,' *New York Times,* 27 Dec. 1993.

47. *Dances with Wolves* press kit, BFIL, 1.

48. Quoted in Keith, 147.

49. Michael Medved, *Hollywood vs. America: Popular Culture and the War on Traditional Values* (New York: HarperCollins, 1992), 3. Although Medved's book was published two years after the release of *Dances with Wolves,* he had been working as a movie critic for a long time, and we can thus assume that his views had been part of popular debate about the movies throughout the late 1980s.

50. Medved, 4.

51. For a detailed discussion of this phenomenon, see Charles Lyons, *The New Censors: Movies and the Culture Wars* (Philadelphia, PA: Temple University Press, 1997) and Romanowski (1996).

52. In fact, Medved was strongly critical of *Dances with Wolves*, which he viewed as unpatriotic. See Medved, 226.

53. Jim Collins, 'Genericity in the Nineties: Eclectic Irony and the New Sincerity' in Jim Collins, Hilary Radner and Ava Preacher Collins, eds., *Film Theory Goes to the Movies* (London: Routledge, 1993), 257.

54. For more on the epic qualities of *How the West Was Won*, see Hall (1996), 255–260.

55. Medved, 183.

56. Undated, anonymous *Variety* review, quoted in John Walker, ed., *Halliwell's Film, Video and DVD Guide 2004* (London: HarperCollins, 2004), 884.

57. Quoted in Geoff Andrew, "Indian Bravery," *Time Out* 9 Jan. 1991, 16.

58. Quoted in Sid Field, *Four Screenplays: Studies in the American Screenplay* (New York: Dell, 1994), 256.

59. Hall, 255.

60. Ibid. For a more elaborate extrapolation of the epic film's thematic 'work,' see James Russell, "Foundation Myths: DreamWorks SKG, *The Prince of Egypt* (1998) and the Historical Epic Film," *New Review of Film and Television Studies* 2, no. 2 (Nov. 2004), 240–241.

61. Hugh Brogan, *The Penguin History of the USA* 2nd ed. (London: Penguin, 1999), 70.

62. See Greg Evans, "Orion creates epic pitch for *Dances with Wolves*," *Variety* 5 Nov. 1990, unpaginated clipping, *Dances with Wolves* file, AMPAS.

63. *Dances with Wolves* press kit, 1.

64. Details of Costner, Blake and Wilson are cited above.

65. Roger Ebert, rev. of *Dances with Wolves*, *Chicago Sun-Times* 9 Nov. 1990, 20, and Jami Bernard, rev. of *Dances with Wolves*, *New York Post* 9 Nov. 1990, 35.

66. Details of this were presented on a press release from Orion Studios, dated 30 Jan. 1991. Obtained from the *Dances with Wolves* clippings file, NYPL.

67. Sheila Benson, rev. of *Dances with Wolves*, *Los Angeles Times* 9 Nov. 1990, Calendar, 1.

68. David Denby, rev. of *Dances with Wolves*, *New York* 19 Nov. 1990, 107; M. S. Malone, rev. of *Dances with Wolves*, *Christian Science Monitor*, 7 Dec. 1990, 12; and David Ansen, rev. of *Dances with Wolves*, *Newsweek* 19 Nov. 1990, 67.

69. Shaun Usher, rev. of *Dances with Wolves*, *Daily Mail* 8 Feb. 1991, 28.

70. Altman, 35.

71. Ibid., 38.

72. Neale, 33.

73. Financial data from Box Office Mojo, http://www.boxofficemojo.com/?movies/?id=unforgiven.htm.

74. Financial data from Box Office Mojo, http://www.boxofficemojo.com/?movies/?id=tombstone.htm and http://www.boxofficemojo.com/?movies/?id=wyattearp.htm. See also Neale, 33.

75. Financial data from Box Office Mojo, http://www.boxofficemojo.com/?movies/?id=lastofthe mohicans.htm.

76. Financial data from Box Office Mojo, http://www.boxofficemojo.com/?movies/?id=far andaway.htm.

77. Financial data from Box Office Mojo, http://www.boxofficemojo.com/?movies/?id=gettysburg.htm.

78. See David Gritten, "Grim. Black and White . . . Spielberg?" *Los Angeles Times* 9 May 1993, Calendar 70.

79. The reviewer also commented on the striking similarity to Stanley Kubrick's *Spartacus* (1962). Brian Lowry, rev. of *Braveheart*, *Variety* 22 May 1995, 91.

80. See comments made by Gibson in *Mel Gibson's Braveheart: A Filmmaker's Passion* on 2001 DVD release of *Braveheart*.

81. John Brodie, "Oscar win vindicates kilt trip," *Variety* 1 Apr. 1996, 1 and 71.

82. Paramount was the original distributor and arranged a co-production deal with Fox as the budget increased. As part of the deal, Paramount retained domestic distribution rights, while Fox distributed overseas (Finler, 5). Financial data from Box Office Mojo, http://www. boxofficemojo.com/?movies/?id=braveheart.htm.

83. The 2003 MPAA report does have figures for 1995 but notes that, in 1993, the average negative cost of a major studio release was $29.9 million. Anon., *U.S. Entertainment Industry: 2003 MPA Market Statistics*, obtained via application to http://www.mpaa.org/useconomicreview, 17.

-3-

Steven Spielberg, the Holocaust and *Schindler's List* (1993)

Steven Spielberg's *Schindler's List* was released in 1993 to widespread critical acclaim. *Newsweek*'s effusive review declared, "Spielberg's very nature as a filmmaker has been transformed; he's reached within himself for a new language, and without losing any of his innate fluency or his natural born storytelling gift, he's found a style that will astonish both his fans and those detractors who believed he was doomed to permanent adolescence."[1] *Variety* argued that *Schindler's List* "evinces an artistic rigour and unsentimental intelligence unlike anything the world's most successful filmmaker has demonstrated before."[2] David Denby, in *New York Magazine*, wrote, "[I]t is as if [Spielberg] understood for the first time why God gave him such extraordinary skills."[3] Only a handful of reviews explicitly labelled the film an 'epic,' but many noted the epic nature of both the story and the project.[4] Nevertheless, like Kevin Costner's *Dances with Wolves* (1990), the film was an important contribution to the emergent epic cycle. *Schindler's List* was quickly packaged as an educational experience for young people, and the film sparked debates amongst critics, audiences and academics. In the process, Spielberg assumed a position equivalent to both public servant and historian—precisely the role, in fact, that many epic filmmakers had also self-consciously adopted in the 1950s and 1960s. As we will see, the subsequent reestablishment of the intellectual prestige surrounding the mainstream Hollywood epic had a profound effect on the perceptions of filmmakers, the industry and audiences, which further encouraged the revival of the genre.

As we saw in chapter 1, Spielberg, like Kevin Costner, had fond memories of the epics of the roadshow era, which informed his later career. As well as his passion for *Ben-Hur*, Spielberg had repeatedly expressed great admiration for David Lean's *The Bridge on the River Kwai* (1957) and *Lawrence of Arabia* (1962). A fascination with history, especially that of World War II, informs almost all of Spielberg's films. Although elements of *Schindler's List* reflect a deep understanding of, and nostalgia for, vanished cinematic forms, the film derived much of its cultural weight from an exacting, and sometimes disturbing, depiction of real historical events. Kevin Costner had sought to recapture a cinematic past with *Dances with Wolves*. By contrast, *Schindler's List* was an attempt to provide a brutally accurate representation of the actual past—the Holocaust and the experiences of Oskar Schindler.

During production of *Schindler's List*, Spielberg told the *Hollywood Reporter*, "It will be the most authentic film I have made."[5] After its release, he claimed, in the *Los Angeles Times*, "The film is a remembrance. I wouldn't have done it if I didn't think a story like this would remind people, in a way that people really don't want to remember, that these events occurred only 50 years ago. And it could happen in all its monstrosity again."[6] His comments indicate that *Schindler's List* was conceived of as an act of public commemoration, which would also educate contemporary audiences about the past. The resulting film was imbued with the kind of intellectual depth, visual sophistication and cultural prestige that, critics claimed, had previously been lacking in Spielberg's work. It also provided a model for other filmmakers interested in creating sincere socially and politically committed mainstream movies about the past.

Hollywood's appreciation for *Schindler's List* can be gauged by the film's performance at the Academy Awards, where it won seven Oscars, including those for Best Picture and Best Director. Furthermore, *Schindler's List* was the most commercially successful epic released since *Dances with Wolves*. Although it did not perform quite as well as Costner's film, *Schindler's List* grossed $96 million in domestic receipts and a further $221 million overseas.[7] The unusually high overseas revenues hinted at a pattern that would recur as the revival of the epic continued. Just as they had in the roadshow era, the most successful epics of the 1990s have generated an unusually high percentage of revenues in the international market, a phenomenon discussed in chapter 6. In general terms, the outstanding financial success of the film was yet another example of the epic's growing economic viability.

In choosing to address the Holocaust, Spielberg's epic was heavily influenced by a broader memorial discourse centred on memories of the Holocaust that had been growing in prominence in America since the 1960s. In 1999, the historian Peter Novick observed that "the Holocaust has, in recent decades, moved from the margins to the centre of how American Jews understand themselves and how they represent themselves to others."[8] Alan Mintz has noted that, over time, "important sectors of the [non-Jewish] American public did come to view the Holocaust as an issue that belongs on the American agenda, and wheels were set in motion that eventually brought about the creation of the Washington museum and other broadly supported sites of memorialization."[9] For Mintz, and for many other scholars, popular culture, in the form of movies and television, played an important role in privileging the Holocaust in American public debate. The television series *Holocaust* (1978) and *War and Remembrance* (1988), discussed in chapter 2, had both contributed to this phenomenon, and Jeffrey Shandler has demonstrated that the Holocaust increasingly permeated public consciousness in more subtle forms through many other television shows of the 1960s and 1970s.[10] The formation, in 1978, of a presidential commission on the memorialisation of the Holocaust eventually led to the opening of the United States Holocaust Museum in Washington, D.C., in the early 1990s, which seemed to cement the process sometimes known as the 'Americanisation of the Holocaust.'[11]

The reasons for an apparently disproportionate American preoccupation with the plight of European Jews during the war have been the subject of fierce debate. Key contributory factors include the capture of Adolf Eichmann in the 1960s and the growing political and military travails of the Israeli state (which has always had close political, social and cultural ties with America).[12] However, this chapter is not intended to account for the 'Americanisation of the Holocaust,' nor does it engage with aesthetic debates about the 'representability' of the Holocaust.[13] It is, as ever, focused on the conditions of film production and seeks to demonstrate how Spielberg's film, generally regarded as an important intervention in public debate, increased the standing of the epic in Hollywood by demonstrating the capacity of mainstream film to contribute to elite cultural and political debates about the past.

The first section of this chapter examines Spielberg's prior releases and biography for traces of the impulse that would lead him to make *Schindler's List*. The second section looks at the production history of the film, and the third examines Spielberg's depiction of the Holocaust in more detail. The fourth links Spielberg's vision of the past to broader questions of virtue, charity and responsibility. We will see that *Schindler's List* is partly the product of an educational agenda (effectively illustrating and explaining the Holocaust in the manner of a straightforward narrative history), but it is also an emotional experience designed to shape audience responses to the past (through the character of Oskar Schindler).

1. Spielberg, Hollywood and World War II

Throughout his career Spielberg has returned repeatedly to World War II as both a setting and subject for his films. According to Joseph McBride, two of the first films that Spielberg ever made as a boy on his father's Super 8 cine-camera were wartime adventures—*Fighter Squad* in 1960, when he was thirteen, and *Escape to Nowhere* in 1962.[14] Prior to the release of *Schindler's List*, Spielberg once said of the war, "I love that period—My father filled my head with war stories. I have identified with that period of innocence and tremendous jeopardy all my life. It was the end of an era, the end of innocence, and I have been clinging to it for most of my adult life."[15] Like so many children born in the 1940s and 1950s, Spielberg is the son of a war veteran, and World War II was to have a lasting impact on his work. Since *Jaws* (1975), almost all of Spielberg's films exhibit some connection to World War II. Towards the end of *Jaws*, the obsessive shark hunter Quint (Robert Shaw) delivers a monologue about the sinking of the USS *Indianapolis* shortly after it had delivered the Hiroshima bomb that explicitly links Quint's harrowing wartime memories to his obsession with sharks.[16] Alternatively, Spielberg's *1941*, released in 1979, was a comedy set shortly before America's entry into the war, charting the ensuing social panic after a Japanese submarine is sighted off the coast of southern California. The film was one of Spielberg's rare flops, in both critical and commercial terms. Nevertheless, Spielberg continued to produce films with war themes or settings, finding greater success with the Indiana Jones films—all of which took place against the rise of Nazism and saw Indiana Jones (Harrison Ford) coming face-to-face with Nazi troops, scheming SS officers and even Hitler himself in *Indiana Jones and the Last Crusade* (1989).

Γ *Empire of the Sun* (1987) was Spielberg's first attempt to produce a more recognisably epic account of the war (which is to say, a serious depiction of pivotal events). The film was an adaptation of J. G. Ballard's semi-autobiographical account of his own childhood in the concentration camps of wartime Shanghai, which Spielberg was originally slated to produce (through his Amblin production company), while his hero, David Lean, would direct. Spielberg once said of Lean's *Lawrence of Arabia* (1962), "More than any other single movie in my memory, that was the one movie that sort of decided my fate," and in the 1980s, Spielberg had become heavily involved in a project to restore Lean's desert epic.[17] Collaborating with Lean must have been the realisation of a lifelong dream, and as a result *Empire of the Sun* can, in its original form, be understood as a nostalgic production in the manner of Costner's *Dances with Wolves*. In both cases, filmmakers were revisiting childhood obsessions. However, it quickly became apparent that Lean was not as easy to work with as Spielberg might have imagined, and as the production process rolled on Lean dropped out, leaving Spielberg to direct.[18]

Spielberg's *Empire of the Sun* traces the adventures of Jim (Christian Bale), the eleven-year-old son of a British family living in Shanghai. When the Japanese invade, Jim is separated from his parents and incarcerated in a concentration camp. In a typically 'Ballardian' inversion, the war, for Jim, becomes a site of adventure and liberation from parental control. He quickly finds that the relaxed social order of the camp allows him a far greater degree of responsibility than his earlier existence, and he also becomes increasingly obsessed with the Japanese fighter pilots stationed nearby. Although his experiences are not always pleasant, much of the film's novelty is derived from Jim's upbeat, even enthusiastic response to the destruction and privation surrounding him.[19] Furthermore, Jim's indifference to suffering, and his adulation of the enemy, seems to comment critically on the boyish, nostalgic obsession with the trappings of war evinced in Spielberg's earlier movies. Spielberg himself viewed the film as transitional and said of it, "I'm trying to grow up by increments, I'm trying very gently to step up to a different kind of movie."[20]

Empire of the Sun performed poorly at the box office, appearing to provide studios and industry personnel with further evidence that epic historical films were unpopular with cinemagoers in the 1980s. However, the ongoing success of epics on television, and the subsequent popularity of epic films in the 1990s, suggests that the relative failure of *Empire of the Sun* had less to do with its putative 'epicness' than with certain formal problems. Speaking retrospectively, David Lean said of the project: "I worked on it for about a year, and in the end I gave up because I thought it's bloody well written and very interesting, but it hasn't got a dramatic shape. I must say a bit of what I felt, I felt about [Spielberg's] film, too."[21] Later, *Variety*'s review of the finished film criticised what it saw as an uneasiness of tone and declared, "Spielberg delves deeply into the well of seriousness and comes up with about half a bucket."[22] *Variety*'s criticisms, and Spielberg's assertion that he had been building towards an 'adult' project, emphasise a widely held critical perception at the time that, for all their commercial success, Spielberg's films were ultimately immature and juvenile. Spielberg's growing interest in epics has to be understood in the context of a growing critical disparagement, which directly equated Spielberg's growing popularity with the supposed frivolity, and cultural 'worthlessness', of his films.

In his article 'The New Hollywood', Thomas Schatz has argued that *Jaws* "marked the arrival of the New Hollywood [because it] recalibrated the profit potential of the Hollywood hit, and redefined its status as a marketable commodity and cultural phenomenon."[23] For Schatz, *Jaws* initiated a new trend towards high-cost, high-return blockbusters. In fact, the blockbuster trend had been a dominant feature of Hollywood's production strategies since the roadshow era, as we saw in chapter 1. Nevertheless, Spielberg is often viewed by critics as the key instigator of a shift towards highly budgeted, easily marketable, family-oriented 'event' movies (much like the major hits of the roadshow era). In attempting to classify what he perceives as Spielberg's 'malign' influence on Hollywood in the 1980s and 1990s, the academic critic Wheeler Winston Dixon has argued that Spielberg's films, and the majority of Hollywood releases influenced by his work, have been characterised by "visuals over content, excess before restraint, spectacle rather than insight."[24] Such negative views of Spielberg were neatly summarised in the otherwise positive *Christian Science Monitor* review of *Schindler's List*:

> Most of his biggest hits, from *Jaws* to *Jurassic Park*, resemble widescreen video games—full of snap and crackle, but intellectually empty and emotionally thin. When he has tried his hand at an adult theme, as in *The Color Purple* and *Empire of the Sun*, he has approached his ambitious material with the same 12-year-old mind that presides over his empty-headed blockbusters.[25]

David Thomson described Spielberg as "the junior mechanic as movie director," whose success is proof that contemporary Hollywood "is not a place for artists."[26] In each case, Spielberg was criticised by some, at least, for producing unenlightened, artistically and thematically shallow films, which exhibited little in the way of culturally resonant or meaningful content. By the late 1980s, Spielberg himself appeared genuinely concerned with such criticism and responded to the suggestion that his films failed to deal with 'adult' issues by saying, "I just feel that I'll make that grown-up movie when I am grown-up enough to make it."[27]

As the next section will demonstrate, *Schindler's List* had a long history as a film project and should not be understood purely as a reaction to critical distain. In part, the success of *Dances with Wolves* may well have opened up the possibility of funding for another of Spielberg's epic visions of World War II. However, the serious, controversial nature of the film did appear to directly address negative perceptions of Spielberg's work. With *Schindler's List* he set out to tackle a sensitive subject with immediate personal resonances. Furthermore, the film was a story of Jewish suffering and public benevolence that resonated both with Spielberg's lowly critical position and, more important, his background as an American Jew. Critical disdain may have encouraged Spielberg to 'prove' his seriousness as a filmmaker, but his decision to revisit the Holocaust was an essentially personal act—a consequence of his upbringing and sense of identity. Like so many epics of the early 1990s, the origins of *Schindler's List* lie more in biography than in economics.

2. Judaism and the Origins of *Schindler's List*

For much of his early working life, Spielberg exhibited an ambivalence about his religious heritage that can be traced back to his childhood.[28] His father, Arnold Spielberg, had been brought up in the Jewish communities of Cincinnati, where Steven Spielberg was born. When he was two, the family moved to New Jersey. Arnold Spielberg was an electronic engineer working in the putative computer industry, and as his career advanced it became necessary to move farther and farther into the Midwest in pursuit of the technology industries that eventually settled in California. In this regard, Arnold Spielberg's life is fairly representative of the broader postwar Jewish experience in America, when the discriminatory social boundaries of earlier periods began to weaken.[29] Arnold's upward social mobility necessitated a move away from ethnically inclusive urban districts on the East Coast, and the Spielberg family were brought into contact with predominantly Gentile America. In the process, the young Steven Spielberg was made very aware that his Jewishness marked him as different.

The Spielberg family moved from Cincinnati to New Jersey, then to Phoenix, Arizona, when Steven Spielberg was ten, and finally to Saratoga, California, when he was seventeen. At each stage of this journey, Spielberg claimed to have encountered increasing levels of anti-Semitic bullying. McBride reports that, even in New Jersey, Spielberg felt uncomfortable with his faith and avoided discussion of Jewish traditions.[30] Spielberg later told the *New York Times* that during his time at school in Arizona and California, "I was embarrassed, I was self-conscious, I was always aware I stood out because of my Jewishness. In high school I got smacked and kicked around. Two bloody noses. It was horrible."[31] Although his family had attended synagogue when he was a child, Spielberg apparently stopped going when he reached his teens. Presumably this was partly the result of encounters with anti-Semitism, but other reasons cannot be discounted, including a simple disengagement with religion that characterised a sizable proportion of his generation.[32]

Unlike many other Jewish families, the Spielbergs had lost no close relatives in the Holocaust, although Arnold Spielberg once estimated that between sixteen and twenty more distant relatives died in the death camps.[33] His son reported, "In a strange way my life has always come back to images surrounding the Holocaust [which] had been part of my life just based on what my parents would say round the dinner table. We lost cousins, aunts, uncles. I grew up with stories of Nazis breaking the fingers of Jews."[34] Spielberg's experiences were, in this regard, fairly representative of postwar Jewish attitudes toward the Holocaust. According to Peter Novick, "[N]obody in these years seemed to have much to say on the subject, at least in public," and remembrance of the Holocaust remained an essentially a private affair.[35]

Although he was not practising his faith in the early stages of his career, many of Spielberg's films contain elements that seem related to his religious upbringing and heritage. The concern with race that informs both *The Color Purple* (1985) and *Amistad* (1997) may well derive from Spielberg's sense of himself as an ethnic artist. Even in his more popular films, references to Judaic myths and traditions recur. *Raiders of the Lost Ark* (1981) is centred on the quest to find and protect a holy Jewish artefact from the Nazis. In the film's final sequence, the Ark of the Covenant, which contains the remnants of the Ten Commandments, is opened, and the wrath of God is unleashed on the Nazis. The god of the Hebrews is revealed as real (although not at the expense of Christianity) and takes literal, physical revenge on the future perpetrators of the Holocaust. In 1986, Spielberg produced the animated film *An American Tail* (directed by Don Bluth), which was loosely based on the life of his great-grandfather Fievel. *An American Tail* told the story of a mouse, also named Fievel, trying to make his way as an immigrant in nineteenth-century America, in much the same way as Fievel Spielberg had done. Although the film provided little overt commentary on Spielberg's Judaic heritage, it demonstrated a willingness to engage with Jewish immigrant history in mainstream, family-oriented films. However, it was with *Schindler's List* that Spielberg underwent what Yosefa Loshitzky has described as "'rebirth' as a Jewish artist."[36]

In interviews given to promote the film, Spielberg was suddenly keen to discuss his newfound commitment to Judaism. He explained that making *Schindler's List* had helped him feel proud of being a Jew, after a long period of equivocation.[37] His wife, the actress Kate Capshaw, converted, and their children were being raised according to Judaic tradition. Spielberg's decision to make *Schindler's List* can therefore partly be understood in spiritual terms, in similar fashion to the epics of the 1950s and 1960s that also spoke to Judeo-Christian religious beliefs. Furthermore, Spielberg's return to his faith again reflects broader trends in American society. As social historian Robert D. Putnam has shown, religious belief and church/synagogue attendance has been increasing since the late 1980s (a phenomenon that clearly impacted on the revival of the epic and is discussed in greater detail in chapter 7).[38] Like Spielberg's earlier films, the spiritual elements of *Schindler's List* also make overt references to Jewish religious traditions in a manner that closely links the film to key releases of the roadshow period.

Thomas Elsaesser has argued that Spielberg's "Schindler can be seen as a Moses figure, leading his people out of Egyptian captivity."[39] At one point in *Schindler's List*, the brutal camp-commandant Amon Goeth (Ralph Fiennes) asks of the central character (played by Liam Neeson), "Who are you? Moses?" As well as engaging with one of the key myths of Judeo-Christian tradition, oblique references to Moses connect several of Spielberg's films to the dominant cinematic account of the Moses story: Cecil B. DeMille's 1956 version of *The Ten Commandments*. In 1998, Spielberg's studio, DreamWorks SKG, produced a remake of DeMille's film, apparently at Spielberg's suggestion (as chapter 5 will demonstrate). Furthermore, the Ark of the Covenant, which drives the narrative of *Raiders of the Lost Ark*, supposedly contains the remains of the tablets that Moses brought down from Mount Sinai. In *Close Encounters of the Third Kind* (1977), an ordinary man finds himself compelled to visit another 'holy mountain' where he communes with apparently 'divine' aliens. Early in the film, Roy Neary (Richard Dreyfuss) actually watches *The Ten Commandments* on television with his young family. From the earliest moments of his career, then, the Moses story seems to have resonated with Spielberg, and it offers an interesting insight into his work. In DeMille's film, Moses initially denies his faith, then experiences a spiritual reawakening and is inspired to carry out great acts of benevolence. It is not difficult to see parallels in Spielberg's career that might draw him towards the Moses story, and *Schindler's List* clearly bears the imprint of this fascination. However, one must be wary of drawing too many direct comparisons. *Schindler's List* had not originated directly with Spielberg, and for the most part the finished film offered little in the way of spiritual consolation. Instead, *Schindler's List* had originated with the 'Schindlerjuden', those Jews who had been saved from the Nazi death camps by Oskar Schindler.

Poldek Pfefferberg was one such individual. He had been living in Kraków when the Germans invaded, and his black market connections brought him into contact with Oskar Schindler, who employed him in his camp and ensured that Pfefferberg survived. After the war, Pfefferberg moved to America, changed his name to Poldek Page, and set up business as a luggage salesman in Los Angeles. Over the course of the next forty years, he worked to see Schindler's story transformed into a movie and thus made known to a wider audience. His first attempt to get a movie made in the 1960s failed, but in 1980, the Australian writer Thomas Keneally walked into Page's Beverly Hills store, and Page told Keneally, "I have a story for you for the theme of a book."[40] Keneally agreed, and *Schindler's Ark* (*Schindler's List* was the U.S. title) was published several years later. The book was a critical success, winning the prestigious Booker Prize, and movie rights to the project were purchased by Sid Sheinberg, president of MCA-Universal. Sheinberg was hoping that Spielberg would direct, and in 1983, the company placed full-page advertisements in the trade newspapers announcing the 'association' of Steven Spielberg with *Schindler's List*.[41] Spielberg has since claimed that he didn't feel ready to make the film in 1983, and he told Poldek Page that he would make *Schindler's List* in ten years—when he was sufficiently 'grown-up.'[42] Whether by accident or design, he was true to his word.

Throughout the 1980s, *Schindler's List* hovered in the background of Spielberg's other projects.[43] On more than one occasion Spielberg attempted to interest other directors in the film, only to withdraw the offer before firm commitments were made. As a result, Martin Scorsese, Roman Polanski and Billy Wilder were all associated with Schindler's story at one time or another, but Spielberg was never willing to let the project slip away entirely. The final decision that he was ready to make the film came at the beginning of the 1990s. Spielberg explained:

There was CNN reporting every day on the equivalent of Nazi death camps in Bosnia, the atrocities against the Muslims—and then this horrible word 'ethnic cleansing', cousin to the 'final solution'.

I thought, My God, this is happening again . . . and on top of all that comes the media giving serious airtime and print space to the Holocaust deniers. . . . And I suddenly turned to Kate, who was asleep, and I said, I'm doing *Schindler's List* as my next film.[44]

As historian Samantha Power has shown, the Holocaust was repeatedly evoked as a reference point during media discussion of the Bosnian war.[45] A report that appeared in *Newsday* in July 1992 described the transport of Muslim civilians as being "like Auschwitz" and quoted a Muslim student, who said, "We all felt like Jews in the Third Reich."[46] Furthermore, projects of Holocaust remembrance were becoming increasingly visible throughout the preceding decade, as work by Novick and others has demonstrated, and the growing visibility of the Holocaust in popular debate, particularly amongst American Jews, presumably helped to strengthen Spielberg's belief that *Schindler's List* was an important and culturally 'necessary' story to tell again.[47]

Although Sid Sheinberg had purchased the project for Spielberg, the studio was concerned about its financial viability. As a result, Universal only agreed to fund *Schindler's List* if Spielberg made *Jurassic Park* first; presumably, studio heads felt confident that *Jurassic Park*, a best-seller adaptation of a very different nature, would prove a surefire box office hit in Spielberg's hands, thus compensating for the potential risk that a three-hour, black-and-white Holocaust epic represented.[48] As a result, Spielberg, like Kevin Costner, enjoyed a considerable degree of economic and creative autonomy on the film. Later he would explain that making *Schindler's List* was something he felt he *had* to do. He told *Newsweek*, "Perhaps indecently, I'm making this film for myself, for the survivors, for my family—and for people who should understand the meaning of the word 'Holocaust.'"[49] He also expressed concerns about the nature of the film in the *New York Times*:

Some days I feel preachy. Sometimes I think this is going to be an important movie. Other days I think it's going to be an anecdote of an important moment in history. In the end, I think I don't care. I have to make the movie—the subject matter dwarfs the habitual worries. This is the one movie I wanted to make for the survivors, for the Schindlerjuden and people who should learn more.[50]

Schindler's List, then, was conceived of as an educational experience, and the next section will explain what Spielberg said to 'people who should learn more.'

3. The Holocaust in *Schindler's List*

Schindler's List begins with a colour prologue showing a contemporary Jewish family preparing for the Seder (or Passover) feast. After World War II, the ritual prayers of the Seder festival were amended to include commemorative references to those Jews who died in the Holocaust.[51] Thus, for Jewish viewers the film is immediately placed within a framework of commemorative ritual.[52] The film then cuts to black-and-white scenes of Jews arriving in the Polish city of Cracow shortly after the German invasion of 1939. As a group of Nazi officials begins to take down their details, the screen is given over to a montage of faces and a typed list of names. Then Spielberg cuts to Oskar Schindler charming a group of Nazi officers at a nightclub. Effectively, Schindler and the Jews are shown to operate in separate social and economic spheres at the beginning of the film. Schindler's world of glittering nightclubs, beautiful women and powerful industrialists contrasts spectacularly with the bleak poverty and privation experienced by the Jews. However, the two are brought together by the machinery of war and genocide, and, in the process, Schindler is slowly transformed from an uncaring entrepreneur to a benevolent hero.

Subsequent scenes provide a carefully constructed overview of the Holocaust's development from abstract policy (embodied by the increasing levels of institutionally mandated social regulation) to practice (the systematic killing of Jews in the ghettos and then the death camps at Plaszow and Auschwitz-Birkenau). As the grim narrative unfolds, various sequences in the film work to meet Spielberg's educative, as well as commemorative, aims. Schindler's story effectively allows Spielberg to present an explanatory account of the Holocaust, which incorporates all the major, academically recognised, historical occurrences throughout the period of Nazi rule in Poland. Thus, the film comes to work as a kind of historical account in and of itself—with key scenes providing a visual 'illustration' of historical events. So, the opening sequence depicts the initial implementation of SS head Reinhard Heydrich's 1939 dictate ordering all Polish Jews to come to the cities and make themselves known to the newly arrived authorities.[53] Various historians, notably Yisrael Gutman, have explored the implementation of this policy and its broader social ramifications.[54] Although accounts differ as to the degree of foresight involved in the early stages of the Holocaust, most writers on the period have identified this moment as the beginning of the Holocaust for Polish Jews.[55] It is therefore significant that Spielberg's film also begins with these moments, because the *specific* story of Oskar

Schindler is immediately presented as part of a *broader* historical account of the Holocaust.

As the film progresses, the treatment of the Polish Jews at the hands of the Nazis becomes more extreme and more violent. In an early sequence where Oskar Schindler goes to visit the Jewish council, casually brushing past a massive queue of dispossessed Jews with the self-assurance of one who has never faced real privation, he stops to observe Nazi soldiers humiliating an elderly Jewish man on the street. Despite its limited screen time the scene serves to illustrate the slow but steady adoption of public violence towards Jews that quickly became a socially accepted means of intimidation in Nazi-occupied Poland. As the historian Daniel Jonah Goldhagen has written, the common practice of "Germans forcibly cutting Jews' beards and hair . . . were physical attacks of fearsome symbolic content that began in the first months of the Nazi period and continued to its end. Such 'public defamation' and humiliation expressed the Germans' eliminationist intent."[56] At the Jewish council Schindler overhears more accounts of public humiliation at the hands of the Nazis, which stress the increasing frequency of such assaults.

Meanwhile, Oskar Schindler sets about establishing his factory using Jewish funds, Jewish labour and Jewish expertise in the form of accountant Itzhak Stern (Ben Kingsley), who will ultimately run Schindler's business. The sudden decline in the social status of the Jews effectively allows Schindler to take advantage of their frozen capital (which they can no longer spend on their own); their black-market connections (which have been forced upon them as they have been excluded from the regular economy); and their physical labour (which has become the property of the Nazi Party). Thus, Schindler's rise in status is directly linked to Nazi efforts to 'dehumanise' Jews in preparation for their campaign of genocide. As Jews lose control of their property, labour and even their bodies, the opportunities available to Schindler increase proportionally. Thus, the film makes clear that Schindler's particular story of entrepreneurial success is entirely attributable to the reallocation of resources away from Jews whose 'personhood' was being steadily eroded by the Nazi state.

The Nazis' dehumanising project intensifies when the Jews of Cracow are forcibly evicted from their homes and moved to Nazi-circumscribed ghettos. (To further illustrate the connection between Nazi policy and Schindler's status, Spielberg cuts from a wealthy Jewish family leaving their luxurious apartment to Schindler taking up residency in the next scene.) 'Ghettoisation' occurred across Poland in 1940 and 1941, in accordance with Heydrich's orders.[57] Once Schindler has founded his factory he relies on Jewish labour from the ghettos to man his machines. Unbeknownst to him, Stern includes some of the more vulnerable Jews in his workforce and ensures their good treatment. Shortly afterwards, Stern himself narrowly avoids being sent to a labour camp in the east and is rescued at the last moment by Schindler. Stern has been placed on board a train crammed with other Jews, heading to some mysterious destination in the east. As Schindler negotiates his release, the camera pans through to a restricted area where clerks are scavenging through the luggage of the Jews, hinting at the sinister nature of their destination. As Susan R. Horowitz has noted, in this sequence "the heaps of possessions stand in for the corpses of their owners, providing a bearable metonymic representation of atrocity."[58] Then, a group of workers on their way to Schindler's factory are co-opted into shovelling snow by a passing brigade of Nazi soldiers, who shoot one elderly employee. Each scene demonstrates the gradually worsening situation of the Jews and the slow exacerbation of the Holocaust, allowing viewers access to the broader currents of history at the margins of the film's narrative.

Unbeknownst to Schindler, SS officer Amon Goeth (Ralph Fiennes) arrives in Cracow charged with the job of removing Jews from the ghetto and relocating them to Plaszow forced labour camp, on the outskirts of the city. In an extended scene of destruction, Goeth and his men quickly overrun the ghetto and force out the inhabitants. Any who attempt to escape are killed. According to Thomas Keneally's account, over 4,000 Jews were murdered on 13 March 1943.[59] Again, the move to Plaszow was representative of a sudden shift in the climate of victimisation, and Goeth's camp is a place of astonishing, but not historically inaccurate, cruelty. Goeth punishes perceived misdemeanours with death and often kills his charges at random. At various points, the unfit or elderly are sent to their deaths, parents are separated from their children, and workers are killed to make way for new inmates. Plaszow stands in for a camp system that emerged across Germany's Eastern European territories at this time—which has been described as the "largest institutional creation of Germany during its Nazi period . . . where the true nature of the evolving regime was being forged."[60] According to Goldhagen, the labour camps were "a site of the freest self-expression, where Germans could become masters who were not hemmed in by the bourgeois restraints which Nazism was rapidly superseding with a new anti-Christian morality."[61] The experiences of the Jews in *Schindler's List* move quickly from a curtailment of individual liberty, to public humiliation, to physical restriction, to imprisonment and finally to an enforced loss of identity and extermination in the camps; in the process, the experiential history of the Holocaust is revealed.[62]

In the film, the final stage of this journey occurs when Plaszow is being dismantled towards the end of the war, and all remaining inmates are sent to the death camp at Auschwitz-Birkenau. At this point Schindler has written a list of Jews he wants to save, but an administrative error causes some of 'his' Jews to be inadvertently sent to their deaths. The Schindlerjuden find themselves at the historical end point of the Holocaust, the most notorious site of the Nazis' industrial campaign of murder, and, in attempting to present as complete a picture of the past as possible, Spielberg's camera actually follows Schindler's workers, naked and terrified, into the Auschwitz gas chambers. Although they receive a last-minute reprieve, the sequence concludes with the image of a line of Jews being ushered into the underground facility at Auschwitz-Birkenau, while a chimney belches smoke in the distance, in a shot clearly intended to act as a metaphor both for the camp's murderous purpose and the ultimate goals of the Holocaust.

Several critics have complained that in all of these sequences, Jewish characters remain relatively marginal players in an undistinguished mass, in contrast to the more rounded depictions of Oskar Schindler and Amon Goeth. For instance, J. Hoberman has written that the film reduces the Jews to the status of "supporting parts in their own cataclysm."[63] In an article subtitled 'The Feminisation of the Jew in *Schindler's List*', Judith E. Doneson expresses concern that the film served to "portray, in some manner, Christian/Gentiles attempting to save the lives of weak, passive Jews."[64] During a roundtable discussion that appeared in the *Village Voice* shortly after the release of the film, the comic book artist and writer Art Spiegelman put these concerns in more direct terms when he stated that, "The problem for me is there weren't any Jews in the picture."[65] The film certainly does tell the story of the Holocaust at a collective level, but I would argue that the narrative remains obsessively focused on the names and experiences of individual Jews. The list is repeatedly used as a means of establishing identity, and Jewish characters are remarkably well rounded given their limited screen time. Several individuals in particular are focused on throughout, including Itzhak Stern, Poldek Pfefferberg (Jonathan Sagall), Goeth's maid Helen Hirsch (Embeth Davidtz), and in several scenes, an unnamed girl in a red dress.[66] Their experiences effectively 'humanise' the historical overview of the Holocaust that Spielberg presents.

Ultimately, then, *Schindler's List* presented an account of the Holocaust that can be loosely compared to more academically inclined, narrative history. Spielberg's film sought to represent key historical events and make history accessible at an experiential level. On release it sparked a barrage of academic comment, which acknowledged the film's status as a historical account but also as a key text in the 'Americanisation of the Holocaust.' Alan Mintz has astutely summarised the reception of the film:

> Ordinary viewers, the popular media and communal organisations saw in the film a momentous breakthrough. [It was] held to be capable of imparting an awareness of the Holocaust to millions of people who would otherwise remain ignorant of the event; and was further credited with success in 'moving' people, that is making the imparted knowledge affecting, in ways that more austere works of art had failed to do. The detractors were intellectuals and academics who argued that *Schindler's List* had absorbed the catastrophe into the sentimental and melodramatic conventions of popular entertainment and in doing so had betrayed the event.[67]

Both positive and negative responses to the film were brought together in Yosefa Loshitzky's collection of academic writing, *Spielberg's Holocaust*.[68] In this book, and elsewhere, the work of explaining how *Schindler's List* relates to the 'Americanisation of the Holocaust' has already been done. *Schindler's List* constitutes an important entry into the modern epic cycle precisely because it united a serious intellectual project with what Mintz describes (in the above quote) as "the sentimental and melodramatic conventions of popular entertainment." Spielberg's contribution to what David Eldridge has called "Hollywood's historical consciousness" marked him out as a "public historian," in similar fashion to Wyler, DeMille and the other filmmakers responsible for the 1950s epic cycle.[69] Spielberg himself seemed keen to adopt the role of valued social commentator when he told one interviewer that, after *Schindler's List*, "I want to go back and forth between entertainment and socially conscious movies," implicitly suggesting that *Schindler's List* could not be understood within the frame of popular entertainment.[70] It was, instead, a valuable and much needed social experience.

4. Virtue in *Schindler's List*

Ultimately, Oskar Schindler's story is significant because it is exceptional, hence some of the criticisms noted above. During the war, few ordinary

Germans took the sort of heroic measures to save Jews that Schindler had.[71] The focus on a 'good German' can therefore seem both perverse and misleading. Why, then, did Spielberg favour this particular account of the Holocaust? In fact, the Oskar Schindler story (especially as it appears in the film) provided more than simple access to the historical events of Holocaust. It also offered viewers a clear responsive framework through which they could interpret the past. In essence, Oskar Schindler's moral journey encouraged viewers to undertake a related moral journey of their own. As Richard Maltby has argued, the goal of most Hollywood cinema is to provide viewers with a coherent and satisfying emotional experience.[72] *Schindler's List* is no exception, and much of the film's extraordinary power to move viewers is derived from the relatively conventional narrative at its heart.

The details of this emotional journey become apparent when one compares the presumably historically 'accurate' novelistic account of Schindler's life offered by Thomas Keneally to the version of the Schindler story presented in Spielberg's film. The cinematic Schindler often differs markedly from the historical figure. Although Keneally acknowledged that Schindler's motivations could never be fully understood, he attempted to account for his wartime actions by looking to his youth, when he was close friends with a Jewish family.[73] He also suggested repeatedly that, by some accident of birth or upbringing, Schindler seemed incapable of extreme emotions such as hatred or guilt, a combination of qualities that somehow made him the right man, in the right place, at the right time. Furthermore, in Keneally's account, Schindler was far more immediately proactive than the figure featured in Spielberg's film. The real Oskar Schindler was attempting to shield his Jewish workers from Nazi aggression from the beginning of the war, and in 1940 he made a dangerous trip to meet with Zionist activists in Budapest.[74] Keneally also depicted Schindler as an early ideological objector to Nazism. By contrast, Spielberg's Schindler is, at the beginning of the film, a self-absorbed Nazi Party member with little interest in Nazi policy, who initially exhibits no real awareness of, or concern for, Jewish suffering. Indeed, he starts out as an exploitative character, not massively different from the Nazi military elite. Unlike the figure presented in Keneally's novel, the cinematic Schindler then undergoes a profound moral transformation. This epiphany brought the film particular praise, and it was widely held as evidence of Spielberg's newfound maturity that he had not explained, in simple terms, what caused Schindler to change.[75] In fact, the suggestion that Schindler underwent some moment of profound moral adjustment is a fiction invented specifically for Spielberg's film.

Spielberg was not merely attempting to explain the past—his version of the Schindler story also presented viewers with a model for reacting *to* the past. So, Schindler begins the film as a disinterested observer. Furthermore, he is a Gentile alien with no personal connection to the events at hand. In this regard, he is a perfectly fitting proxy for the many western Gentiles watching the film at the end of the twentieth century. Like them, Schindler is initially ignorant about the Holocaust. However, through exposure to the reality of systematic killing, he is shocked, chastened and then transformed into a morally decent saviour figure who leads at least some of the Jews from slavery and murder into a promised land of relative safety.

Throughout the first half of the film, Schindler consistently *observes* rather than *acts* (usually relying on others to take action for him). Often his position in the spatial organisation of the film signals his status as an onlooker. The opening scenes show him watching the arriving Nazi officers, and later he uses Jewish capital to set up Deutsche Emailwaren Fabrik (DEF); he employs Stern to manage the business, Poldek Pfefferberg to obtain items on the black market and favours a Jewish workforce because they are cheap. Although Schindler is exploiting the Jews, he never shows any distaste in his dealings with them. Instead he treats them with exactly the same calculating self-interest that characterises his relationship with the Nazis, and as a result he barely tolerates Stern's attempts to use the factory as a sanctuary. The spatial organisation of the DEF plant situates him in an office perched high above the factory floor, where he enjoys his cognac, fine food and the company of his beautiful secretaries, all the time watching the workers below. Later, when Schindler is approached by a Jewish woman hoping to have her parents transferred to his factory, he appears as a shadowy figure observing her from above.

Schindler finds himself in a similar position when he inadvertently witnesses the liquidation of the Cracow ghetto from a nearby hillside. His spatial position is, again, that of an observer positioned above the action, with a perfect and all-encompassing view. This scene was another invention for the film. Keneally notes that the real Schindler was aware of the forthcoming 'aktion' in the ghetto, and that he stayed away, drinking cognac and raging at his own inability to prevent the Nazi purge.[76] By contrast, the cinematic Schindler is, at this point, still apparently unaware of the Nazis' plans, and a riding trip with his girlfriend brings him to the facing hillside by accident. Much of the following sequence is then presented in point-of-view shots from Schindler's perspective, including one camera trick that focuses the viewer's eye on a little girl whose red dress catches Schindler's eye. The sudden use of colour is apparently designed to bring the audience view in line with Schindler's subjective vision of events. For a moment, viewers see, and presumably feel, what Schindler sees and feels—a shock of recognition, a momentary awareness of one figure in amongst the destruction.

Schindler's position in these scenes offers a viewpoint for viewers to adopt, but it also seems to parallel Nazi attempts to regulate the Jewish presence in Eastern Europe. Within the film, related comparisons are also drawn with the character Goeth, who, in various scenes, is presented as Schindler's mirror image—literally, in one sequence, where shots of the two men shaving are intercut. Curiously, Goeth's villa is also positioned above Plaszow camp in almost exactly the same fashion as Schindler's office. Unlike Schindler, however, Goeth involves himself immediately with events below by taking potshots at passing Jewish workers. Still, towards the end of the film, Schindler describes Goeth in terms that apply equally well to himself—a crook, a ladies' man, a drinker, even a Nazi camp overseer reliant on Jewish labour. However, there is one crucial difference: Goeth does not 'change.' Schindler, by contrast, becomes a very different kind of active participant in events after witnessing the ghetto massacre.

At the moment he witnesses the Nazi killing in the Cracow ghetto, it seems that Schindler is forced to confront the murderous nature of the Holocaust. Afterwards, he begins to subvert Nazi plans in small but significant ways. He convinces Goeth to let him run his own smaller camp at the DEF plant, which quickly becomes a haven from Goeth's arbitrary cruelty. He provides Stern, who is unable to leave Plaszow, with small valuables to facilitate the transfer of particularly vulnerable Jews over to Schindler. He also tries to influence Goeth's behaviour and at one point tells him, "Power is when we have every justification to kill and we don't." Goeth admires Schindler's self-control but will not stop killing. When Schindler realises this, he begins to take more direct action. Goeth becomes obsessed with his maid, Helen Hirsch, but cannot bring himself to act upon his desires with anything other than violence. Spielberg cuts between one particularly brutal attack, which in effect embodies Goeth's inability to express desire, and scenes of Schindler flirting with a showgirl in a glitzy nightclub. To further emphasise the difference between the two men, in the next scene Schindler pointedly kisses one of the female Jewish workers at his own birthday party and, as a result, finds himself briefly imprisoned and questioned by the Nazi authorities. The juxtaposition of these two scenes suggests that Schindler has finally reached the point where he is willing to publicly transgress the enforced social restrictions of the Holocaust in a manner that Goeth, the only other Nazi character with any real screen time, cannot.

Repeatedly, the cinematic Schindler is forced to watch the humiliation, dehumanisation and mass killing that characterised the nightmarish lived reality of the Holocaust. The act of observation transforms him from a witness to a man of action. Schindler gradually begins to implicate himself in the acts of humanistic benevolence that had previously been carried out by proxy. At one point he hoses down the sweltering occupants of a waiting train himself, to the consternation of watching Nazi officials. As the war draws to an end, it becomes apparent that Plaszow and DEF will close, and all the occupants will be sent to the death camps. When Stern asks Schindler what he will do afterwards, Schindler replies, "I'm going home. I've got more money than one man could spend in a lifetime." Following a sleepless night, he decides to use the money for benevolent purposes. Schindler convinces Goeth to sell him his workers, at exorbitant fees, and 'Schindler's list' is written. When Stern realises the high cost that Schindler is paying for every Jew, Stern tells him, "The list is an absolute good. The list is life. All around its margins lies the gulf."

Schindler is therefore changed by the act of witnessing the historical 'reality' of the Holocaust. Of course, what Schindler experiences is exactly what the audience experience. Much like Schindler, viewers are asked to watch the historical atrocities of the Holocaust occur, perhaps with a loved one at their side, perhaps enjoying some light refreshments in the darkened cinema, just as Schindler does in his factory. Even Schindler's riding trip is an essentially pleasurable outing that becomes a far more serious and disturbing experience when he is exposed to the killings in the Cracow ghetto, just as the pleasurable experience of cinemagoing is subverted by Spielberg into a far more harrowing encounter for viewers of *Schindler's List*. Much like Schindler, audiences are supposed to be moved, educated and perhaps even *changed* by the events they witness.

One might also say that Goeth provides an alternative response—gleeful immersion in the scenes of killing and cruelty—which is repeatedly, and rightly, coded in the film as wicked and perverse. But it should be acknowledged that this *is* a potential audience response—violent extended action sequences are the modus operandi of many Hollywood films, and action movie fans are usually thought to enjoy the visceral thrill of watching violent spectacle. The opposed responsive model offered by Goeth, then, is one of the ways that the film discourages more frivolous responses. By bearing witness to the Holocaust, Spielberg's Schindler moves from indifference to committed action. Like the film's audience, Schindler is forced to watch a series of disturbing historical events, calculated to provide an accurate and historically exhaustive overview of the Holocaust's nature and progression. His responses provide a model response that audiences are encouraged to imitate.[77]

Spielberg hoped that *Schindler's List* would present the Holocaust to audiences in such a way as to profoundly affect their view of the world and to modify their behaviour. The focus on Schindler's story provides experiential access to the Holocaust, but it also suggests that the appropriate reaction to witnessing such events is to act decisively to end them (or, at least, to support such action). As a result, Spielberg's film can be related back to the immediate context of the Bosnian war, which, he had claimed, had been a vital spur to producing *Schindler's List*.

During production, the Bosnian war had become a common fixture in the American news media, and the newly elected president Bill Clinton had publicly stated his determination to end a perceived policy of 'ethnic cleansing', being perpetrated upon indigenous Muslims by Bosnian Serb forces.[78] In February 1993, Secretary of State Warren Christopher described the American action in response to the Bosnian war as "an early and crucial test" of Clinton's government.[79] However, as time passed, the Clinton regime seemed reluctant to take direct military action. Samantha Power has demonstrated that the government quickly shifted from categorising events in Bosnia as a form of genocide with links to the Holocaust to a form of internal civil war that outsiders could not resolve.[80] An unwillingness to act was partly a response to the belief that a majority of ordinary American citizens opposed committing American forces. Defence Secretary William Perry claimed that there was "no support, either in public or in the Congress, for taking sides in this war as a combatant, so we will not."[81] However, Power quotes surveys that suggest that a sizable majority theoretically supported intervention. As Power explains, "[B]y the time of Clinton's inauguration in January 1993, some 58 percent of Americans believed military force should be used to protect aid deliveries and prevent atrocities."[82]

Regardless of government actions and the reliability of individual surveys, it was certainly the case that 1993 was a time when many Americans firmly believed that intervention was necessary to prevent (or at least curtail) genocide in Eastern Europe. Spielberg can be counted amongst them. In addition, we have seen that the Holocaust had become a vital feature of the American cultural landscape, and acts of Holocaust remembrance were often used as an opportunity to stress America's commitment to preventing similar atrocities in the future.[83] Spielberg's film must be understood in this context. It was a Holocaust memorial that reflected, at a deep thematic level, an attempt to promote an interventionist attitude towards current atrocities. It asked audiences to leave the auditorium feeling that they had observed the Holocaust and should, like Oskar Schindler, act to prevent another one from occurring.

The message seemed to reach the highest echelons of American society. At an AIDS charity event held in 1993, President Bill Clinton "talked about the film, which he had seen at a special screening the previous evening, and urged everyone to see it. Describing it as 'an astonishing thing' he explained how *Schindler's List* had helped him understand the nature of human suffering and its appropriate response."[84] Although Samantha Power has argued that Clinton subsequently failed to respond with any appropriate haste to human suffering in Bosnia, the President of the United States had been affected at some level by Spielberg's film. No better illustration of the cultural capital attached to Spielberg's historical epic could be provided.

Before the liquidation of the ghetto begins, Amon Goeth gathers his troops together and tells them, "Today is history. Today will be remembered. Years from now the young will ask with wonder about this day. Today is history and you are a part of it." The speech explicitly emphasises the historical reality of the disturbing scenes that follow, and in the process notifies audiences that the film itself 'is history,' that the film should 'be remembered' and that the audience 'is part of it.' Spielberg wanted audiences to learn from the past and apply these lessons to the present.

Finally, Schindler's journey could be said to parallel Spielberg's. Clifford J. Marks and Robert Torry have argued that "the film tells the story of [Schindler's] successful transformation from a Nazi Industrialist, profiting from an evil system, into a doer of great deeds, even though his quest to save lives runs the risk of infuriating the Nazi hierarchy. Spielberg's own career is loosely analogous."[85] By making *Schindler's List*, Spielberg was transformed, in the public eye at least, from a popular entertainer to a benevolent artist. The film was often presented as a considerable financial risk for investors, formulated out of a personal connection to the period. Furthermore, focusing on Schindler implicitly stressed the guilt of all those who did not act to save the Jews, and, one might add, those who did not act to end injustices in the present. This analogy can be extended to examine the way that the film spoke to, and implicitly challenged, Hollywood filmmakers. *Schindler's List* was a mainstream hit, but it was also a politically and culturally resonant polemic. Spielberg demonstrated that Hollywood movies in the 1990s could be a suitable and successful forum for public remembrance and political debate.[86] The focus on Schindler's actions was an implicit attack on bystanders who had failed to engage with the world around them. In a related fashion, the making of *Schindler's List* could be construed as a challenge to contemporary Hollywood to produce more meaningful, challenging movies.

Even at the time of its release, several figures within the industry recognised the challenge to Hollywood that the film represented. Jeffrey Katzenberg, head of filmed production at Disney, claimed:

> I think *Schindler's List* will wind up being so much more important than a movie. It will affect how people on this planet think and act. At a moment in time, it is going to remind us about the dark side, and do it in a way in which, whenever that little green monster is lurking somewhere, this movie is going to press it down again. I don't want to burden the movie too much, but I think it will bring peace on earth, good will to men. Enough of the right people will see it that it will actually set the course for world affairs.[87]

Katzenberg was convinced, however erroneously, that Spielberg's film would prove a potent political and social tool, so long as it was seen by the 'right people.' Although the belief that films possess such profound social power may have been overstated in light of real political events, the impact of such assumptions on the development of the historical epic cycle in the 1990s should not be understated.

Critical responses to the film often stressed the extent to which *Schindler's List* defied established Hollywood conventions. The *Los Angeles Times* review noted, "Not only is the subject matter different for Spielberg, the way it is treated is a departure both for him and for the business as usual standards of major studio releases."[88] Alternatively, England's *New Statesman* observed that "Spielberg rigorously expunges any sense of Hollywood and its conventions."[89] In many ways, however, the reverse is true. Rather than transcending Hollywood convention, *Schindler's List* championed the defining characteristics of the defunct Hollywood historical epic in much the same way as *Dances with Wolves* had done. Spielberg looked to the cinema of his youth to produce a serious, yet accessible, historical narrative. Parallels can be drawn with Henry Noerdlinger's defence of *The Ten Commandments*—a historical film "made for the widest possible dissemination, to be understood by all the peoples of the world who have seen it or will see it."[90] Like that other story of Jewish suffering and exodus, *Schindler's List* must be understood as a profound contribution to an emergent epic cycle.

Conclusion

In his new role as a social historian of sorts, in 1994 Spielberg founded the 'Survivors of the Shoah Visual History Foundation.' The project was Spielberg's attempt to document the recollections of Holocaust survivors and can be understood as an extension of his agenda with *Schindler's List*—to place the Holocaust on record in a publicly accessible forum. The 2004 DVD release of the film featured nothing in the way of conventional 'extras,' such as commentaries, production reports and other superfluities. Instead it was accompanied entirely by material collected by the Shoah Foundation. The DVD contents stressed the film's historical veracity over its fictional nature and linked it to other acts of recollection and remembrance. The packaging insisted that *Schindler's List* was more than an ordinary movie.

With *Schindler's List* Spielberg had shown that a mainstream Hollywood filmmaker could achieve an elevated and powerful position in American culture without sacrificing popularity or financial standing in the film industry, and other filmmakers were undoubtedly affected by his example. It is no coincidence that an increasing number of filmmakers were attracted to epics in the next few years, and, more important, they were able to achieve studio funding for their maverick projects. For instance, Mel Gibson's *Braveheart* (1995) told a thematically similar story of an enslaved and subjugated people fighting for liberty. Anthony Minghella's *The English Patient* (1996) was another critically and commercially successful vision of World War II, featuring Ralph Fiennes in the title role. The impact of *Schindler's List* was, however, most clearly visible in Spielberg's subsequent releases, including *Amistad* (1997), *Saving Private Ryan* (1998), and the television series *Band of Brothers* (HBO, 2001), as well as the film that marked the apotheosis (and end) of the maverick epic subcycle, James Cameron's *Titanic* (1997). All of these films were attempts to represent, and spark collective memorialisation of, some tragic moment from the past, in a manner that spoke to the dominant concerns of the present.

Schindler's List helped to reestablish the prestige of the epic format, thus increasing the likelihood that powerful filmmakers and investors might support the cycle. Furthermore, the popular success of the film suggested again that there was a large audience for such releases, viewers who clearly demanded more from their movies than pure escapism. In America and Europe, Universal released the film gradually, allowing word of mouth to build while *Schindler's List* was screened in a handful of city centre theatres, before widening release. One marketing executive for Universal's European distribution arm, United International Pictures (or UIP), said that the company wanted to treat the film "as a serious event," aimed at "a more intelligent, more upmarket, 25-year-old–plus" target audience.[91] Anecdotal evidence and the film's exceptional box office returns suggest that *Schindler's List* did indeed attract older viewers who rarely visited the cinema, another factor that invited industrial imitation.

The release schedule, presumed audience demographic and core aims of *Schindler's List*, to educate, edify and enlighten, all extended the agendas that had characterised the epics of the roadshow era. The next chapter explores the development of Spielberg's 'socially conscious' moviemaking project, but it also asks what conclusions can be drawn about the generation of filmmakers that pioneered the revival of the epic in the early 1990s, through examination of Spielberg's other great 1990s war epic, *Saving Private Ryan*.

Notes

1. David Ansen, rev. of *Schindler's List*, *Newsweek* 20 Dec. 1993, 113.

2. Todd McCarthy, rev. of *Schindler's List*, *Variety* 13 Dec. 1993, reprinted in George Perry, *Steven Spielberg: The Making of His Movies* (London: Orion, 1998), 136.

3. David Denby, rev. of *Schindler's List*, *New York* 13 Dec. 1993, 82.

4. See Jonathan Romney, rev. of *Schindler's List*, *New Statesman and Society* 18 Feb. 1994, 33, as well as Susan Stark, "Spielberg Triumphs with His Forceful Epic of the Holocaust's Unlikely Hero," *The Detroit News* 25 Dec. 1993, and Anon., "Spielberg Tells a Powerful Holocaust Tale," *Houston Chronicle* 15 Dec. 1994, both reprinted in Thomas Fensch, ed., *Oskar Schindler and His List* (Forest Dale, VT: Paul S. Eriksson, 1995), 182 and 171 respectively.

5. Steven Spielberg, quoted in Anon., "Film Shorts," *Hollywood Reporter* 31 Jan. 1992, unpaginated, held in 'Schindler's List' clippings file, AMPAS.

6. Steven Spielberg, quoted in David Gritten, "Grim. Black and White . . . Spielberg?" *Los Angeles Times*, Calendar, 9 May 1993, 8.

7. Financial data obtained from the Internet Movie Database, http://www.uk.imdb.com/ title/tt0108052/business.

8. Peter Novick, *The Holocaust and Collective Memory* (London: Bloomsbury, 1999), 201.

9. Alan Mintz, *Popular Culture and the Shaping of Holocaust Memory in America* (Seattle: University of Washington Press, 2001), 16.

10. Jeffrey Shandler, *While America Watches: Televising the Holocaust* (Oxford: Oxford University Press, 1999).

11. See Mintz, 23.

12. See Novick, 127–206, and Sara R. Horowitz, "The Cinematic Triangulation of Jewish American Identity: Israel, American and the Holocaust," in Hilene Flanzbaum, ed., *The Americanization of the Holocaust* (Baltimore, MD: Johns Hopkins University Press, 1999), 142.

13. The taboo on representation of the Holocaust (or 'Bilderverbot,') has been used by the documentary maker Claude Lanzmann and others to heavily criticise Spielberg's fictional account. See Miriam Bratu Hansen, "*Schindler's List* Is Not *Shoah*: Second Commandment, Popular Modernism, and Public Memory," in Yosefa Loshitsky, ed., *Spielberg's Holocaust: Critical Perspectives on Schindler's List* (Bloomington: Indiana University Press, 1997), 83.

14. Joseph McBride, *Steven Spielberg: A Biography* (London: Faber and Faber, 1997), 64.

15. Steven Spielberg, quoted in McBride, 64.

16. There is some disagreement over the authorship of this speech. See Carl Gottleib, *The Jaws Log* (New York: Newmarket, 2001).

17. Steven Spielberg, quoted in Susan Royal, "*Always*: An Interview with Steven Spielberg," in Lester D. Friedman and Brent Notbohm, eds., *Steven Spielberg: Interviews* (Jackson: University Press of Mississippi, 2000), 136.

18. Kevin Brownlow, *David Lean, A Biography* (London: Richard Cohen, 1996), 702.

19. This was a key feature of Ballard's novel; see J. G. Ballard, *Empire of the Sun* (London: Flamingo, 1994).

20. Steven Spielberg, quoted in Myra Forsberg, "Spielberg at Forty: The Man and the Child," in Friedman and Notbohn, 131–132.

21. Brownlow, 702.

22. *Variety* review, reprinted in George Perry, *Steven Spielberg: The Making of His Movies* (London: Orion, 1998), 131.

23. Thomas Schatz, "The New Hollywood," reprinted in Stringer (2003), 24.

24. Wheeler Winston Dixon, "Twenty-Five Reasons Why It's All Over," in Jon Lewis, ed., *The End of Cinema as We Know It: American Film in the Nineties* (New York: New York University Press, 2001), 361.

25. David Sterrit, rev. of *Schindler's List*, *Christian Science Monitor* 15 Dec. 1993, 16.

26. David Thomson, *The New Biographical Dictionary of Film* 4th ed. (London: Little Brown, 2002), 828.

27. Steven Spielberg, quoted in Forsberg, 134–135.

28. This brief overview of Spielberg's relationship to Judaism has been drawn from McBride.

29. This trend is discussed in Mintz, 6.

30. McBride, 55.

31. Steven Spielberg, quoted in Bernard Weinraub, "Steven Spielberg Faces the Holocaust," *New York Times* 12 Dec. 1993, Section 2, 1.

32. See Wade Clark Roof, *A Generation of Seekers: The Spiritual Journeys of the Baby Boom Generation* (San Francisco, CA: Harper, 1993), 63–99.

33. McBride, 22.

34. Steven Spielberg, quoted in McBride, 44.

35. See Mintz, 36–60, and Novick, 104.

36. Yosefa Loshitzky, "Introduction," in Loshitzky, 12.

37. See Jack Matthews, rev. of *Schindler's List*, *Newsday*, 15 Dec. 1993, 59.

38. Robert D. Puttnam, *Bowling Alone: The Collapse and Revival of American Community* (New York: Touchstone, 2000), 65–79.

39. Thomas Elsaesser, "Subject Positions, Speaking Positions: From *Holocaust, Our Hitler* and *Heimat* to *Shoah* and *Schindler's List*," in Vivian Sobchack, ed., *The Persistence of History: Cinema, Television and the Modern Event* (New York: Routledge, 1996), 177.

40. This incident is recounted in Franciszek Palowski, *Witness: The Making of Schindler's List,* trans. Anna and Robert G. Ware (London: Orion, 1999), 6. See also Thomas Keneally, *Schindler's Ark* (London: Hodder and Stoughton, 1982), 13.

41. Deborah Caulfield, "And Other Relationships," *Los Angeles Times* 7 Mar. 1983, unpaginated clipping held in the *Schindler's List* file at AMPAS.

42. McBride, 426.

43. Ibid.

44. Steven Spielberg, quoted in McBride, 426.

45. Samantha Power, *"A Problem From Hell," America in the Age of Genocide* (London: Flamingo, 2002), 247–327.

46. Roy Gutman, "Like Auschwitz," *Newsday* 21 July 1992, quoted in Power, 272.

47. Novick, 207–221.

48. McBride, 416.

49. Steven Spielberg, quoted in Andrew Nagorski, "Spielberg's Risk," *Newsweek* 24 May 1993, 61.

50. Steve Spielberg, quoted in Jane Perlez, "Spielberg Grapples with the Horror of the Holocaust," *New York Times* 13 Jun. 1993, 16.

51. Novick, 104 and 187.

52. I use *ritual* in the spiritual sense here, rather than as an ideological phenomenon.

53. See Daniel Jonah Goldhagen, *Hitler's Willing Executioners: Ordinary Germans and the Holocaust* (London: Abacus, 1997), 145.

54. See Yisrael Gutman, "The Response of Polish Jewry to the Final Solution," in David Cesarani, ed., *The Final Solution: Origins and Implementation* (London: Routledge, 1994), 152–153.

55. See Gutman, 153; Goldhagen, 143–145; and much of Christopher R. Browning, *The Origins of the Final Solution: The Evolution of Nazi Jewish Policy 1939–1942* (London: William Heineman, 2004).

56. Goldhagen, 93.

57. For details of this policy see Michael Burleigh, *The Third Reich: A New History* (London: Pan Macmillan, 2000), 580.

58. Sara R Horowitz, "The Cinematic Triangulation of Jewish American Identity: Israel, American and the Holocaust," in Hilene Flanzbaum, ed., *The Americanization of the Holocaust* (Baltimore: John Hopkins University Press, 1999), 123.

59. Keneally, 208.

60. Goldhagen, 171–172.

61. Ibid., 172.

62. For details of this changing agenda, see Christopher R. Browning, *Nazi Policy, Jewish Workers, German Killers* (Cambridge: Cambridge University Press, 2000), 26–88.

63. J. Hoberman, rev. of *Schindler's List*, *Village Voice* 21 Dec. 1993, 63.

64. Both quotes in Judith E. Doneson, 'The Image Lingers: The Feminisation of the Jew in *Schindler's List*' in Loshitzky, 140.

65. Art Spiegelman, comments made in J. Hoberman et al., "*Schindler's List*: Myth, Movie and Memory," *Village Voice* 29 Mar. 1994, 26.

66. Scenes with the girl in red have been criticised by some critics for 'sentimentalising' the purge of the ghetto. See David Thomson, "Presenting Enamelware," *Film Comment* Mar.–Apr. 1994, reprinted in Fensch, 94.

67. Mintz, 126.

68. Loshitzky, cited above.

69. David Eldridge, *Hollywood's History Films* (London: IB Tauris, 2006), 6 and 8.

70. McBride, 441.

71. Daniel Jonah Goldhagen points out the staggering infrequency of principled German dissent at the time, which he describes as "the voices of lonely criers in a desolate night," in Goldhagen, 124.

72. Richard Maltby, *Hollywood Cinema* 2nd ed. (Oxford: Blackwell, 2003), 71.

73. Keneally, 191.

74. Ibid., 175.

75. See, for example, Terrence Rafferty, "A Man of Transactions," *New Yorker* 20 Dec. 1993, 129.

76. Keneally, 135–147.

77. Thomas Elsaesser has also noted that the film suggests a "preferred reading" for viewers. See Elsaesser (1996), 177.

78. Power, 277 and 294.

79. Warren Christopher, quoted in Power, 295.

80. Power, 305.

81. William Perry, quoted in Power, 305.

82. Power, 294.

83. See quotes from presidents Carter, Reagan, Bush, and Clinton in Power, xxi.

84. Jeffrey Shandler, "Schindler's Discourse: America Discusses the Holocaust and Its Mediation, from NBC's miniseries to Spielberg's film," in Loshitzky, 163.

85. Clifford J. Marks and Robert Torry, "'Herr Direktor': Biography and Autobiography in *Schindler's List*," *Biography* 23, no. 1 (Winter 2000), 53.

86. Mintz, 125–158, makes a similar point about the impact of the film.

87. Jeffrey Katzenberg, quoted in Steven Schiff, "Seriously Spielberg," reprinted in Friedman and Notbohm, 174.

88. Kenneth Turan, rev. in *Los Angeles Times* 15 Dec. 1993, Calendar, 1.

89. Jonathan Romney, rev. in *New Statesman and Society* 18 Feb. 1994, 33.

90. Henry Noerdlinger, Letter to Art Arthur, dated 8 Nov. 1956, 'The Henry S. Noerdlinger Collection,' Folder 6, AMPAS.

91. Claudia Eller, "Will 'List' Speak for Itself?" *Los Angeles Times* 22 Nov. 1993, F5.

–4–

The Baby Boomers, Remembrance and
Saving Private Ryan (1998)

y 1998, the historical epic had become an occasional but highly recognisable feature of Hollywood's production schedules. That year's list of Best Picture Academy Award nominees was made up entirely of historical films with epic dimensions. The eventual winner, *Shakespeare in Love* (1998), had been in competition with *Elizabeth* (1998), *The Thin Red Line* (1998) and Steven Spielberg's *Saving Private Ryan*. Although Madden's historical romantic comedy was clearly the least 'epic' in thematic or stylistic terms, all were described by certain sectors of the press as 'epic' movies.[1] Spielberg's account of the 1944 Normandy invasion ultimately won five Academy Awards, including Best Director. In 1997, James Cameron's *Titanic* had won eleven Oscars at the ceremony, equalling the record set by William Wyler's *Ben-Hur* in 1959, while in the previous year, Anthony Minghella's *The English Patient* had won both Best Picture and Best Director. When *Saving Private Ryan* was released, the emergence of a new epic cycle was becoming apparent at the Academy Awards (a ceremony designed to reward the 'best' that Hollywood had to offer) and also at the box office. More and more filmmakers were evidently following the lead of the maverick writers, directors and producers by producing popular epics of their own.

At the beginning of 1998, it was generally assumed by industry insiders that one of two mega-blockbusters would predominate at the American box office that year, either *Armageddon* (1998), an asteroid impact drama produced by Jerry Bruckheimer, or *Godzilla* (1998), a giant lizard disaster movie from the director of *Independence Day* (1996).[2] Shockingly, *Saving Private Ryan* would become the highest grossing domestic release of 1998, taking $216 million in North America and a further $263.3 million overseas.[3] In conjunction with the success of *Titanic* (the highest gross-ing Hollywood film ever released if figures are not adjusted for infla-tion) in 1997, the unexpected and outstanding commercial dominance of Spielberg's film helped to facilitate a shift from the occasional produc-tion of epics on an experimental basis to an industry-wide reorienta-tion of production strategies, discussed in greater detail in the next two chapters. However, the film remained the product of personal obses-sions and interests. In fact, most of the filmmakers responsible for the 'maverick' epics of the 1990s worked independently from one another and were often driven by intimate, personal concerns, which ran coun-ter to presumed economic logic. Why, then, did so many of the most successful filmmakers of the late 1980s and early 1990s suddenly feel compelled to produce roughly similar epics (characterised by a nos-talgia for the 1950s) at roughly the same time? And why did modern audiences respond so fervently to these films, when the few epics of the 1980s had failed to achieve anything like the same degree of popular commercial success?

This chapter looks at the filmmakers behind the maverick epics of the early 1990s in *collective* terms. Spielberg, Costner, Cameron, Gibson, et al., were all members of a bloated generational group sometimes known as the 'baby boom', and in this chapter we will see that the shared cul-tural experiences of these 'baby boomers' played a vital role in shaping their perceptions of the historical epic as a cinematic institution. As the baby boomers reached maturity, broader demographic shifts—both in their own social status and in their relationship to other generations—seems to have contributed to a popular belief that the historical epic was once more a relevant form of cinematic expression. In particular, Steven Spielberg is perhaps the most representative filmmaker of the baby boom generation, and it is therefore no coincidence that he has done more than any other to popularise the epic once again. Furthermore, *Saving Private Ryan*'s awed focus on the generation of Americans who fought in World War II seemed to dramatise precisely the intergenera-tional address that characterised so many other epics. The first section of the chapter locates Spielberg and his work in the context of generational change in America since 1946. The second section looks more broadly at the impact of the baby boom on film trends, and preferred genres, since the 1960s. The third section goes on to examine *Saving Private Ryan* in relation to these trends. As we will see, the narrative of Spielberg's film directly addresses questions of memory and responsibility that resonate across the epics of the 1990s.

1. Spielberg and the Baby Boom

Steven Spielberg was born in 1946, the first year of the post–World War II baby boom, when American troops returned from Europe, started families and began the work of rebuilding their lives. Prior to World War II, general levels of fertility in America had been declining steadily since the late nineteenth century. However, in 1946, the number of children being born on a year-by-year basis suddenly increased, and high birth rates were sustained well into the middle of the 1960s.[4] In 1932, the annual number of live births in the United States had dropped to 2.3 million; by 1956, it had soared to an unprecedented 4.2 million.[5] Birth rates dropped decisively again in 1964 and bottomed out at well below the 'replacement rate' of 2.2 births per mother in the early 1970s.[6] This sudden sustained increase in birth rates, followed by a sudden decline, created the baby boom, a massive group of Americans who grew to maturity in the latter half of the twentieth century and whose impact has been felt in all areas of American endeavour.

Establishing precise dates for the beginning and end of the baby boom has been the subject of some debate. Slow upward fluctuations of the birth rate during World War II have led some to argue that the baby boom began as early as 1943 and was finished by 1961.[7] Others set the dates slightly later, between 1946 and 1964, the demarcation used in this study.[8] However, it must be stressed that the boundaries between baby boomers and those born in the years immediately preceding and succeeding the boom are fluid, particularly when it comes to cultural experiences. Nevertheless, the baby boom was a huge, clearly demarcated generational 'cohort,' a term that refers to "individuals who were born in the same year or period and who will thus experience all of the various stages of the life cycle at about the same time," in the words of Diane J. Mancunovich.[9] Herbert S. Klein notes that "because this boom in births was immediately followed by a return to low fertility, which some have called the 'baby bust,' it has meant that those born in this period were a well-defined cohort that could be easily identified as they grew older."[10] Those born during the baby bust and afterwards (1964–1977) are sometimes known as 'Generation X.' Since 1977, fertility levels in America have again increased, in a phenomenon known as the 'echo boom,' a cohort made up of the children of baby boomers.[11] Like so many events of the last sixty years, the emergence of the similarly bloated echo boom generation can be understood as a symptomatic consequence of the baby boom. Just as the baby boomers were part of a disproportionately large group, so their offspring formed another large cohort, all growing up at roughly the same time.

As Klein has explained, various factors facilitated the emergence of the baby boom, including

> [n]ew levels of family income, new availability of federal credit to the middle and lower classes for home ownership, the introduction of cheap mass-produced tract housing, and increasing economic mobility due to the movement to higher status employment on the part of the younger population. . . . The space and income for providing for more children was now available, and Americans responded to these opportunities by lowering the age at which they married, beginning their families at an earlier age, and opting for marriage more frequently.[12]

The America that Spielberg grew up in was a more populous and affluent society than it had ever been.[13] Although the postwar period was marked by major international conflicts, particularly the initiation and exacerbation of the Cold War, the conclusion of World War II signalled an end to extremes of economic hardship that had plagued America in preceding decades and facilitated a transformation in both the social climate and urban environment of the country. The population began to move to large suburbs (thereby contributing to the shifts in movie attendance discussed in chapter 2), and the American economy expanded at an unprecedented rate.[14] After the Great Depression in the 1930s and the hardships of the war, new markets for American goods were opening up as they had never done before, and levels of prosperity and employment soared.[15]

These factors all had some bearing on Steven Spielberg's early life. His father, Arnold, had fought in the war and was aged twenty-nine when Steven was born. He belonged to a cohort that has been labelled both the 'GI generation' and, more recently, the 'greatest generation.'[16] The greatest generation were born between 1901 and 1924 and had, in their youth, endured both the Great Depression and the Second World War.[17] Like many members of his generation Arnold had been to college on the GI Bill after World War II and was therefore qualified to pursue a successful career as an electronic engineer. As the previous chapter noted, this caused him to move his family westwards through a series of newly established, increasingly prestigious and increasingly non-Jewish suburbs.

Spielberg's early life, and the America he depicted in many of his early movies, offers an exemplary model of the baby boomer experience, regardless of ethnicity. Like many of his contemporaries, Spielberg grew up in a predominantly suburban world, in circumstances of relative prosperity. Despite the difficulties posed by moving from city to city, as well as his parents' divorce and his occasional encounters with anti-Semitism, biographers generally agree that Spielberg's life was not marked by any exceptional hardships.[18] The world of suburban normality that Spielberg inhabited during his formative years was exactly the environment he sought to recapture in *Close Encounters of the Third Kind* (1977) and *E.T.: The Extra-Terrestrial* (1982), in which suburbia acts as the starting point for elaborate flights of fancy, much as it did for the young Spielberg. The increased prosperity of the 1950s meant that a large number of consumer durables, from TV to automobiles, were suddenly within the grasp of the American consumer. Billions of dollars were spent fitting out the American home. Indeed, Lizabeth Cohen has argued that in the 1950s Americans were increasingly encouraged to view consumer spending as an act of civic responsibility.[19]

The most significant of these new technological developments, for Spielberg at least, was the widespread adoption of television. From the moment he was exposed to the television screen, Spielberg, like so many other baby boomers, was provided with a springboard for his own imaginative adventures. Joseph McBride describes television as "the single most persuasive cultural influence on Spielberg," although the budding director also grew up reading comic books and pulp sci-fi novels and, as noted in the last chapter, using his father's cine-camera to film amateur World War II action movies.[20] The last of these, *Escape to Nowhere*, won first prize in Arizona's Canyon Films Junior Film Festival in 1962. Like many other young people Spielberg also went to the movies a great deal (as the statistics quoted in chapter 1 support), where he was exposed to the epics he would later class as such pivotal moments in his filmmaking career.

To a greater or lesser degree, the broad elements of Spielberg's formative experiences were shared by many other filmmakers of the baby boom. James Cameron was born in 1954, in Kapuskasing, Canada. He was also the son of an electrical engineer who moved his family several times pursuing work, also eventually ending up in California. Cameron, too, loved movies, comic books and pulp sci-fi, and he got his first 16mm cine-camera in his teens.[21] Other baby boomer filmmakers such as George Lucas (born 1944), Kevin Costner (1955), Robert Zemeckis (1952), Ron Howard (1954), Edward Zwick (the director of *Glory* in 1989, *Legends of the Fall* in 1994 and *The Last Samurai* in 2003, born 1952), and Jeffrey Katzenberg (head of animation at DreamWorks, and a central figure in the next chapter, born 1950) were all growing up in the suburbs of America at the same time and having similar experiences.[22] The same could be said of producer Jerry Bruckheimer, who was responsible for *Pearl Harbor* (Michael Bay, 2001) and was born in 1945. Even the experiences of Mel Gibson (born 1956), whose family moved from New York to the suburbs of Australia in 1968, are probably not so far removed from those of his fellow American baby boomers. All of the filmmakers who contributed to the revival of the epic, in its maverick incarnation and afterwards, were baby boomers who had been exposed to the same movies, the same TV shows, and were all affected by the same political and social shifts at roughly the same age. When they entered the film industry, these baby boomers would come to reflect on their own experiences in a manner that would lead directly to the revival of the historical epic.

2. The Baby Boom and American Film Culture

The historical epic is often claimed to have disappeared at the end of the roadshow era because the Hollywood majors began producing a higher number of lower budget movies aimed at people in their teens and twenties. These were explicit, artistically inclined productions partly facilitated by a relaxation of censorship regulations, such as Mike Nichol's *The Graduate* (1967), Arthur Penn's *Bonnie and Clyde* (1967) and Dennis Hopper's *Easy Rider* (1969). I have tried to show in chapters 1 and 2 that the epic remained popular with many viewers throughout the 1960s and 1970s, and that Hollywood's actions were a response to overproduction rather than a change in public taste. However, it remains the case that edgier, more violent and sexually explicit films increased in popularity throughout the period often referred to as 'the New Hollywood,' or 'the Hollywood Renaissance.'[23] Many critics and scholars view 1967–1976 as a high point in Hollywood's aesthetic history. The target audience for the canonical films of this period were baby boomers, who were then beginning to reach their late teens and early twenties.[24] The shift towards edgier subjects, with limited mainstream appeal, can be understood as an early cinematic sign of the baby boom's growing significance. However, baby boomers themselves did not assume positions of creative control in the film industry until the end of the Hollywood Renaissance.

Instead, Peter Krämer has argued that the 1960s and 1970s were marked by a rapid turnover of different generations within the film industry. The group Krämer identifies as the 'Studio Generation'—including

Cecil B. DeMille (born 1881), William Wyler (1902) and David Lean (1908)—were dying out, to be replaced by younger filmmakers who had learned their trade working on television.[25] This 'TV Generation'—again, Krämer's term—included Arthur Penn (born 1922), Mike Nichols (1931), Sydney Pollack (1934) and William Friedkin (1935) amongst others. During the early 1970s, they were joined by a group sometimes known as the 'movie brats,' which included Martin Scorsese (born 1942), Francis Ford Coppola (1939), John Milius (1944), Brian De Palma (1940) and Peter Bogdanovich (1939).[26] The films produced by the TV generation and movie brats clearly appealed to the youthful baby boomers. However, when baby boomers began to achieve creative control in the late 1970s, the films they produced were often very different from the work of their immediate precursors. Spielberg and his sometime collaborator George Lucas are generally considered the exemplary filmmakers of the baby boom, and yet they favoured family-friendly blockbusters and accessible action movies over the complex, self-conscious 'mature' films of the Hollywood Renaissance. Instead, Thomas Schatz describes their work as "increasingly plot driven, increasingly visceral, kinetic and fast paced, increasingly reliant on special effects, increasingly 'fantastic' (and thus apolitical), and increasingly targeted at younger audiences."[27]

Other key filmmakers of the baby boom, who produced similar work, included directors such as Robert Zemeckis, Ron Howard, Joe Dante, teen comedy specialist John Hughes (born 1950), writer/director Lawrence Kasdan (1949) and writer/producer/director James Cameron. In front of the camera baby boomers made up the majority of stars, including Mel Gibson, Tom Hanks (born 1956), Tom Cruise (1962), Eddie Murphy (1961), Meryl Streep (1949), Sigourney Weaver (1949), Richard Gere (1949), Arnold Schwarzenegger (1947) and Sylvester Stallone (1946). Throughout the 1980s, their films came to predominate at the box office, and, according to Stephen Prince, the most popular genres of the 1980s were 'science fiction/fantasy' and 'comedy' movies.[28] We can add to this 'action-adventure' films, such as *Top Gun* (1986) and *Die Hard* (1988), as well as 'family-adventure' films such as *E.T.: The Extra-Terrestrial*, *Back to the Future* (1985), *The Goonies* (1985) and *Who Framed Roger Rabbit* (1988).[29] As we have seen, many key releases, including *Star Wars* (1977), *Close Encounters of the Third Kind* (1977) and even *Ghostbusters* (1984), told stories of apocalyptic historical events occurring in fantasy settings, which can retrospectively be understood as fantasy epics. The trend suggests that many baby boomer filmmakers shared an interest in narratives of epic import, but it was some time before they began to produce overtly serious historical epics as a matter of course.

In the 1980s, space remained for more experimental, exclusive films at the margins of production schedules, but the industry was increasingly driven by expensive blockbusters targeted at young people and families, and in the 1990s, the trend for family films intensified.[30] According to Peter Krämer, "[C]hildren's and family films are at the very heart of today's media conglomerates and indeed today's popular culture, because the majority of the most popular and more profitable films and multimedia franchises are primarily (but not exclusively) 'kid's stuff.'"[31] Again, this shift in preferred material is linked to the actions and collective experiences of the baby boomers. After 1977, the echo boom began to emerge, and birth rates increased. Spielberg's first child was born in 1985, and, by 2004, he had six children. In accordance with general trends, many more of the filmmakers discussed in this book have had children of their own during the 1980s and 1990s. So, the baby boomers entered the film industry at a time when the number of children and families across America was increasing. Their films understandably reflected the growing importance of the child and family market.

Furthermore, many of the films produced by the baby boomers demonstrated a desire to reexamine and reflect on their own formative historical experiences. Daniel Marcus has argued that throughout the 1980s and 1990s baby boomers looked to the 1950s and 1960s as a meaningful site of political and ideological debate. Marcus suggests that "during the early 1980s Conservatives associated the 1950s with stable family structures, free-market mechanisms and American dominance in international affairs. They characterised the social movements of the 1960s as responsible for the destruction of natural hierarchies."[32] The presidency of archconservative 1950s movie star Ronald Reagan served to consolidate this process. However, Marcus goes on to argue that, in the late 1980s and early 1990s:

> Cultural producers created a myriad of representations of historical events that served, at times, as the major challenge to the nostalgic discourse of conservatism. Films and television programs offered depictions of 1960s experiences that celebrated and questioned American involvement in Vietnam, revisited the civil rights movement, and traced changes in baby boomer lifestyles from the 1960s to the 1980s. In addition, with the solidification of baby boomers

as prime adult consumers, nostalgia for 1960s childhoods became a new element in advertising and other cultural appeals.[33]

Chief amongst these was Robert Zemeckis's 1994 hit *Forrest Gump*, a film described by the critic J. Hoberman as "a boomerography."[34]

Through the eventful life of its title character, *Forrest Gump* offered viewers of all ages a potted history of the baby boom. The framing narrative of the film sees Tom Hanks's character relaying the story of his life to various passersby. We quickly discover that Forrest Gump has inadvertently found himself present at almost every major event in American history since the 1950s. As a boy in Alabama he inspires Elvis; at college he encounters political radicalism and the emergence of the civil rights movement; as a young man he meets John F. Kennedy moments before his assassination; he goes on to fight in the Vietnam War, and later he shares his opinion of Vietnam with thousands of peace protestors in Washington (although the microphone breaks, and viewers never hear Forrest's assessment, in a neat attempt to avoid partisan comment); he encounters hippies, Black Panthers and drug addicts in a seedy 1970s New York; he spends an eventful night at the Watergate Hotel; then, finally, he has a son with his long-lost childhood sweetheart, shortly before she begins to show symptoms of a mysterious virus. When the film ends, Forrest is a single father, coping with the responsibility of raising and educating his son.

Forrest Gump can be clearly understood as the work of a baby boomer filmmaker seeking to relay the formative cultural experiences of his generation onwards to future generations. As Forrest tells his story, so Zemeckis sought to tell the story of the baby boomers, in what should be understood as an epic account, which treats the baby boom as a meaningful and significant cultural event. The film provided older viewers with an opportunity for reflection, but it also allowed young people to better 'understand' their parents. In 1994, audiences of all ages were extremely receptive to the project, and *Forrest Gump* went on to become the highest grossing release of the year, with a $330-million domestic gross and a $305-million overseas gross.[35] It won six Academy Awards, including Best Picture, Best Director, Best Actor and Best Adapted Screenplay. Despite the fact that reviews were mixed, *Forrest Gump* nevertheless engaged a large number of viewers, all keen to reminisce on the experiences of baby boomers.[36]

A variety of other films, in a range of genres, grew out of a similar impulse. *New York Times* critic Janet Maslin noted that the renewed success of the Disney Corporation's animated division depended, at least in part, on "recalling baby boomers' fond memories of the traditional Broadway score."[37] One might add that they also recalled baby boomers' fond memories of Disney's earlier animated movies. Spielberg produced several movie adaptations of popular 1960s TV shows, including *The Flintstones* (1994) and *Casper: The Friendly Ghost* (1995). Meanwhile, action movies like *The Fugitive* (1993) the *Mission: Impossible* franchise (1996; 2000; 2006), *Lost in Space* (1998) and *Dragnet* (1987), also reformulated popular TV shows from the 1950s and 1960s for a modern audience. Even Disney's 2004 epic *The Alamo* was a related attempt to revisit their successful 1950s TV series (and subsequent cinema release) *Davy Crockett and the River Pirates* (1956). Invariably, academic critics have sought to account for this obsessive recycling of the past by invoking "postmodernism"—the theoretical paradigm described by Fredric Jameson as "an attempt to think the present historically in an age that has forgotten how to think historically in the first place."[38] However, it seems to me equally important to focus on the specific experiences and actions of the baby boomers themselves, where the traces of broader cultural movements can be seen in practical terms. In each case, filmmakers were seeking to revisit their formative cinematic experiences at a moment when many had young children of their own.

Most parents are forced to reflect on their own upbringing when they have children, and the baby boomers were no exception. In fact, social historians Neil Howe and William Strauss have argued that much of American generational history must be understood as a series of linked historical reactions, as one generation attempts to improve on the parenting efforts that marked their own childhood.[39] This means keeping positive elements and attempting to avoid perceived mistakes. It goes without saying that the results are usually somewhat mixed. Nevertheless, elements of this process were reflected in the films that the baby boomers chose to make when they became parents. Daniel Marcus has demonstrated how the nostalgic productions of the 1980s and 1990s films fit into political debates, but I wish to stress that a primary reason why baby boomers have been attracted to the 1950s and 1960s as a representational space, and as a source of cinematic inspiration, is because they had been children then.[40] Now that they have responsibility for a new generation of children, like Forrest Gump at the end of Zemeckis's film, the baby boomers have looked to their past.

Initially, family films with nostalgic dimensions were favoured—familiar genres, remakes, even elegiac narratives concerned with youth and childhood. However, as baby boomers and echo boomers have aged, public interest in serious subjects has increased. Throughout their own youth, epics had been presented to baby boomers as the most resonant and educational films that Hollywood had to offer. Even very young baby boomers were likely to have encountered roadshow epics on television. Perhaps unsurprisingly, concerted and widespread attempts to revive the epic occurred with increasing frequency as the children of the echo boom were reaching an age when they might be receptive to attempts to explain the world around them. Such films could also be addressed to members of Generation X, who had grown up in a world without historical epics. Spurred on by their responsibilities to their own children, a series of key baby boomer filmmakers set about making movies that spoke to both of these younger generations. Even filmmakers without children of their own were reaching an age where they were beginning to reflect on their cultural legacy, and their prestige epic projects can be understood as the result of a similar impulse.

At a narrational level, the maverick epics of Costner, Spielberg, Gibson, Cameron and others were often clearly marked by a nostalgic desire to return to some elysian past associated with childhood. For instance, *Dances with Wolves* was a journey into the American past, but it was also a journey into the cinematic past (in the form of the western epic) and even into Costner's boyhood dreams. *Schindler's List* was an attempt to pass on historical knowledge to future generations, but it was also an attempt to revive the epic—a defunct mode of filmmaking perceived by many baby boomers as valuable and necessary. Spielberg's *Saving Private Ryan* made the generational address of the contemporary epic explicit. It was described by Thomas Doherty in *Cineaste* as "a final, *fin de siecle* act of generational piety."[41] In it, Spielberg sought to honour the sacrifices made by his parents' generation and ensure that the experiences of the greatest generation remained alive in the minds of younger viewers. However, the next section will argue that the account of the past that he offered was closely tied to his experiences as a member of the baby boom.

3. Generations in *Saving Private Ryan*

At the very beginning of *Saving Private Ryan,* an elderly man (played by Harrison Young) is shown making his way through the graves of the American Cemetery at Colleville-sur-Mer in Normandy. Although the film does not make it explicit, the cemetery overlooks the sector desig-nated 'Fox Green' on Omaha Beach. A mile to the west is 'Dog Green' sector, where the main historical narrative of the film will shortly begin. In the present, the elderly American, accompanied by his wife and family, makes his way to a grave and is then overcome by emotion. His middle-aged son, a baby boomer who stands amongst his own gaily dressed teen-aged children, calls out 'Dad?!'—the only spoken line in the sequence. The camera then focuses on his father's face, and the sound of crashing waves can be heard. A cut takes the audience to the nearby beach, on the morning of 6 June 1944, and the Normandy landings begin.

No names are spoken in the introductory scenes, and no obvious character traits are exposed. The younger members of the family remain entirely undistinguished. They have no close-ups, and, aside from the son's single line, which establishes his relationship to the older man, they remain silent. The family can therefore be understood as an iconic stand-in for similar generations of viewers watching *Saving Private Ryan* in movie theatres. Like the audience they represent, the family watch in awed silence as the old man remembers his wartime experiences. Unlike the audience, they cannot accompany him into the past.[42] The sequence immediately serves to place *Saving Private Ryan* in the context of generational memory, and what follows is clearly intended to both recreate and memorialise the events of World War II in such a way as to enlighten and edify generations who had not fought.

The project was made explicit in the film's marketing. Spielberg told *American Cinematographer* that he was attracted to Robert Rodat's script for *Saving Private Ryan* because "I think that World War II is the most significant event of the last 100 years; the fate of the Baby Boomers and even Generation X was linked to the outcome."[43] Spielberg, Tom Hanks, Matt Damon and historical consultant Stephen Ambrose went on a five-city university speaking tour to explain the film to younger Americans (and, in the process, to provide a very definite context for viewing).[44] The film was, Spielberg told assembled industry players at a preliminary screening in Los Angeles, intended "to honor . . . the men who put an end to the Holocaust and saved Western Civilization."[45] Thus, the greatest generation was immediately presented as a group who had, like Oskar Schindler, acted to curtail the Holocaust, and Spielberg classified their deeds as a vital model of self-sacrifice for future generations.

Spielberg's view of World War II was shared by many members of his generation. Survey work carried out by sociologists Howard Schuman and Jacqueline Scott in the United States has suggested that political opinion and identity is shaped during one's late teens and early twenties.[46] When generational cohorts break down along clearly demarcated lines, as they have done in America since World War II, it is possible to see broad patterns in political opinion shared by the majority of the generational group. Although the baby boomers are divided over many issues, the view of World War II as a 'good' war is one such point of consensus.

Schuman and Scott asked a representative sample of Americans to name the most important historical events of the last fifty years and to justify their decisions. Perhaps unsurprisingly, the most mentioned event was World War II, followed by the Vietnam War. When the results were filtered according to age it became clear that although those born after World War II still rated it as profoundly important, their understanding of its significance was markedly different from those who had actually lived through it. Members of the greatest generation chose World War II but never discussed broader geopolitical issues. Instead they tended to remember the privations of war and their own experiences of combat and global travel. By contrast, the baby boomers argued forcefully that World War II had been a 'good' war, a war worth fighting for moral reasons. Schuman and Schultz identified the Vietnam War, with its very different political resonances, as the root cause of this interpretative mismatch:

> It is primarily the Vietnam generation that looks back on World War II as the "good war" that we fought and won—not those who lived during the war itself! These Vietnam generation representatives are nostalgic for a world they have never known directly, in contrast to the world of their youth during the divisive late 1960s and early 1970s.[47]

Of the filmmakers discussed in this book, only Oliver Stone, the director of *Platoon* (1986), *JFK* (1991) and *Nixon* (1995), as well as *Alexander* (2004), had actually fought in the Vietnam War, while Spielberg, Cameron and Gibson experienced the war as a media event.

Consequently, Michael Hammond has suggested that *Saving Private Ryan* is indebted to filmic accounts of the Vietnam War. Hammond quotes Spielberg's declaration that "without Vietnam I could never have made *Ryan* as honestly as I did, because Vietnam sort of showed everybody, and sort of prepared audiences to accept war for what it was."[48] Hammond goes on to note that in *Saving Private Ryan*, "The impact of the Vietnam experience can be noted in the lack of emphasis placed on the enemy as agent of the conflict. The middle section may be construed as a Vietnam platoon film, the mission of which does not make sense to those involved on the ground."[49] The work of Schuman and Scott suggests that the legacy of the

Vietnam War is also visible at a deeper thematic level. By constructing World War II as a 'just' war, a war worth commemorating for moral reasons, Spielberg was giving voice to a conception of the war that united members of his generation. The men may not understand their mission, but the framing narrative places their actions in context as vital acts of generational benevolence.

Reviewers, many of them presumably also baby boomers, often wholeheartedly embraced Spielberg's attempts to honour the greatest generation and stressed the need for other acts of generational remembrance. Shortly after its release, the *New York Times* ran an article headed 'Long Delayed Lessons About Fathers at War,' in which William McDonald ruminated on the way that *Saving Private Ryan* had brought him closer to his own father.[50] A similar story was repeated by *New York Post* columnist Rod Dreyer in a piece about a depressed friend who had been reconciled with his father after seeing the film.[51] As Marouf Hasian, Jr., has noted, "Watching *Saving Private Ryan* became a cultural event where different generations sometimes saw the movie together and then discussed some of the pain and trauma that came with remembrance."[52] These included baby boomers and their parents, but many of Spielberg's comments indicate that the film was also aimed at younger people whose lives had not been lived in the wake of the war.

Although he made several public statements that the film was definitely not suitable for younger children, Spielberg nevertheless tempered these entreaties by saying, "I believe that if you can drive a car and fight in a war you should see it."[53] He viewed the film as a moral and educational 'rite of passage.' Star Tom Hanks went further and said, "There are some young kids, I think, that have seen so much violence on television and movies that need to see this."[54] England's *Independent* newspaper noted that "*Ryan*, like *Schindler's List* before it, has been sold as an essential learning experiences for young audiences."[55] In this way, the film extended the 'socially conscious' moviemaking project that Spielberg had initiated with *Schindler's List*. Where that film had honoured European Jewry, *Saving Private Ryan* clearly sought to honour the sacrifices of a generation of Americans.

At the end of the 1990s, Americans were becoming increasingly interested in the experiences of the men and women who had fought in, and lived through, the Second World War. The early part of the decade had seen the fifty-year anniversaries of the Pearl Harbor attack, D-day and VE-day, and World War II had increased in prominence as a result. A growing concern with the ordinary participants was neatly summarised in NBC news anchor Tom Brokaw's 1998 book, *The Greatest Generation*, which presented the wartime experiences of various Americans in awed tones. In his introduction, Brokaw traced the origins of his interest in the period back to his memories of reporting on the fortieth anniversary of D-day, which he saw as the defining experience of the greatest generation.[56] Brokaw's book was published at around the same time as the release of Spielberg's film and quickly became a best seller.[57] Spielberg had also cited Stephen E. Ambrose's books *D-Day, June 6, 1944: The Climactic Battle of World War II* (published 1995) and *Band of Brothers: E Company, 506th Regiment, 101st Airborne from Normandy to Hitler's Eagle's Nest* (published 1993) as central inspirations for his film.[58] Ambrose acted as a historical consultant on *Saving Private Ryan*, and *Band of Brothers* was later made into a television series by DreamWorks, which employed the same stylistic and narrational techniques as *Saving Private Ryan*.[59] Like Brokaw's, Ambrose's books reproduced the stories of ordinary American soldiers and became best sellers in the wake of *Saving Private Ryan*.[60] All of these works resulted from a desire to memorialise American experiences of the war in popular forms that had a generational basis. Krin Gabbard has argued that *Saving Private Ryan* "uncritically idealised the role of the United States in World War II at a time when many Americans were experiencing the death or imminent death of a parent or grandparent."[61]

The 'greatest generation' quickly replaced the 'GI generation' as the common designation for those Americans born between 1901 and 1924.[62] Although it was less massive than the baby boom, the greatest generation nevertheless constituted a large generational cohort.[63] However, by the late 1990s, it had been estimated that around 1,000 of the 6.3 million surviving World War II veterans were dying each day, a process that was certain to intensify in the future.[64] Their deaths provoked a degree of reflection writ large across the public sphere because their baby boomer children were so numerous. *Saving Private Ryan* invited baby boomers, and subsequent generations, to remember and honour the sacrifices made by their parents in a manner that spurred public reflection.

Clearly, Spielberg's interest in the period was also linked to his preoccupation with the Holocaust. Peter Ehrenhaus has argued that scenes featuring the Jewish character Mellish (Adam Goldberg) "instantiates the failure of America to act—as a predominantly Christian nation—upon their commitment to help save European Jewry ... [and] the quest to save Private Ryan instantiates the moral tenet [from *Schindler's List*] 'whoever saves one life, saves the world entire.'"[65] As we have seen, Spielberg did not view the greatest generation as guilty bystanders; rather they were in some sense 'Schindler-esque' figures, who had, however unwittingly, fought to stop the Holocaust. In the process, the greatest generation had performed an act of unassailable virtue, which, in *Saving Private Ryan*, translated into a multifaceted vision of committed self-sacrifice in a narrative that encouraged younger viewers to compare themselves to the greatest generation (just as *Schindler's List* encouraged identification with Schindler). To this end, the visual and thematic organisation of the film proved viewers with access to the terrible wartime experiences that their parents or grandparents might have endured.

Saving Private Ryan's graveyard prologue is followed by an exacting recreation of the second wave of American landings on Omaha Beach—the landfall that saw the heaviest fighting on D-day. Geoff King has claimed that the opening sequence "is represented as something like a solid 'slab' of recreated reality, seeking to immerse the viewer in the appalling chaos of events."[66] Various techniques are used to heighten the sense that the audience is immersed in real combat. The film stock has been bleached of colour, camera shutter rates vary to create jarring changes in pace, blood frequently splatters across the lens, and the camera moves jerkily forward, as if the audience were seeing through the eyes of one of the men hurrying up the beach. Although these techniques should highlight the presence of the camera, Michael Hammond has argued that they ultimately serve to bring the action closer to the audience.[67] Hammond maintains that the shocking violence of the film is intended to generate feelings of empathy and understanding for members of the greatest generation, by recreating the sort of traumas they had had to endure. In these scenes Spielberg ensures that "the older generation has been spoken for, and at the same time, is allowed to remain silent."[68]

According to Spielberg, the sequence was intended to be shocking and to "create a kinship between the audience and the citizen soldier . . . to put the audience inside those landing craft."[69] In yet another interview, he explained, "This isn't the kind of movie you see and then go to a bistro and break bread talking about it. I think the audience leaves the theatre with a little bit of what the veterans left that war with."[70] Reviewers were quick to praise the sequence, and the *New York Post* described it as "one of the most astounding passages ever committed to celluloid."[71] Throughout the marketing of the film, the awed and sometimes shocked responses of D-day veterans were presented as indicative of the sequence's accuracy, while their apparent gratitude to Spielberg emphasised the moral necessity of his memorialising project.[72] One can extend such points to explore how the opening scenes implicitly reflect on Spielberg's position as a filmmaker of the baby boom.

By foregrounding the physical presence of the camera, Spielberg emphasises his presence as an interpreter of the past. In essence, the audience sees through Spielberg's eyes, who has placed himself in the thick of the fighting, amongst the soldiers, and is telling viewers what the elderly Ryan will not, and perhaps cannot, tell his children, as Michael Hammond has observed. This seems to embody the generational position of the baby boomers, caught between their own parents, for whom World War II was a grim reality, and their children, for whom the war is a story in history books. *Saving Private Ryan* assumes that the baby boomers have a responsibility to pass on the memories of their parents. Like *Schindler's List* it challenged viewers, and presumably other filmmakers, to engage in acts of generational remembrance. The camerawork in the opening sequence makes Spielberg's stance explicit. Unlike the baby boomer son in the prologue, Spielberg stands closer to the greatest generation and speaks for them to subsequent cohorts.

At a thematic level the film's narrative presents a story of duty and indebtedness that closely mirrors Spielberg's memorialising project. The opening scenes were considered so effective (and affecting) that many reviewers found the rest of the film quite disappointing. Stanley Kauffman said that it "begins as a monumental epic; then it diminishes, and, by its finish, is baffling."[73] The *Village Voice* agreed, calling the central narrative "merely a banal war movie with a forced premise and clichéd characters."[74] Other reviews were less vitriolic but frequently similar in sentiment.[75] The story proper begins in the aftermath of D-day, when Captain Miller (Tom Hanks) is instructed to lead a small unit of soldiers to find James Ryan (Matt Damon), whose three brothers have all been killed in action. Ryan is to be rescued for the sake of his mother. The story is one of generational piety. Miller and his men are acting to honour a member of their parents' generation, exactly like Spielberg. Their search becomes the spur for a peripatetic journey through Normandy, used to illustrate different aspects of the invasion, which function in much the same fashion as the Holocaust history in *Schindler's List*. Sequences include close quarters fighting in a ruined French town, a lethal assault on a machine-gun battery, life at a makeshift camp, the aftermath of a American glider crash and, finally, intensive urban combat in the fictional town of Ramelle, where Ryan is found.

Along the way the audience learns that Miller is a midwestern schoolteacher, described in *Variety* as "a decent man of the sort America was theoretically supposed to produce, and perhaps did during the generation in question."[76] The rest of the unit is staffed by Sergeant Horvath (Tom Sizemore); the New Yorker Reiben (Edward Burns); the Italian American Caparzo (Vin Diesel); the Jew Mellish; Jackson, a devout but deadly Southern sniper (Barry Pepper); the medic Wade (Giovanni Ribisi); and the cowardly translator Upham (Jeremy Davies). In the final firefight, all but Upham and Ryan are killed, and Miller's final words to Ryan are "Earn this." The film then returns to the present, and the audience realises that the old man is Ryan, and the grave he has come to visit is Miller's. Ryan turns to his wife, with tears in his eyes, and says, "Tell me I'm a good man. Tell me I've lived a good life." She responds, "You are." The elderly Ryan recognises the debt he owes to the men who died, and his reaction provides a template for the audiences' emotional and intellectual responses. Viewers are asked to leave the auditorium feeling that their lives have also been lived in the wake of such sacrifices, however distantly.

A concern with the consequences of sacrifice pervades *Saving Private Ryan*. The mission to find Ryan is repeatedly queried, as characters ask why they should risk their lives to save one man. Privately, Miller discusses the question with his sergeant and explains, "When you end up killing one of your men, you tell yourself it happened so you could save the lives of two or three or ten others. And that's how simple it is. That's how you rationalise making the choice between the mission and the men." Horvath responds, "Except this time the mission is a man." In the final battle, the bridge at Ramelle is not saved by Miller but by passing Allied bombers, apparently rendering the sacrifice of his men unnecessary. Hasian has observed that such scenes led a handful of reviewers to complain that "the film was not commemorative enough and that it should have been more respectful of World War II veterans."[77] A key complaint seems to have been that *Saving Private Ryan* "shrinks from an explanation of any kind, with the ultimate effect of seeming insensitive to the enormity of the fascist threat and the convictions of those who died," in the words of one reviewer.[78] However, the conclusion of the film stresses that Miller and his men die in order to rescue Ryan. They sacrifice themselves so that a younger man, arguably a surrogate for younger viewers in the audience, might live. In the process they offer a model of self-sacrificing benevolence that critical commentators in the late 1990s, including Spielberg, saw as a defining quality of the greatest generation.

Furthermore, the mission to rescue Ryan involves a group of older, more experienced men saving a younger man. Or, to put it another way, one 'generation' of men, made up of Miller, Horvath, et al., are sacrificed so that another generation, represented by the youthful Ryan and also the cowardly Upham, might survive. Ryan and Upham could therefore be said to stand in for the young people in the audience both in figurative terms (their lives are built on the sacrifices of others) but also in literal terms (they are played by members of Generation X—Matt Damon was born in 1970, Jeremy Davies in 1969). Significantly, although the characters played by Tom Hanks and Tom Sizemore would have been members of the greatest generation, the actors are baby boomers. Like Spielberg, then, Hanks and the other actors are re-creating the experiences of their parents' generation, in order to educate their children. In the case of Tom Hanks, this paternal project was made all the more explicit when his son Colin Hanks went on to play one of the few surviving GIs in the spin-off television series produced by Hanks and Spielberg, *Band of Brothers* (a title which itself suggests generational unity).

In his review, David Denby notes that Upham, who collapses in fear during the final firefight, "represents the audience—he's terrified—and when he freezes at the crucial instant, he forces us into a moment of grim self-recognition."[79] Spielberg admitted that Upham "was me in the movie. That's how I would have been in war."[80] At a key moment, Upham can merely observe as his compatriots are killed. He occupies the same position that Spielberg's cameras have adopted from the start. He is with the men, but not one of them, and he survives. Like Ryan, like Spielberg, and like the audience, he is part of a generation that lives on beyond the war but remains eternally indebted to those who did not. Thus, *Saving Private Ryan* tells the story of one generation rescuing another in microcosm, and, in related fashion, younger audiences are explicitly asked to feel that they, too, have been rescued by men like Miller.

In the concluding scenes, the elderly Ryan leans close to Miller's grave and says, "My family is with me today, they wanted to come with me. To be honest with you I wasn't sure how I'd feel coming back here. Every day I think about what you said on the bridge. I hope that in your eyes I earned what you and your men did for me." The scene is constructed so that Ryan's family stand in the background, but Ryan himself is separated from them in the foreground. Between them looms the white cross of Miller's grave, which acts as an emblem of the horrifying memories that divide Miller from his children but also of the sacrifice made for him. Spielberg's film bridges that gap. It presents the wartime experiences of the greatest generation as a vital model of noble self-sacrifice that subsequent generations ought to remember. The director was seeking to pass on what he perceived as vital, morally elevating historical information about the vanishing greatest generation, in the form of a historical epic. However, the work of Schuman and Scott suggests that Spielberg's understanding of the war as a site of necessary sacrifice was the product of his own experiences as a baby boomer. In its concern with generation debt, and the necessity of World War II, *Saving Private Ryan* clearly reflects a baby boomer's perspective on history.

Conclusion

In 2002, a *Hollywood Reporter* article entitled "Big Pictures: Sword and sandals films are back in style," claimed that, "After *Saving Private Ryan* the young audience suddenly discovered a thing called World War II, and now that that's run its course, they are going after other big period pieces."[81] Of course, the revival of the epic can be traced back further, but the release of *Saving Private Ryan* in 1998 represented a turning point. It inspired production of a series of movies that dealt with World War II in a similar fashion, including *Pearl Harbor* (2001), *Enemy at the Gates* (2001), *Captain Corelli's Mandolin* (2001) and *Windtalkers* (2002). In each case these films quite consciously attempted to honour the sacrifices of those who fought.

More recent conflicts were the subject of *We Were Soldiers* (2002) and *Black Hawk Down* (2001), which owed a stylistic and thematic debt to Spielberg's film. They honoured the soldiers who had sacrificed themselves in two generally underrepresented conflicts, the Vietnam War and American intervention in 1990s Somalia, and each depicted the soldiers themselves as noble, self-sacrificing heroes with an exemplary commitment to a set of moral ideals (however suicidal the ideals became in application). *We Were Soldiers* in particular was an attempt to correct negative perceptions of the baby boomers who had fought in Vietnam, and thus could be understood as another key baby boomer epic. At the time, the actor Josh Hartnett, who starred in both *Pearl Harbor* and *Black Hawk Down*, told an interviewer, "One of the main reasons that I made two military movies so close to one another is that at the moment, for whatever reason, they're pretty much making all military movies in Hollywood. You just have to take your pick among them."[82]

Other epics with a more historically distant wartime setting included *The Messenger: The Story of Jean of Arc* (1999), the Civil War drama *Ride with the Devil* (1999), and the War of Independence epic *The Patriot* (2000), also written by *Saving Private Ryan* screenwriter Robert Rodat.

Even the reconstructed roadshow epic *Gladiator* (2000) owed a clear stylistic debt to Spielberg. Director Ridley Scott explained, "Steven really threw down the gauntlet with *Ryan*. To me that movie put everyone who makes films on notice that if you're going to see a battle, you had better take people right there and have metal whizzing past their ears."[83] The view of war presented in the majority of these films was, like Spielberg's, a vision of a 'good' war. The soldiers who fought were always acting for the greater good, even when they did not understand the specifics of their missions.

So, one of the reasons why baby boomers were attracted to such epic films was because the genre had been presented to them as a versatile means to comment on the past in their own youth. When they were having children, and beginning to think about their cultural legacy in the 1990s, a series of filmmakers risked money and reputation to rework, and ultimately revive, the dormant epic tradition. Over the course of this chapter, we have seen how the maverick epics of the 1990s functioned as a long-delayed response to the roadshow epic. After 1998, epics were being green-lighted more frequently than at any time since the early 1970s. Although *Saving Private Ryan* was clearly the product of Spielberg's particular cinematic agenda, it was also a calculated feature in the production schedules of DreamWorks SKG, and Spielberg had certainly not struggled to find funding, as he had with *Schindler's List*. The next chapter moves away from a focus on highly motivated baby boomer filmmakers to examine industrial perceptions of the epic. Why did it make sense for an economically motivated institution like DreamWorks SKG to favour historical epics in its production schedules at the end of the 1990s?

Notes

1. See, for example, discussion of these films in Emanuel Levy, *Oscar Fever: The History and Politics of the Academy Awards* (New York: Continuum, 2001), 151.

2. Peter Bart, *The Gross: The Hits, the Flops—The Summer That Ate Hollywood* (New York: St. Martin's Griffin, 2000), 160.

3. Financial data from Box Office Mojo, http://www.boxofficemojo.com/movies/?id=saving privateryan.htm.

4. By 'fertility' I mean "the number of births in a given year relative to the number of women of childbearing age," Diane J. Mancunovich, *Birth Quake: The Baby Boom and Its Aftershocks* (Chicago: University of Chicago Press, 2002), 3.

5. Louise B. Russell, *The Baby Boom Generation and the Economy* (Washington, D.C.: The Brookings Institution, 1982), 2.

6. Herbert S. Klein, *A Population History of the United States* (Cambridge: Cambridge University Press, 2004), 177.

7. Neil Howe and William Strauss, *Millennials Rising: The Next Great Generation* (New York: Vintage, 2000), 414.

8. Russell, 1 and Mancunovich, 2.

9. Mancunovich, 3.

10. Klein, 175.

11. Ibid., 186.

12. Ibid., 176.

13. See Douglas T. Miller and Marion Novak, "The Precarious Prosperity of People's Capitalism," in Robert Griffith, ed., *Major Problems in American History Since 1945: Documents and Essays* (Lexington, MA: D.C. Heath, 1992), 213–226.

14. Miller and Novak, 226.

15. Ibid., 220–221.

16. The key text on the greatest generation is Tom Brokaw, *The Greatest Generation* (New York: Delta, 1998).

17. Howe and Strauss, 327.

18. See Joseph McBride, *Steven Spielberg: A Biography* (London: Faber and Faber, 1997), 11–111.

19. Lizabeth Cohen, *A Consumer's Republic: The Politics of Mass Consumption in Postwar America* (London: Vintage, 2004), 123.

20. McBride, 62.

21. Christopher Heard, *Dreaming Aloud: The Life and Films of James Cameron* rev. ed. (Ontario: Doubleday, 1998), 3–10.

22. Although Lucas's birthdate places him outside the dates that I use to delineate the baby boom, he is included here because his films seem to have perfectly captured the tastes of baby boomers rather than preceding generations. For a very brief sketch of influences on Spielberg, Cameron, Lucas, and Zemeckis, see Tom Shone, *Blockbuster: How I Learned to Stop Worrying and Love the Summer* (London: Simon and Schuster, 2004), 1–6.

23. Books on the Hollywood Renaissance include Robert Kolker, *A Cinema of Loneliness: Penn, Stone, Kubrick, Scorsese, Spielberg, Altman* 3rd ed. (Oxford: Oxford University Press, 2003); Peter Biskind, *Easy Riders, Raging Bulls: How the Sex, Drugs and Rock 'n' Roll Generation Saved Hollywood* (New York: Simon and Schuster, 1998); James Bernardoni, *The New Hollywood: What the Movies Did with the New Freedoms of the Seventies* (Jefferson, NC: McFarland, 1991); and Peter Lev, *American Films of the '70s: Conflicting Visions* (Austin: University of Texas Press, 2000), and *Peter Krämer, The New Hollywood: From Bonnie and Clyde to Star Wars* (London: Wallflower, 2005).

24. See Robert Sklar, "'The Lost Audience': 1950s Spectatorship and Historical Reception Studies," in Melvyn Stokes and Richard Maltby, eds., *Identifying Hollywood's Audiences* (London: BFI, 2000), 81–91.

25. Peter Krämer, "The 'New Hollywood', 1967–1977," unpublished MS obtained from author.

26. Michael Pye and Linda Myles, *The Movie Brats: How the Film Generation Took Over Hollywood* (New York: Holt, 1979).

27. Thomas Schatz, "The New Hollywood," in Julian Stringer, ed., *Movie Blockbusters* (London: Routledge, 2003), 29.

28. Stephen Prince, *A New Pot of Gold: Hollywood under the Electronic Rainbow, 1980–1989* (Berkeley: University of California Press, 2000), 288–298.

29. For more on the burgeoning popularity of 'action-adventure' at this time, see Neale (2000), 52–60. 'Family-adventure' is a term coined by Peter Krämer in his article, "'Would You Take Your Child to See This Film?' The Cultural and Social Work of the Family Adventure Movie," in Steve Neale and Murray Smith, eds., *Contemporary Hollywood Cinema* (London: Routledge, 1998), 294.

30. Tino Balio, "Hollywood Production Trends in the Era of Globalisation, 1990–99," in Steve Neale, ed., *Genre and Contemporary Hollywood* (London: BFI, 2002), 165.

31. Peter Krämer, "'The Best Disney Film Disney Never Made': Children's Films and the Family Audience in American Cinema since the 1960s," in Neale (2002), 196.

32. Daniel Marcus, *Happy Days and Wonder Years: The Fifties and Sixties in Contemporary Cultural Politics* (New Brunswick, NJ: Rutgers University Press, 2004), 6.

33. Ibid., 7.

34. J. Hoberman, rev. of *Forrest Gump*, *Village Voice* 12 Jul. 1994, 41.

35. Financial data from Box Office Mojo, http://www.boxofficemojo.com/?movies?id=forrest gump.htm.

36. Daniel Marcus argues that *Forrest Gump* "confirmed [conservative] views of the American past," in Marcus, 196. Like many of his assessments, it seems to me that Marcus ignores the specific political agendas informing film production in favour of sweeping classifications of films as 'conservative' or 'liberal.' For example, *Dances with Wolves* (1990) could be seen as deeply 'conservative' in its nostalgia for an uncorrupted past, but a 'liberal' rejection of colonialist, patriarchal Anglo-American values also informs its production. The film clearly fits into multiple political frameworks. By assuming that any release, including *Forrest Gump*, is an unproblematic reflection of the contemporary political climate, Marcus sometimes fails to adequately explore the more nuanced and specific political agendas informing film production.

37. Janet Maslin, "Target: Boomers and Their Babies," *New York Times* 24 Nov. 1991, B2, quoted in Balio (2003), 171.

38. Fredric Jameson, *Postmodernism, The Cultural Language of Late Capitalism* (Durham, NC: Duke University Press, 1990), ix.

39. Howe and Strauss, 33–70.

40. Marcus, 150–206.

41. Thomas Doherty, "Saving Private Ryan," *Cineaste* 24, no. 1 (Winter 1998), 68.

42. Michael Hammond, "*Saving Private Ryan's* 'Special Affect'," in Yvonne Tasker, ed., *Action and Adventure Cinema* (London: Routledge, 2004), 164. Helpfully, Hammond also insists that the film "belongs firmly in the category of epic war film" (Hammond, 153).

43. Quoted in Stephen Pizello, "Five-Star General," in *American Cinematographer* Aug. 1998, 45. It must be noted that Spielberg could well be using 'Generation X' to describe members of the echo boom, as well.

44. Andrew Hindes, "'Private Ryan's' Saving Grace," *Variety* 20 Jul. 1998, 6.

45. Steven Spielberg, quoted in Army Archerd, "Just For Variety," *Variety* 23 Jul. 1998, 2.

46. Howard Schuman and Jacqueline Scott, "Generations and Collective Memories," *American Sociological Review* 54 (June 1989), 361. What follows is a précis of their work, and I have only cited direct quotations.

47. Schuman and Scott, 374.

48. Steven Spielberg, quoted in Michael Hammond, "Some Smothering Dreams: The Combat Film in Contemporary Hollywood," in Neale (2002), 70. Spielberg also discussed the formal influence of Vietnam movies in David Ansen, "Saving Private Ryan," *Newsweek* 13 Jul. 1998, 52.

49. Hammond (2002), 70.

50. William McDonald, "Long Delayed Lessons About Fathers at War," *New York Times* 26 Jul. 1998, Section 2, 1 and 16. The *New York Times* was a particularly vocal contributor to this debate at this time, and several other articles were run that made very similar points about the generational value of Spielberg's film. See, for example, Anon., "Spielberg's War," *New York Times* 28 Jul. 1998, A14; and Vincent Canby, "Saving a Nation's Pride of Being," *New York Times* 10 Aug. 1998, E1 and E3.

51. Rod Dreyer, "What 'Ryan' Teaches," *New York Post* 11 Jan. 1999, 40.

52. Marouf Hasian, Jr., "Nostalgic Longings, Memories of the Good War, and Cinematic Representations in *Saving Private Ryan*," *Critical Studies in Media Communication* 18, no. 3 (Sept. 2001), 346.

53. Steven Spielberg, quoted in Mike Goodridge, "Selling Private Ryan," in *Screen International* 24 Jul. 1998, 6.

54. Tom Hanks, quoted in Michael Tunison, "Spielberg at War," *Entertainment Today* 24 Jul. 1998, 6.

55. Andrew Gunbel, "How Spielberg's D-Day hit movie was secretly hyped," *Independent on Sunday* 2 Aug. 1998, unpaginated clipping held in the *Saving Private Ryan* clippings file, AMPAS.

56. Brokaw, xvii–xxx.

57. See Anon., "Behind the Bestsellers," *Publisher's Weekly* 4 Jan. 1999, unpaginated, obtained from http://www.publishersweekly.com/article/CA166351.htm.

58. A particularly insightful assessment of Ambrose's books, and his 'best-seller' status, is John Gregory Dunne, "Virtual Patriotism," *New Yorker* 16 Nov. 1998, 98–104.

59. There was some controversy surrounding Ambrose's role as an advisor. According to the *New York Observer* he was hired after the making of the film, partly to assuage possible accusations of plagiarism like those which had plagued the production of Spielberg's previous epic, *Amistad* (1998). See Frank DiGiacomo, "Steven Ambrose Saves Spielberg's Butt," *New York Observer* 13 Jul. 1998, 1 and 3.

60. See Anon., "Ambrose Backlist Soars," *Publisher's Weekly* 17 Aug. 1998, unpaginated, obtained from http://www.publishersweekly.com/article/CA165959.htm.

61. Krin Gabbard, "Saving Private Ryan Too Late," in Jon Lewis, ed., *The End of Cinema As We Know It: American Film in the Nineties* (New York: New York University Press, 2001), 137. On the same page she added that the public emphasis on the greatest generation may well be an attempt on the part of baby boomers to "reconcile with fathers who may have made real, face-to-face reconciliation difficult."

62. Howe and Strauss, 414.

63. Klein, 157.

64. K. S. O'Donoghue, "Memorial to World War II on Track," *Houston Chronicle* 1 Jul. 1999, 23.

65. Peter Ehrenhaus, "Why We Fought: Holocaust Memory in Spielberg's *Saving Private Ryan*," *Critical Studies in Media Communication* 18, no. 3 (Sept. 2001), 328 and 325.

66. Geoff King, *Spectacular Narratives: Hollywood in the Age of the Blockbuster* (London: I.B. Tauris, 2000), 122.

67. Hammond (2004), 161–163.

68. Ibid., 164.

69. *War Stories: Mark Cousins talks to Steven Spielberg*, BBC2 Documentary, broadcast 13 Sept. 1998, quoted in Hammond (2004), 156.

70. Quoted in Bill Higgins, "Ryan Leaves Them Speechless," *Los Angeles Times*, 23 Jul. 1998, unpaginated clipping held in the *Saving Private Ryan* clippings file, AMPAS.

71. Rod Dreyer, rev. of *Saving Private Ryan, New York Post* 24 Jul. 1998, 35.

72. For an account of these responses, see Hasian, 342.

73. Stanley Kauffman, "War, and More," *New Republic* 17 Aug. 1998, 24.

74. Amy Taubin, "War Torn," *Village Voice* 28 Jul. 1998, 113.

75. See, for example, Kenneth Turan, rev. of *Saving Private Ryan, Los Angeles Times* 24 Jul. 1998, Calendar, 1.

76. Todd McCarthy, rev. of *Saving Private Ryan, Variety* 20 Jul. 1998, 46.

77. Hasian, 346.

78. J. Rothkopf, quoted in Hasian, 347.

79. David Denby, "Heroic Proportions," *New York* 27 Jul. 1998, 44.

80. Steven Spielberg, quoted in C. Caldwell, "Spielberg at War," *Commentary* 106, no. 4 (Oct. 1998), 49.

81. David Foster quoted in Stephen Galloway, "Big Pictures: Sword and sandals films are back in style," *Hollywood Reporter*, 1 Oct. 2002, 19.

82. Josh Hartnett, quoted in Rick Lyman, "Into Summer with a Roar," *New York Times* 25 May 2001, E14.

83. Ridley Scott, quoted in Christopher Noxon, "The Roman Empire Rises Again," *Los Angeles Times* 23 Apr. 2000, 5.

–5–

DreamWorks SKG and
The Prince of Egypt (1998)

In October 1994, Steven Spielberg, Jeffrey Katzenberg and David Geffen called a press conference to announce the foundation of a new movie studio. The three founders labelled themselves a 'dream team' at the event, where Spielberg explained the details of their vision.[1] "Hollywood movie studios," he declared, "were at their zenith when they were driven by point of view and personalities. Together with Jeffrey and David, I want to create a place driven by ideas and the people who have them."[2] The studio was later named DreamWorks SKG (as in Spielberg, Katzenberg and Geffen), a moniker described by Thomas Elsaesser as "brilliantly and nonchalantly candid: the manufacture of dreams that 'work' (i.e., 'function' but also 'do their job')."[3] DreamWorks was to be run by innovative and talented moviemakers, including the most successful American filmmaker of recent years, and it would nurture exciting new projects in a way that the other major financier-distributors were failing to do. DreamWorks SKG's founders were inspired by the same vision that had motivated both UA and Orion. They hoped to reconstruct the studio system of the 1940s as it never was and envisaged a place where filmmakers could produce heartfelt films, with real cultural merit. The studio's mission statement, still featured on the DreamWorks Web site, reflects these ideals and states that the founders' vision "was to create an artist-friendly studio to develop, produce and distribute superior film and music entertainment that would inspire and delight audiences worldwide."[4] Spielberg, Katzenberg and Geffen wanted to produce popular yet meaningful and important movies. In a real sense, they were pursuing a dream.

The studio began releasing movies in 1997, and although a relatively broad production schedule was favoured, in its first few years of operation,

DreamWorks produced a disproportionate number of historical epics, including *Saving Private Ryan* (1998) and the animated musical remake of *The Ten Commandments* (1956)—1998's *The Prince of Egypt*. As previous chapters have demonstrated, Spielberg had played a decisive role in the revival of the historical epic, and it was likely that DreamWorks SKG's output would reflect his preoccupations, as Warren Buckland has argued.[5] However, the studio also consciously used historical epics as a way of establishing its identity. Epics are exactly the sort of educational yet spectacular mainstream films that DreamWorks mission statement presented as the core business of the studio.

The DreamWorks founders, particularly Spielberg, were undoubtedly aware that epics were becoming a commercially viable cycle by the late 1990s, and DreamWorks SKG's production schedule effectively ensured the ongoing public visibility of historical epic films in the months and years following the release of James Cameron's *Titanic* in 1997. As a result, the studio played an important role in the revival of the genre, and its early years of operation merit further study. Of all DreamWorks SKG's early releases, *The Prince of Egypt* is particularly revealing. One of the founders' central aims was to create an animation division that might rival that of Disney. Jeffrey Katzenberg had previously been head of filmed production at the Disney Corporation; during his time there, he had overseen the spectacular revival of investment and public interest in Disney's animated films that began with *The Little Mermaid* in 1989 and climaxed with *The Lion King* in 1994. Katzenberg left Disney in acrimonious circumstances (explored later in this chapter) and established DreamWorks within a matter of months. He then chose to announce the foundation of the studio's animation department by producing a hugely expensive yet solemn and thoughtful animated epic. This chapter examines how DreamWorks used the epic film in general fashion, and *The Prince of Egypt* in particular, to announce and comment upon the foundation of DreamWorks.

The chapter is divided into three sections. The first looks at the industrial conditions of the studio's formation and examines some of the organisational problems that the DreamWorks founders needed to overcome. The second section focuses on *The Prince of Egypt*, looking at the production process and comparing it to DeMille's version of the Moses story. The third section relates the central narrative of the film to the role played by Jeffrey Katzenberg in the establishment of DreamWorks and draws some broader conclusions about the industrial function of historical epics since the roadshow era. The conclusion traces subsequent developments at DreamWorks and looks at some of the epics that the studio has produced since the release of *Saving Private Ryan* and *The Prince of Egypt*. This chapter and the next move away from a focus on individual filmmakers to explore the institutional factors motivating the production of historical epics at the end of the 1990s. Despite the growing economic viability of the genre, it does not necessarily follow that the epics released at this time were necessarily less meaningful or innately personal than earlier releases, as *The Prince of Egypt* demonstrates.

1. The Establishment of DreamWorks SKG

In its first few years of operation, DreamWorks rapidly became well integrated into the American film industry. In 2000, the year of *Gladiator*, the studio boasted a 12.8 percent market share in domestic box office receipts, second only to Buena Vista (Disney), while their average box office take per film was $95 million, far more than their nearest competitor.[6] However, DreamWorks released fewer films annually than their rivals and was not part of a broader multimedia conglomerate.[7] The company did boast music and video games divisions, but movie production and distribution were at the centre of its operation. Nevertheless, the studio was more than a production company. The founders had consciously set out to penetrate the main business of the Hollywood majors—the development, financing and distribution of movies. These activities are generally perceived as prohibitively expensive, which is why control of the industry has remained in the hands of a few major companies since the early twentieth century.[8] Martin Dale has proposed that the most significant of the "formidable barriers to entry into the business [include] high overhead, and the importance of a library and wide production slate."[9] According to Thomas Elsaesser, "[B]y making filmmaking ever more costly and extravagant, [Hollywood] has made sure that the number of competitors has become smaller and smaller. . . . [R]ather like the membership fees to country clubs and golf courses it is designed to keep out the undesirables, the upstarts."[10] To compound these problems the majors often act as an oligopoly, a practice that aids their continued dominance.[11] So, how did DreamWorks overcome these barriers to reach the position that it held in 2000?

In fact, the capital needed to fund DreamWorks SKG's operation appeared remarkably quickly. Within a few weeks of the 1994 press conference, the financial basis of the studio took shape. Between them, the three founders put up $100 million of their own money and received outside investment from Paul Allen, a co-founder of Microsoft, and from Cheil Jedang, a Korean company. Five hundred million was borrowed from Chase Manhattan, $350 million from Bear Sterns, and overdraft facilities were arranged with Chemical Bank.[12] The studio was a private Limited Liability Company, which does not have to declare profits or answer to shareholders. The three founders owned roughly 66 percent of DreamWorks, Paul Allen owned 26 percent, and the remaining 8 percent was divided between other investors.[13] This start-up capital was used to fund several key activities. First, DreamWorks had to put a series of movie projects on the road to production. The projects that received the green light would then need to be paid for. The studio released nine films in its first two years of full operation, which between them had a total negative cost well in excess of $300 million.[14] To make these, an actual production plant—a 'studio' in the traditional sense of the word—was unnecessary, because the industry has tended to rely on leased production premises and equipment since the roadshow era. Nevertheless, DreamWorks unveiled early plans for a multimillion-dollar studio complex to be sited at Playa Vista in Los Angeles. Ultimately, this dream never came to pass because environmentalists raised concerns about the effect that the complex might have on the indigenous flora and fauna.[15] Instead, DreamWorks operated out of offices on the Universal lot. Of course, these have to be rented, and the people who staff them have to be paid. However, one can assume that these expenses pale beside the cost of establishing and operating a distribution network.

As Janet Wasko and other industrial historians have shown, distribution is perhaps the most capital-intensive element of the movie business, and it is also the main operation that drives movie production.[16] Once an infrastructure that can deliver product to theatres has been established, it must remain in almost constant use to cover operating costs.[17] DreamWorks chose to distribute their own films in America but made arrangements with Universal to distribute overseas. There are no available figures that indicate how much it actually cost DreamWorks to establish its domestic distribution network, but Wasko has claimed on average 30 percent of a film's receipts go towards paying the overheads entailed by domestic distribution.[18] The overall cost of establishing and running a studio can therefore be measured in billions, and it is quite remarkable that DreamWorks was able to attract such high levels of investment with apparent ease.

For the established studios, operating capital is partially derived from profits made on current releases but mainly comes from related synergies and judicious use of their film libraries. Martin Dale describes these libraries as "by far the most important component of most film companies' assets. The value of Hollywood's libraries is higher than the total production and promotion cost of the annual film slate, and provides a very bankable asset upon which the majors can obtain finance."[19] The funding that the majors offer is frequently borrowed from banks with which the studio has an established relationship, but the relationship is dependent on the studios' 'bankability'.[20] DreamWorks could offer no visible assets of this sort, yet represented a reasonably safe investment opportunity for related reasons. Spielberg, Katzenberg and Geffen may not have owned the *rights* to any film libraries, but they had been responsible for some huge hits, and consequently their reputations functioned in a similar fashion. Spielberg's status has been comprehensively dealt with in the last two chapters. Jeffrey Katzenberg, on the other hand, is perhaps less well known than Spielberg but had developed a solid reputation in the industry nonetheless. Katzenberg had been responsible for a string of successful movies that had virtually redefined the image of the Disney Corporation during his tenure as production head, culminating in *The Lion King*.[21] Throughout this period, Disney had enjoyed an extremely high market share, and by the time Katzenberg left they had become "joint leader of the industry with [their] arch rival Time-Warner."[22] David Geffen had had a limited (but not unsuccessful) career as an independent film producer but was already a billionaire music mogul. He brought to DreamWorks a reputation as a skilled businessman and an especially formidable deal maker.[23]

So, the DreamWorks troika had been responsible for an enviable library of titles that included some of Hollywood's most successful and prestigious films. Consequently, their reputations were a good indication of their fiscal reliability. They were able to break through financial barriers and establish their studio on the strength of their past successes, which acted as a form of financial security for investors. However, the studio needed more than financial support. DreamWorks also needed product—specifically the founders needed to attract talented, creative filmmakers who could make the meaningful, culturally valuable movies that were central to DreamWorks SKG's mission. Arguably, the studio's early films needed to prove that DreamWorks was the sort of open, nurturing environment described by Spielberg in his press statement, and, for all their success, Katzenberg and Spielberg had certain problems with their reputations as producers within the industry which they needed to overcome.

Through his Amblin production company, affiliated to Universal, Spielberg had already built a reputation as a commercially intuitive producer, notably in the 1980s with *Back to the Future* (1985) and *Gremlins* (1984).[24] However, when the DreamWorks deal was put together, he appeared reluctant to commit completely to the new venture and retained a clause in his contract whereby he could, if he wanted, make films for other companies, as both a director and a producer.[25] Presumably, this resulted from a desire not to lose out on appealing projects owned by other studios, but it sent out a message to the industry that Spielberg was not entirely dedicated to DreamWorks. If it all went wrong, the person whose vision was supposed to inform the working ethos of the studio had a get-out clause.

Jeffrey Katzenberg had related issues to deal with, insofar as creative talent may have been concerned. For all his phenomenal success as a producer, his tenure at Disney had seen the corporation earn the moniker 'Mouschwitz' amongst Disney workers and the trade press.[26] Katzenberg was a hard taskmaster, who expected total dedication from his employees, and as a result he was sometimes seen as an insensitive workaholic. He was also famous within the industry for drafting a memo critiquing the trend for ever more expensive blockbusters and star salaries, which was subsequently leaked to the press.[27] This had compounded his, and Disney's, reputation for penny pinching, although it was complicated by Katzenberg's subsequent decision to bring blockbuster-auteurs Don Simpson and Jerry Bruckheimer under Disney's wing. The memo, and Katzenberg's move to recruit Bruckheimer and Simpson, who went on to produce increasingly expensive blockbusters and became notorious for their overspending, could have been construed as hypocritical, and, worse for DreamWorks, an abandonment of principles.[28] The broad production schedule put together by the studio can be understood as an attempt to address these concerns, as subsequent sections will demonstrate.

DreamWorks SKG's first productions hit the screen three years after the studio was established. They were *The Peacemaker* (1997), *Mousehunt* (1997) and *Amistad* (1997), respectively a political action thriller, a Gothic family comedy and a serious historical epic about slavery. *Mousehunt* and *The Peacemaker* were immediately successful, but Spielberg's film was one of his rare flops. Although all of these releases eventually made their money back, the director had to defer his fee for *Amistad* before the film broke even.[29] In 1998, the studio released six films: *Small Soldiers*, *Deep Impact*, *Antz*, *Paulie*, *The Prince of Egypt* and *Saving Private Ryan*.

Close examination of the directors and writers behind these early projects indicates that, rather than attracting new talent, DreamWorks had initially exploited Spielberg's established relationships, particularly those fostered through Amblin. Mimi Leder, director of *The Peacemaker* and *Deep Impact*, had previously worked on Amblin's television series *ER* and had brought star George Clooney with her. Alternatively, Joe Dante, who directed *Small Soldiers*, had worked with Spielberg on *Gremlins*, and Robert Zemeckis, another Spielberg protégé, put two projects into production, *What Lies Beneath* (2000) and *Cast Away* (2000). The founders must have hoped that other talented filmmakers would see in these films a reason to work with DreamWorks.

On the whole the 1997 releases fall into line with the vision of the studio as a relatively daring creative environment, although commentators at the time tended to view the first few releases as slightly disappointing. *Mousehunt* was the only comic piece, but it exhibited a marked degree of visual stylisation, while *Amistad* was a sombre true story about a group of slaves fighting in the courts for their freedom in nineteenth-century America. *The Peacemaker* was an action film that dealt with the legacy of the recent Balkans conflict, and in the film an effort was made to deal with the complex politics of the time in a serious and sensitive manner. Both of these movies obliquely derived their focus from *Schindler's List*. *Amistad* transferred that film's narrative of institutionally sanctioned slavery, struggles for human rights and eventual escape into an American historical setting. Indeed, the film allowed current generations to honour and remember the terrible hardship endured during the slave trade. Meanwhile, *The Peacemaker*'s focus on the Balkans conflict extended Spielberg's comments that *Schindler's List* had been made as a response to the war in Bosnia.[30]

As the previous chapter has explored, Spielberg also returned to the Second World War in his next film, *Saving Private Ryan*. This, and *The Prince of Egypt*, became the studio's 'signature' releases—projects made directly under the auspices of the studio's founders that most directly embodied the DreamWorks SKG's mandate. A great deal was riding on them in terms of both money and reputation. *The Prince of Egypt* was intended to show that Katzenberg could recapture the success of his Disney films, and that the studio was capable of competing with Disney in the animated market. Furthermore, because the studio's image was closely linked to Spielberg's work, the success or failure of his World War II epic *Saving Private Ryan* was also likely to be considered a good indicator of its health.[31] It is highly significant that these signature releases, which were intended as the best that DreamWorks had to offer, were both historical epics.

According to Andrew Hindes of *Variety*, in 1998, "DreamWorks enjoyed the most auspicious first full year of theatrical releases of any movie company in recent memory. The young studio found both commercial and artistic success by reinventing such shopworn Hollywood genres as the World War II action drama, the sci-fi disaster pic and the animated musical."[32] As noted in the previous chapter, *Saving Private Ryan* became the top-grossing film of the year in the United States, with a domestic box office take of $216 million.[33] It also won the studio's first Academy Awards, while *The Prince of Egypt* was a more modest success, taking $101 million in domestic receipts and a further $117.6 overseas.[34] The studio's other major hits in 1998 included the CGI-animated comedy *Antz* and the asteroid collision drama *Deep Impact*, which had been directed by *The Peacemaker*'s Mimi Leder. *Deep Impact* took $348.6 million in worldwide box office receipts.[35] In comparison with the Jerry Bruckheimer–produced *Armageddon* (1998), *Deep Impact* clearly took an 'epic' stance to the story, inasmuch as it provided a broad view of the asteroid impact as an international, historical tragedy, while *Armageddon* was more clearly an action movie. Of the nine films released in the first years of DreamWorks SKG's operation, three were historical epics (*Amistad*, *Saving Private Ryan* and *The Prince of Egypt*), and two more were entertaining movies that attempted to speak with some degree of gravity on recent or imagined history (*The Peacemaker* and *Deep Impact*).

Obviously, historical epics were just one element in a broader production schedule. With projects like *Small Soldiers* and *Paulie* (respectively, films about talking toys and a talking parrot) DreamWorks had sought to produce the kind of edgy family films that Spielberg had overseen as a producer through Amblin. In later years, the studio also presided over a series of 'gross-out' comedies, including *Road Trip* (2000) and *Old School* (2003). However, historical epics played an important role in establishing a sense of identity during DreamWorks SKG's early years, and the studio subsequently returned to grandiose, edifying epics with *Gladiator* and the television series *Band of Brothers*. In particular, *The Prince of Egypt* was clearly used to identify the studio as a successful and distinctive entrant into the animated market but also to demonstrate what the DreamWorks animated movie might look like. Furthermore, the way that the film used, and transformed, the conventions of the roadshow epic, and the narrative of the Cecil B. DeMille film on which it was based, shows how the studio's epic was tailored for a contemporary family audience.

2. *The Prince of Egypt* and the Epic Tradition

Although *The Prince of Egypt* was produced under the auspices of Jeffrey Katzenberg, the film's press kit placed Spielberg at the moment of its inception, bolstering the image that DreamWorks was a free-thinking environment but also showing that the film had benefited from Spielberg's considerable creative acumen. Katzenberg explained:

> Steven asked what the criteria would be for a great animated film and I launched into a twenty-minute dissertation about what you look for: a powerful allegory that we can relate to in our time; extraordinary situations to motivate strong emotional journeys; something wonderful about the human spirit; good triumphing over evil; music as a compelling storytelling element; and so on. Steven leaned forward and said, "You mean like *The Ten Commandments*?" and I said, "Exactly." [36]

Like other early DreamWorks releases, *The Prince of Egypt* again owes something to *Schindler's List*. Not only does it tell of another vital moment in Jewish history and feature Ralph Fiennes as the villain, but *The Prince of Egypt* returned directly to the Moses story that had subtly informed Spielberg's most prestigious film to date (and many other Spielberg films), as explained in chapter 3. Jeffrey Katzenberg also cited several other sources of direct inspiration, "When we were recruiting, people would come in and I'd show them the Doré illustrated Bible, a book of Monet paintings and some stills from Lean's *Lawrence of Arabia* (1962). I'd say, 'These are our inspirations, I hope we can do them justice.'" [37] The invocation of nineteenth-century Bible illustrator Gustave Doré, the paintings of Claude Monet and David Lean's most famous epic, another film with strong connections to Spielberg, all heaped artistic legitimacy on Katzenberg's film, while the act of remaking *The Ten Commandments* demonstrated that the studio heads knew their popular film history. [38] A comparison of the two movies provides a compelling insight into the ways that DreamWorks integrated thematic features of the roadshow epic and the contemporary family film.

The Bible provides little detail about the early life of Moses, and DreamWorks SKG's film fills in the blanks along similar lines to *The Ten Commandments*. Moses is abandoned in the Nile during a massacre of firstborn Hebrew children and recovered by the Egyptian royal family, who raise him as one of their own. As an adult he is made chief architect of the Empire, overseeing thousands of Hebrew slaves. He then discovers his Hebrew heritage and flees into the desert. After a period of wandering, he encounters the shepherd Jethro and builds a new life after marrying Jethro's daughter. Eventually, he becomes a desert shepherd himself. He is called back to Egypt by God, who appears in the form of a burning bush and demands that Moses free the Hebrews from Egyptian bondage. Moses obeys and comes into conflict with Rameses, the Pharaoh who was once like a brother to him. A series of plagues are brought against the Egyptian empire, at the culmination of which Pharaoh's son is killed, along with all the other firstborn Egyptian children. In despair, Pharaoh capitulates to Moses, and the exodus of the Hebrews begins, but when his despair turns to rage, Pharaoh gives chase. To escape his armies Moses parts the Red Sea, creating a passageway that collapses on Pharaoh's pursuing army. Moses then ascends Mount Sinai and receives the Ten Commandments. At this point, *The Prince of Egypt* ends, whereas in DeMille's film Moses returns to discover the Hebrews in the middle of an idolatrous orgy. God takes his vengeance, and they are doomed to wander the wilderness for forty years. The film then shifts forward to the end of this period, when we see Moses dying on a mountainside just as the promised land appears on the horizon.

Where the two movies differ is in their elaboration of this story. Family relationships form the chief narrative concern of DreamWorks SKG's film, which seeks to explain the central characters' enmity, torment and loss very much in terms of a dysfunctional contemporary family unit. Consequently, *The Prince of Egypt* features a fairly restricted cast of characters, all related in some fashion; Moses (voiced by Val Kilmer) and his adoptive brother Rameses (Ralph Fiennes) are raised by the Pharaoh Seti I (Patrick Stewart) and his queen (Helen Mirren). Later Moses encounters his real brother and sister, Aaron (Jeff Goldblum) and Miriam (Sandra Bullock), his wife, Tzipporah (Michelle Pfeiffer), and father-in-law Jethro (Danny Glover). When the movie begins, Moses is happily enmeshed in his Egyptian 'family'. In DeMille's version, Moses (Charlton Heston) and Rameses (Yul Brynner) are cousins and enemies—jealous rivals for the throne of Egypt and the love of Nefretiri, a pagan femme fatale played by Anne Baxter, whose manipulation of events inadvertently hastens the destruction of Egypt. There is a large cast of secondary characters, including Dathan, a corrupt Hebrew overseer played by Edward G. Robinson; the stone carver Joshua; his lover, Lilia; the sadistic architect Baka (Vincent Price); as well as Moses's adoptive mother, Bithiah, and her handmaiden, Memnet. The interaction of these characters loads the plot with intrigue that sustains its 220-minute running time. Consequently, the narrative is far less focused on family affairs, but it also takes a considerably less restrictive view of what constitutes family entertainment.

According to Derek Elley, "DeMille never resolved the struggle in his films between sexual and devout content," and the occasionally titillating aspects of *The Ten Commandments* are clear evidence of this.[39] During the early stages of preproduction, production code administrator Joseph Breen had expressed particular concern about "the number of scenes throughout the script which require particular care with regard to costumes, especially the women" (thereby reflecting the PCA's increased focus on lewd content over politically controversial subjects).[40] DeMille's scenes of dancing girls, idolatrous orgies, scantily clad Nubian slaves and the lustful plotting of Nefretiri have been used by contemporary critics to suggest that his film was, at times, frivolous. As we have seen, the critic Vincent Canby described *The Ten Commandments* as being "as American as apple pie and the striptease, alternately ceremonial and teasing, stern and giddy."[41] DeMille's approach may have been that of a showman, perfectly happy to show a flash of thigh alongside the more staggering miracles, but he nevertheless claimed to have been primarily motivated by sincere political and spiritual beliefs.

At the beginning of *The Ten Commandments*, DeMille appears at a lectern and informs the audience, "The theme of this picture is whether men are to be ruled by God's law, or whether they are to be ruled by the whims of a dictator like Rameses. Are men the property of the state, or are they free souls under God? This same battle continues in the world today." In his biography DeMille clarified his approach: "[Following] the awful experience of totalitarianism, fascist and communist, the world needs a reminder of the Law of God."[42] Chapter 1 demonstrated that a sizable sector of the audience received the film in this spirit, even if critics have sometimes viewed it as profane. Although it was an animated film, *The Prince of Egypt* was produced with an apparently similar agenda in mind. Katzenberg and the other filmmakers set out wanting to create a meaningful spiritual and artistic experience that might enrich the lives of their viewers. Hence, Katzenberg was keen to claim that *The Prince of Egypt* was "a breakthrough both in terms of its epic style and grownup content."[43] In early publicity he repeatedly stressed that the studio had produced a serious historical epic that would appeal to adults as much as it did children. Primarily, *The Prince of Egypt* asked audiences to identify with Moses in a way that *The Ten Commandments* never managed. It did this by emphasising the familial conflicts at the heart of the story.

As noted in the previous chapter, family films have become a constituent part of Hollywood's release schedules over the last two decades for a variety of reasons, including gradual demographic shifts in the ages and experiences of filmgoers and filmmakers. Peter Krämer has argued that many of the family films produced in the 1980s and 1990s are intended to act positively on the families who see them. He writes, "The cultural work that the films' narratives perform to reconcile family members with each other on the screen translates into a kind of social work performed by the films on the familial units in the auditorium, creating shared experiences and opening up channels of communication."[44] *The Prince of Egypt* performs a similar function. Brotherly and parental love form the lynchpin on which the narrative turns. Moses's family is ripped asunder, and the film documents his journey towards reconciliation. After his return to Egypt, Moses is torn between his duty and his genuine love for Rameses.

As *The Ten Commandments* progresses, Charlton Heston's Moses gradually becomes a distant authoritarian figure, particularly after receiving his divine orders, while the 1990s animated Moses remains defined by his human relationships. In *The Prince of Egypt* he expresses great regret that "things cannot be as they were," and this regret turns to remorse and grief as the plagues take their toll on the Egyptian people. As he cradles the body of his dead son, who has been killed by the 'Angel of Death,' Rameses finally gives Moses permission to depart. When he leaves the palace, Moses collapses and sobs in sympathy for his brother. The animated Rameses is also a noticeably more complex figure than the malicious villain played by Yul Brynner. He is a victim of circumstance, living in the shadow of an oppressive father, with a resulting weight of expectation resting on his shoulders. His struggles to live up to his father's memory set him on a path that ultimately leads to his own destruction and to the collapse of his empire. At one point during the plagues, the animated Rameses cries out, "I will not be the weak link," referring to his father's suggestion, voiced earlier in the film, that "one weak link can break the chain of a mighty dynasty."

Moses has an equally problematic relationship with the old Pharaoh. In the early part of the film Seti is a loving father to Moses, but his adopted son eventually recalls the circumstances that brought him to Seti's palace—a traumatic memory he had previously repressed. A confrontation occurs, and when Moses accuses his father of slaughtering Hebrew children to control the slave population, the old man holds up his hands and says, "Oh, my son. They were only slaves." Moses backs away in horror. The film then documents Moses' attempts to find a new father, who arrives in the form of the monotheistic shepherd, Jethro. Here, the religious dynamics of the Moses story are mapped onto the story of a family. Seti is a father, but he is also a living god, described as "the morning and the evening star," whose idolatrous image appears on sphinxes across the city. According to the film's thematic logic, Moses must abandon this false god (and false father) before the god of Judaism and Christianity will speak to him. The Hebrew god then comes to function as his true father and, the film implies, the father of all who follow Moses. Rameses is presented as misguided rather than wicked, a cog in a malign, idolatrous machine, while Moses is an unwilling vessel of divine vengeance. The film's conclusion then brings Moses back to the bosom of his extended Hebrew 'family', having overcome the terrible barriers to freedom erected by Rameses (whose actions are also the result of an earlier generation's parental failure). Thus, *The Prince of Egypt* preaches intergenerational understanding along the lines proposed by Krämer, in that it presents adult life and familial relationships as a complex, but ultimately navigable, terrain, where the legacy of childhood trauma and familial dysfunction must be carefully negotiated, and the film provides a shared audience experience centred around these concerns. It also actively dramatises the spiritual struggle at the heart of the story, mapping familial elements onto a spiritual story that makes claims to religious significance in a manner akin to DeMille's film.

In its marketing campaign, DreamWorks was careful to stress the sincerity and thoughtfulness of *The Prince of Egypt*. In contrast to the marketing of Disney's animations, no action figures were produced, no product tie-in was arranged with fast-food restaurants, and much was made of the fact that religious scholars of various denominations had been consulted at the start of the project.[45] In part this was a necessary response to the sacred, and potentially controversial, nature of the story, and similar problems had been faced by DeMille forty years before.[46] For some critics the seriousness of the project was a surprising, and not always welcome, feature of the story.[47] However, for DreamWorks it must have been essential. *The Prince of Egypt* was intended to prove that the studio could produce a meaningful and successful animated movie that contrasted with the standard 'Disney model,' a film that might just demonstrate of what the studio was capable. Katzenberg explained, "Walt Disney had a mission statement: 'I make movies for children and the child who exists in each of us.' So I say—with both a nod and a wink—my idea for DreamWorks was that we would make animated movies for adults, for the adult that exists in every child."[48] The studio heads didn't just want to compete with Disney, they wanted to establish their own identity as an animation company, and the historical epic was an eminently appropriate vehicle for these intentions.

The Prince of Egypt asked audiences to empathise with Moses the man, and the biblical story was presented in such a way that it resonated with different generations of a family audience. In the same way, *Saving Private Ryan* asked younger generations of viewers to understand the hardships that their parents or grandparents had once endured. Like Spielberg's film, *The Prince of Egypt* was also designed to address the American film industry. By making an animated epic DreamWorks SKG's founders demonstrated that they could produce a serious, thoughtful and culturally valuable film, the very existence of which seemed to prove that DreamWorks was a studio where such projects could flourish. As the next section will show, this message was also woven into the film's narrative at the level of allegory.

3. DreamWorks as Promised Land

According to the critic Michael Wood:

> The ancient world of the epics was a huge, many-faceted metaphor for Hollywood itself. . . . [T]hese movies are always about the creation of such a world in a movie. The hero of *The Ten Commandments* is not Moses, but DeMille himself, who set up the whole show, the voice of God and the burning bush and the miracles of Egypt included. And the hero of *Ben-Hur* is not Ben-Hur, who only won the chariot race, but William Wyler, the director, the man responsible for providing the chariot race for us.[49]

As we have seen throughout this book, the claim that epics dramatise the circumstances of their production has long been considered to be an integral feature of the form by academic critics, and the introduction argued that the connection between production and content is a defining feature of the epic genre. Vivian Sobchack has extended Wood's point in her assertion that the epic "often formally or literally celebrates and represents the historic struggles under which it produced itself as a mimetic imitation of the historical events it is dramatising."[50] A good example of this can be seen in the marketing of *How the West Was Won* (1962), of which Sobchack writes, "The laborious struggle entailed by the film's production formally repeats the laborious struggle of the American pioneers."[51] Her point is that "a correlation is clearly established here between the present events of a film's production and the past events it is intended to represent."[52] *How the West Was Won* explicitly linked the pioneering technological advances of Cinerama to the 'pioneer spirit' of the American West. *The Prince of Egypt* contains traces of a similar impulse. At the level of allegory it reconstructs the story of the Exodus in a manner that has strong parallels to the story of DreamWorks SKG's foundation. The central figure in this interpretation is not so much Steven Spielberg as animation head Jeffrey Katzenberg.

The precise details of DreamWorks SKG's origins are unclear, but several accounts point to Katzenberg as the chief instigator.[53] In his early years as head of filmed production at Disney, Katzenberg had initially ignored the company's ailing animation department and focused instead on their live-action releases.[54] With *The Little Mermaid* this situation began to change, and Katzenberg gradually became extremely enamoured of animation. Three years later, and with three of Disney's biggest hits behind him, he was unhappy in his position, and he then became embroiled in a bitter dispute with Disney's CEO, Michael Eisner. Eisner's 'second in command', chairman Frank Wells, was killed in a helicopter crash in April 1994. Katzenberg had expected to replace him and claimed that Eisner had promised him the job, which Eisner denied.[55] However, Eisner was reluctant to promote Katzenberg after Frank Wells's death. Instead he let the post remain empty and took on the chairman duties himself.[56] Katzenberg forced his boss into a confrontation over the issue. His contract was up for renewal in September 1994, and he issued an ultimatum threatening to quit if he was not promoted to Wells's position, while Eisner was in the hospital recovering from a heart attack. Eisner's response was equally calculated. He arranged a meeting with Katzenberg, who he told to prepare a memo outlining his vision of the company's future, but the document was never read. When Katzenberg entered Eisner's office he was handed a press release stating that the company was being restructured and that Katzenberg would be leaving.

The next day, Katzenberg departed forever from Disney and began to ponder his next move. He and Spielberg were friends, and they co-owned a chain of sandwich shops called *Dive*. Katzenberg apparently introduced the idea of forming a studio during a consolatory phone call. When the dream began to coalesce, Spielberg contacted Geffen, who had recently sold his record label, and convinced him to come on board.[57] Over the following months and years, the relationship between Katzenberg and his former employers remained strained. He maintained that he was owed royalties from the projects he had initiated while working at Disney, while Eisner claimed that Katzenberg had forfeited his rights to any royalties when he left. Katzenberg began proceedings to sue in 1995, and the case stretched on for four years. In 1999, he received an undisclosed out-of-court settlement, rumoured to be almost $300 million.[58] Eventually, the story of Katzenberg's difficulties at Disney and the subsequent establishment of DreamWorks found its way into *The Prince of Egypt*.

A great many roadshow-era epics revolved around the construction of hugely expensive and spectacular monuments, from the ancient cities of *The Ten Commandments* and the pyramids of *Land of the Pharaohs* (1955) to the eponymous *Bridge on the River Kwai* (1957). *The Prince of Egypt* is no exception. The film's opening sequence shows thousands of Hebrew slaves enduring terrible suffering as they labour on monuments to the greatness of Seti. From the very beginning the Hebrews are associated with construction, and, indirectly, the visual arts. The Hebrews are the stonemasons and sculptors responsible for the beautiful sphinxes and friezes that abound in DreamWorks SKG's ancient Egypt. In the song that accompanies the introductory scenes of backbreaking labour, they sing:

Deliver us,
There's a land you promised us,
Lord of all, remember us here in this burning sand,
Deliver us,
Send a shepherd to shepherd us,
And deliver us to the promised land.

When the song concludes, and Moses is adopted by the Egyptian queen, the narrative moves forward by fifteen years, to a chariot race between the now teenaged Moses and Rameses, who career around the streets of Cairo in a conscious homage to *Ben-Hur*. They race through the Parthenon that was being constructed in the initial scenes. By this time it is virtually complete, but the brothers barely notice the beauty of their surroundings, and at one point they succeed in knocking the nose from a sphinx and are almost crushed in the resulting commotion. At this point, the space that was coded as an area of oppression and labour for the Hebrew slaves becomes a playground for their thoughtless and indolent Egyptian rulers.

Moses is then made 'chief architect' by his brother and put in charge of construction and thus the Hebrew slaves. Soon afterwards, he learns that he is himself a Hebrew, which is revealed in a sequence that clearly links him to the craftsmanship of the slaves. The hieroglyphs on the walls of the Egyptian palace become animated during a dream sequence and, in the process, Moses relives his repressed memories of the massacre that led to his adoption. As his heritage is revealed, Moses is effectively recoded as a member the Hebrew community. The vision is framed in the visual, two-dimensional, animated arts—the hieroglyphs that cover every surface of the slave-built palace. Moses is then unable to continue living as a slave driver and heads off into the desert after killing an Egyptian foreman. His brother offers to forgive him, but Moses feels that a wedge has been driven between them, and he flees.

After a bravura sequence showing Moses's progress through the inhospitable Egyptian desert, he eventually encounters people like himself, who worship the Hebrew god but live in freedom. He joins their community but finds that he cannot remain with them indefinitely, when his divine mission is eventually revealed to him. In accordance with God's will, he finds that he must return to Egypt and lead the rest of his people to freedom in a new state, where they will, presumably, be able to realise their potential as free men (and women) rather than slaves. Moses seeks to achieve his goal through the use of spectacle, when the will of God enables him to create miracles that overwhelm the trickery of the Egyptian magicians. This is illustrated particularly well in a sequence that follows his return to the Egyptian court. To demonstrate the power of his god, Moses transforms his staff into a serpent. The Egyptian priests attempt to do the same, but it is clear that their effects are the result of showmanship and conjuring tricks. Moses, on the other hand, produces 'authentic' spectacles, something evident in the manner through which they are represented on the screen. These spectacles are not mere frivolity. In fact, they have the power to change people's lives.

Throughout the film, moments where the divine intrudes upon the everyday world incorporate three-dimensional computer-generated imagery. The 'fire' on the burning bush is an ephemeral CGI substance, as are the swirling clouds of the 'Angel of Death'. Most spectacular of all is a photorealistic parting of the Red Sea, which apparently took 318,000 work-hours to realise.[59] These scenes are among the most remarkable in the entire film, as the understandably nervous Hebrews hurry between two mountainous walls of ocean, which then come crashing together on their Egyptian pursuers. The CGI used in these sequences has a very different texture from the two-dimensional animation used in the rest of the film, and it lends such moments an intangible sense of authenticity.

Suddenly, something quite literally intrudes onto the screen from another dimension. In this way the animators managed to successfully convey a sense that the divine extends beyond the world of the film. Of course, their approach also linked the miraculous events of the narrative to the technological means of its creation—the transcendental moments of the story are precisely those when the technology of the cinema is at its most visible. Importantly, Moses is the chief purveyor of these divine 'effects'.

The above reading emphasises the allegorical dimensions of the film in order to show that *The Prince of Egypt* is not only about Moses, but it is also about Jeffrey Katzenberg (to paraphrase Michael Wood). The oppressive Egyptian regime can be understood as the Disney Corporation, and the monuments that the Hebrews labour on are movies. Moses' subsequent journey towards enlightenment mirrors Katzenberg's departure from Disney and his involvement with DreamWorks. His creative potential is discovered, and he has to leave, but he returns to free other filmmakers (in the film, Hebrew slaves) and lead them to the promised land—DreamWorks. Moses, and thus Katzenberg, is shown to have changed on his journey, and the brutal Egyptian regime has been abandoned in favour of a simple, free and ennobling existence, to which he will guide all of his people. Where Moses convinces his enemies through divinely inspired spectacle, Katzenberg, of course, has *The Prince of Egypt*. Thus, the film presents the foundation of DreamWorks in allegorical and mythic terms. Along with Spielberg, it is implied, the reformed Jeffrey Katzenberg could lead the filmmaking community to a promised land of unparalleled creative freedom. Because the film is a historical epic, a conscious effort is made to edify and educate the viewer. Like Moses' miracles, to watch the film is to experience something more than mere entertainment. In the process, *The Prince of Egypt* suggests that to work at DreamWorks is to produce films with great social and cultural value, embodied by, but not limited to, the historical epic.

Conclusion

The self-reflexive nature of the roadshow epics that Wood and Sobchack examine is often linked to broader debates about the role of mainstream cinema in the postwar period. This book has documented a related process occurring in contemporary epics. In *Dances with Wolves*, Kevin Costner's efforts to revive the western epic were reflected in John Dunbar's attempts to save the indigenous culture of the American West.

Alternatively, Spielberg's quest to make *Schindler's List* was mirrored in Oskar Schindler's acts of public benevolence. However, such allegories only serve to reflect individual commitments. *The Prince of Egypt* is closer in spirit to the epics of the roadshow era, because it clearly demonstrates that the allegorical narrative drive of the epic film can serve a practical, industrial function. The production of a heartfelt animated epic confirmed DreamWorks SKG's commitment to high quality, culturally worthwhile projects, while the film itself allegorically resolved potential problems with Katzenberg's image and presented the studio as an enterprising, free-thinking environment. *The Prince of Egypt* clearly demonstrated DreamWorks SKG's commitment to 'ideas and the people who have them' and made a conscious entreaty to such people. Therefore, *The Prince of Egypt* confirmed what DreamWorks was capable of, and asked both filmmakers and audiences to come along for the ride. Its influence can be seen in the performance and nature of the studio's subsequent animated and live-action releases.

Although *The Prince of Egypt* earned a total worldwide gross of $218.6 million and can therefore be counted as a hit, it was not a colossal success on the scale of the epics discussed elsewhere in this book. Nevertheless, DreamWorks continued to produce animated movies with historical, at times epic, settings. In 2000, the studio released *The Road to Eldorado*, an animated swashbuckling comedy set in sixteenth-century South America, which was followed, in 2002, by *Spirit: Stallion of the Cimarron*, the story of a free-spirited horse (whose thoughts are voiced by Matt Damon) and his life in the American West. Essentially, *Spirit* was a western told from the horse's point of view, but its focus on the ravages wrought by Anglo conquerors, and the beneficence of the American Indians, at times bore close comparison to *Dances with Wolves*. Moreover, Jeffrey Katzenberg again compared this film to *Lawrence of Arabia*, noting that *Spirit* "takes on the great American landscape and tries to bring it to life and make it a character—and that is part of what Lean did with *Arabia*."[60]

In 2003, *Sinbad: Legend of the Seven Seas* presented a version of the mythic Arabic story, which, somewhat incongruously, placed the famous swashbuckling sailor (voiced by Brad Pitt) amongst a panoply of ancient Roman gods. Arguably, the ancient-world elements included in *Sinbad* were part of an attempt to introduce a more clearly epic tone, which brought the film closer to the ancient-world epics of the roadshow period. Like all of DreamWorks SKG's other two-dimensional animated releases since *The Prince of Egypt*, the film was not particularly successful at the box office.[61]

However, DreamWorks enjoyed colossal success with the computer-animated *Shrek* (2001)—another film that seemed to take a swipe at Katzenberg's former employers, and in 2004, *Shrek 2* took an astonishing $436.5 million in domestic box office receipts alone.[62] The arch yet accessible tone of the *Shrek* films was also duplicated in DreamWorks SKG's *Shark Tale* (2004). Following the success of *Shrek 2*, DreamWorks SKG's animated division separated from the parent company and became a public concern, overseen directly by Katzenberg.[63] DreamWorks Animation (as it is now known) appears to have found its greatest successes, and its 'brand identity,' by abandoning the sober, consciously resonant terrain of the historical epic in favour of more knowing, ironic family entertainments, which can be widely exploited in other markets, unlike *The Prince of Egypt*. Nevertheless, in interviews Jeffrey Katzenberg has continued to claim that he thinks *The Prince of Egypt* is his company's best film, and under his guidance further entries in the *Shrek* franchise will apparently develop epic dimensions of their own.[64]

DreamWorks SKG's live-action releases seem to provide some evidence that the founders have successfully established exactly the sort of working environment they set out to create. Within the industry, DreamWorks apparently established a more recognisable brand identity than any other studio except Disney—partially through the eclecticism of its product. According to a 2002 *Variety* article, "DreamWorks *has* defined itself: It consistently refuses to pigeonhole itself while it taps into disparate creative energies."[65] Although it continued to rely on Spielberg's established links with long-term stalwarts like Robert Zemeckis and Lawrence Kasdan, the studio also fostered many new relationships, which have resulted in some of its most popular films. For instance, Sam Mendes' *American Beauty* (1999) won several Oscars in 2000, including Best Picture. Although this was an example of DreamWorks exploiting new talent rather than attracting established filmmakers, the studio's relationship with this young English theatre director was a good indicator of its ongoing interest in relatively highbrow projects, and it was perhaps significant that the director stayed with DreamWorks for his next production, *The Road to Perdition* (2002).

DreamWorks was also keen to recruit another well-regarded British talent, animator Nick Park, for the critically acclaimed and financially successful *Chicken Run* (2000). Park is one of animation's great auteurs, and his relationship with DreamWorks was another example of the studio actively pursuing talents with a unique cinematic vision and unclear box office appeal. Other established Hollywood talent attracted to the studio has included Cameron Crowe, Michael Mann and Woody Allen. If anything, the deal with the prolific but rarely successful Allen embodied the studio's stated commitment to 'ideas and the people who have them.' However, as the new millennium wore on, DreamWorks SKG's relative instability, and its limited production schedule, sent the company's fortunes into decline. In October 2004, DreamWorks Animation separated from its parent and began trading as a publicly owned company (29 million shares were initially made available at $28 per share).[66] As a result, many of the biggest hits released under the DreamWorks logo were no longer earning revenue for the original company. Increasingly, DreamWorks focused their activities on Spielberg's movies, as the aim to nurture talent failed to pay off. Then, in December 2005, Paramount Pictures purchased the studio for a reported $1.6 billion (a figure that includes DreamWorks SKG's debts, estimated at approximately $400 million).[67] In March 2006, Paramount sold the rights to DreamWorks SKG's film library for a reported $900 million—thus marking the effective end of DreamWorks SKG's existence as an independent institution. However, DreamWorks Animation continues to trade successfully (although it operates more in the vein of a production company than a true financier-distributor today, following the collapse of DreamWorks SKG's domestic distribution network).[68]

Despite the ultimate failure of the DreamWorks 'dream,' the studio's early production schedules ensured the epic's visibility at the end of the 1990s and led to some of the most successful entries in the cycle, including *Saving Private Ryan*, *The Prince of Egypt*, and, in 2000, Ridley Scott's *Gladiator*—perhaps the studio's most successful epic. The next chapter explores how the release of *Gladiator* finally cemented the epic film in production schedules across the industry. However, while the film sparked an increase in epic releases from all of the other majors, it marked the end of DreamWorks SKG's sustained investment in the genre.

One can argue that the novel strategy of favouring epics had served its purpose for DreamWorks, creating an image of stability (by evoking memories of movies with 'classic' status) and innovation (by pursuing a trend that was considered relatively marginal until the late 1990s). As the other majors began to duplicate the production schedules that had brought the studio to industrial predominance within a few years, DreamWorks searched out other projects that might continue to reflect its commitment to meaningful, cutting-edge entertainment—but the studio failed to recapture the creative zeitgeist to quite the extent that it had done with its epics. The next chapter explains the widespread industrial adoption of epic films that followed the pioneering efforts of

DreamWorks SKG's founders and the maverick filmmakers who had preceded them. Until the end of the 1990s, epics were generally produced on a tentative, experimental basis. Despite a steadily expanding assortment of successes, the Hollywood majors took a long time to begin favouring epic films as a routine element of production schedules. Chapter 6 uses DreamWorks SKG's last major epic hit, *Gladiator*, to explain how the conditions of the film marketplace changed in such a way as to ensure the survival of the genre.

Notes

1. The moniker of 'Dream Team' seems to have informed the naming of the studio, which was made public shortly after the October press conference. As a descriptive term it remains in use in the trade press. See Geraldine Fabrikant and Rick Lyman, "Dreaming in Tighter Focus," *New York Times* 25 September, 2000, C1.

2. Steven Spielberg, quoted in Tom King, *David Geffen: A Biography of New Hollywood* (London: Random House, 2000), 532.

3. Thomas Elsaesser, 'The Blockbuster: Everything Connects but Not Everything Goes' in Jon Lewis, ed., *The End of Cinema as We Know It: American Film in the Nineties* (New York: New York University Press, 2001), 13.

4. DreamWorks SKG Web site, http://www.dreamworks.com/jobs/index2.

5. Warren Buckland has made precisely this point and argued that the studio's early releases were closely allied to Spielberg's aesthetic and thematic preferences. See Warren Buckland, "The Role of the Auteur in the Age of the Blockbuster: Steven Spielberg and DreamWorks," in Julian Stringer, ed., *Movie Blockbusters* (London: Routledge, 2003), 95.

6. Fabrikant and Lyman, C1.

7. Paul F. Duke, "D'Works: What Lies Beneath?" *Variety* 24 Jul. 2000, 68.

8. Joel Finler remarks that "five of the original eight Hollywood majors continue to be leading players in the new millennium" (Joel W. Finler, *The Hollywood Story* 3rd ed. [London: Wallflower, 2003], 1).

9. Martin Dale, *The Movie Game: The Film Business in Britain, Europe and America* (London and New York: Cassell, 1997), 23.

10. Elsaesser (2001), 17.

11. Janet Wasko, *How Hollywood Works* (London: Sage, 2003), 81.

12. Fabrikant and Lyman, C17.

13. Wasko, 77.

14. The Internet Movie Database gives budgetary data for all of DreamWorks SKG's first nine releases except *Paulie* (John Roberts, 1998). Without *Paulie*, DreamWorks releases cost $305 million before marketing costs are factored in. See the Internet Movie Database, http://www.uk. imdb.com/List?productioncompanies=DreamWorks.

15. Dan Cox, "Dream Schemes, Pricey new studio ready to roll out first pix," *Variety* 18 Sep. 1997, unpaginated article obtained from Variety Online http://www.variety.com.

16. Wasko, 223.

17. See Barry D. Reardon, "The Studio Distributor," in Jason E. Squire, ed., *The Movie Business Book* 2nd ed. (London: Fireside, 1992), 310–319.

18. Wasko, 92.

19. Dale, 25.

20. Wasko, 34.

21. For more on Katzenberg during this period see Ron Grover, *The Disney Touch: Disney, ABC and the Quest for the World's Greatest Media Empire* rev. ed. (New York: McGraw-Hill, 1997).

22. Dale, 12.

23. For details of Geffen's involvement and his career prior to the establishment of DreamWorks, see King, 170–306.

24. There had, however, been problematic aspects here as well. In the early 1980s, it was widely claimed that Spielberg had interfered too much in the production of Tobe Hooper's *Poltergeist* (1982) and been too distant during the production of *Twilight Zone—The Movie* (1983).

25. Spielberg has only taken up this opportunity once, to direct *The Lost World: Jurassic Park* (1997), a project to which he had committed before DreamWorks released its first films. Subsequently, all of Spielberg's films have been either produced or co-produced by DreamWorks.

26. See Kim Masters, *The Keys to the Kingdom: How Michael Eisner Lost His Grip* (New York: HarperCollins, 2000), 250–265.

27. The memo appeared in the trade press as Anon., "The Teachings of Chairman Jeff," *Variety*, 24 Sept. 1990, 24.

28. For more on Bruckheimer and Simpson's time at Disney, see Charles Fleming, *High Concept: Don Simpson and the Hollywood Culture of Excess* (London: Bloomsbury, 1998).

29. Nick Madigan, "Studio Report Card 1997: DreamWorks," *Variety* 12 Jan. 1998, unpaginated clipping, 'DreamWorks' file, NYPL.

30. Quoted in Joseph McBride, *Steven Spielberg: A Biography* (London: Faber and Faber, 1997), 427.

31. This is visible in the reception of the film by the trade press, who viewed the film as a surprising but much needed hit. See Andrew Hindes and Dan Cox, "Antz Colony Cranks It Up," *Variety*, 19 Oct. 1998, 1, and Jon Elson, "Can 'Saving Private Ryan' Save DreamWorks?" *New York Post*, 13 Jul. 1998, 37.

32. Andrew Hindes, "Studio Report Card 1998: DreamWorks," *Variety*, 12 Jan. 1999, unpaginated clipping, 'DreamWorks' file,' NYPL.

33. Finler, 362.

34. Financial data obtained from Box Office Mojo, http://www.boxofficemojo.com/movies/ ?id=theprinceofegypt.htm.

35. Financial data from the Internet Movie Database, http://www.uk.imdb.com/ box-office/alltimegross?region =worldwide.

36. Quoted in *The Prince of Egypt* press kit, AMPAS, 3.

37. Quoted in *The Prince of Egypt* press kit, 6.

38. In inflation-adjusted figures DeMille's film is the fifth highest grossing of all time (according to the Box Office Mojo chart, http://www.boxofficemojo.com/alltime/adjusted). Sumiko Higashi has attributed its peculiar cultural resonance in the United States to an annual Easter telecast of the film, which has become an American tradition. Sumiko Higashi, "Antimodernism as Historical Representation in a Consumer Culture: Cecil B. DeMille's *The Ten Commandments*, 1923, 1956, 1993," in Vivian Sobchack, ed., *The Persistence of History: Cinema, Television and the Modern Event* (New York: Routledge, 1996), 107.

39. Derek Elley, *The Epic Film: Myth and History* (London: Routledge and Kegan Paul, 1984), 36.

40. Joseph L. Breen, letter to Luigi Laraschi, dated 29 Aug. 1954, '*The Ten Commandments*' file, MPAA Collection, AMPAS.

41. Vincent Canby, "For DeMille, Moses' Egypt really was America," *New York Times* 25 Mar. 1984, 19.

42. Cecil B. DeMille and Donald Hayne, *The Autobiography of Cecil B. DeMille* (London: W. H. Allen, 1960), 376.

43. Bernard Weinraub, "Moses and Rushes," *New York Times*, 10 Apr. 1998, E14.

44. Peter Krämer, "Post Classical Hollywood" in John Hill and Pamela Church Gibson, *The Oxford Guide to Film Studies* (Oxford: Oxford University Press, 1998), 295.

45. See Anon., "Prince Gets the Royal Treatment," *Daily News, New York*, 13 Dec. 1998, 'Extra' section, 12; and Weinraub (1998), E14.

46. DeMille and Hayne, 394.

47. J. Hoberman, rev. of *The Prince of Egypt, Village Voice* 22 Dec. 1998, 127; and Jack Matthews, rev. of *The Prince of Egypt, Newsday*, 18 Dec. 1998, B7.

48. Jeffrey Katzenberg, quoted in Serena Davies, "Filmmakers on Film," *Daily Telegraph* 10 Jul. 2004, Arts and Books, 19.

49. Michael Wood, *America in the Movies, or, "Santa Maria, It Had Slipped My Mind!"* (London: Secker and Warburg, 1975), 173.

50. Sobchack (1995), 293.

51. Ibid., 288.

52. Ibid.

53. See, for example, McBride, 444–448.

54. The somewhat anecdotal account that follows has been pieced together from several popular biographies and accounts of the period. See Grover, Masters and Michael D. Eisner and Tony Schwartz, *Work in Progress* (London: Penguin Books, 1999).

55. Grover, 259.

56. In 2004, Eisner was stripped of the chairman post. See Jill Goldsmith and Carl DiOrio, "Mike Slipped a Mickey," *Variety* 4 Mar. 2004, 1.

57. John Baxter, *Steven Spielberg* (London: Harpercollins, 1996), 400.

58. Masters, 436.

59. Kenneth Turan, rev. of *The Prince of Egypt, Los Angeles Times* 18 Dec. 1998, Calendar, 1.

60. Jeffrey Katzenberg, quoted in Davies, 19.

61. *The Road to El Dorado* took $50.8 million in domestic receipts, according to the Internet Movie Database, http://www.uk.imdb.com/title/tt0138749/business>; *Spirit: Stallion of the Cimarron* $73 million, http://www.uk.imdb.com/title/tt0166813/business; and *Sinbad: Legend of the Seven Seas* $26.3 million, http://www.uk.imdb.com/title/tt0165982/business.

62. Financial data from the Internet Movie Database, http://www.uk.imdb.com/title/tt0298148/business.

63. Jill Goldsmith and Nicole Laport, "D'Works Does Splits," *Variety* 21 Jul. 2004, unpaginated, obtained from http://www.variety.com/article/VR1117908068.

64. See Davies, 19.

65. Dade Hayes, "So How Does the Dream Work?" *Variety* 10 Jul. 2002, 1.

66. Financial data from Warren Buckland, *Directed by Steven Spielberg: Poetics of the Contemporary Hollywood Blockbuster* (New York: Continuum, 2006), 27.

67. Jill Goldsmith, "Wall Street Backs DreamWorks deal," *Variety* 12 Dec. 2005, unpaginated, obtained from http://www.variety.com/article/VR1117934475.

68. Steven Zeitchik and Jill Goldsmith, "Par sells DreamWorks library to Soros," *Variety* 19 Mar. 2006, unpaginated, obtained from http://www.variety.com/article/VR1117940016.

~6~

Gladiator (2000)
and the Film Marketplace

Whenever the gladiators in Ridley Scott's *Gladiator* (2000) fight, they put themselves in terrible danger. Each tournament is little more than entertainment for its audience, but for the gladiators it is always a battle to the death. As their owner, Proximo (Oliver Reed), puts it, "I did not pay good money for your company. I paid it so I might profit from your death." To be a gladiator, therefore, is to be in constant peril. For Maximus Decimus Meridius (Russell Crowe), a Roman general forced into slavery and eventually into the arena, the danger is especially great. The Emperor Commodus (Joaquin Phoenix) despises Maximus and ensures that the odds are always stacked against him. The only protection Maximus has is the love of the crowd and the strength of his belief that Commodus must be deposed and the values of the Roman republic restored. Each time Maximus enters the arena he has more to lose. The audience is fickle in its affections, and he may not survive the bout. If he dies, so will his dream, and other gladiators will quickly appear to take his place. In essence *Gladiator* is an epic about entertainment, but the entertainment it depicts is of lethal import for those who participate.

In this way *Gladiator* seems to dramatise the filmmaking climate from which it emerged. According to economist Arthur DeVany, every week at the box office we see

> ... an evolving dynamic tournament among movies. Motion pictures lead unpredictable and brief lives. They are tested each week by the audience against a changing cast of competitors. The motion picture theatrical market is an accelerated stress test and when a

156

movie breaks, its run is over. Fallen competitors are replaced by new contenders.[1]

The risks involved might be more financial than mortal, but the theatrical film marketplace is the stage for tournaments not unlike the gladiatorial battles of *Gladiator*. Movie theatres constitute the first, most important arena of a tournament that will eventually spread into other so-called ancillary markets. Week in and week out, reputations and financial stability in Hollywood are determined by the whims of the audience. In the tournament every movie represents an enormous risk for its makers and financiers, but none more so than historical epics. At least, that is what Hollywood lore would have us believe.

By the year 2000, historical epics were more visible than at any time since the 1960s. The maverick epics had given way to a new group of industrially sanctioned productions, but epic films were still viewed by Hollywood commentators as perilous investments. In the months before its release, *Variety* described *Gladiator* as a "high stakes" project, an expensive, "ultra bloody," R-rated movie, premiering unusually early in the year, with a historical setting that might well prove "B.O. [box office] poison."[2] *Gladiator* was considered a phenomenal risk, and it was by no means alone. Reporting on the revival of the form, *Variety* continued to claim:

> Hollywood should take a history lesson from the recent past. By the early1960s audiences had tired of the genre and . . . even big-scale epics like the 1963 *Cleopatra* proved disastrous. Historical epics may have become some of Hollywood's biggest hits, but they have also contributed to its biggest failures.[3]

As we have seen, the habit of classifying epics as potentially lethal cinematic hazards dates back to *Cleopatra* and was reinforced by the failure of Michael Cimino's *Heaven's Gate* in 1980. However, previous chapters have demonstrated that epics remained relatively popular with audiences in the 1960s but had been stymied at the box office by overproduction and overspending. The genre was also a common fixture of television schedules well into the 1980s. Nevertheless, the film industry seems to have retained a belief that epics are dangerous investments in spite of the revival of interest amongst both filmmakers and audiences.

Production schedules at the end of the 1990s were increasingly at loggerheads with presumed industry wisdom. Despite proclamations of doom amongst Hollywood commentators, more money was being invested in epics than at any time since the late 1960s. There was growing disparity between what was said regarding the epic and observable trends in the American film industry. This chapter will explain why, at the turn of the millennium, it started to make economic sense for the industry to collectively participate in the revival of the historical epic. Epic films began to feature in the production schedules of all the major studios because the market conditions that had worked against the production of epics in the past had changed.

Gladiator was both an end point and a spur for this revival. It was viewed by many critics as a sudden, unexpected and entirely unprecedented attempt to revive the historical epic single-handedly. Variety editor Peter Bart described it as a novel attempt to "reinvent the costume epic."[4] The Variety review described it as the first "historical/biblical/war epic" since 1964, and England's Observer claimed, "[I]t's hard to figure out why anyone would want to make this film now. After all, it's 36 years since the last of the great toga epics."[5] The Los Angeles Times described it as "an epic adventure that marks Hollywood's return to the era so lavishly portrayed in classics like Ben-Hur and Spartacus."[6] Even the film's press kit played on its novelty and opened with the declaration, "It has been four decades since chariots raced across movie screens in epic dramas of a time long past. Now, director Ridley Scott brings the glorious battles of the ancient Roman arena back to the big screen in a sweeping story of courage and revenge."[7] On Gladiator's release, Variety claimed with some confidence that "even if the film is a big hit, it's unlikely that the genre will come back in any significant way due to the high costs involved."[8] This prediction proved incorrect. Following the success of Gladiator, the epic became a constituent feature of production schedules across the industry.

It is possible to identify several distinct subcycles within the mass of epic films emerging at this time. First, there were historical epics produced before Gladiator, which attempted to capitalise on the success of Titanic and Saving Private Ryan. These were followed by a second subcycle produced in response to Gladiator's success, which continued to be released well into 2004. There was also a third, related cycle of fantasy/science fiction epics in production throughout the period. This chapter seeks to understand these trends and places them in an economic, operational and logistical context. The first section looks at the various epics in production or on release at the turn of millennium, including Gladiator. Rick Altman's producer's game is used to explain the widespread adoption of the form. The second section examines the production of Gladiator and provides a brief analysis. Ridley Scott's film seems to comment quite overtly on the public function of entertainment, and thus can be interpreted as a commentary on the position of epics in contemporary film culture. The third section then traces the impact of *Gladiator* on production schedules but, more important, draws some conclusions about the film marketplace itself. Over the last twenty years, the accentuated risk often associated with epics has been neutralised. Historical epics now have the opportunity to triumph in an arena of ancillary revenue streams that afford returns undreamt of in the roadshow era or even in the 1980s.

1. The Epic at the Millennium

The epics released at the turn of the millennium were a series of closely connected productions, each of which was designed to capitalise on the phenomenal, sometimes unprecedented, success of the various 'maverick' epics released earlier in the decade. The process of imitation, interpretation and adaptation that distinguished the post-1998 epic subcycle can be understood using Rick Altman's 'producer's game' (the conceptual model outlined in chapter 2). Altman has claimed, "The first step in genre production is the creation of a reading position through critical dissection, the second is reinforcement of that position through film production, and the third is broad industry acceptance of the proposed reading position and genre."[9] At the end of the 1990s, the second and third steps of this process occurred, and 'acceptance' can be measured in the establishment of commonly used terms that reflect a consensus on the qualities of an epic. As Steve Neale has argued, "The institutionalisation of any generic term is a key aspect of the existence of any genre."[10]

It is important to recognise that *Gladiator* was not the daring, innovative product it was sometimes classed as by the trade press. Like the majority of epics that emerged in the late 1990s, *Gladiator* was an example of the profit-oriented, collaborative filmmaking that tends to dominate mainstream film production in Hollywood. However, this does not mean that it lacked thematic resonance, and the epics that emerged at this time are good examples of the "collective expression" that Alan Lovell and Gianluca Sergi have argued is integral to the modern blockbuster.[11]

In 1999, Luc Besson's medieval epic *The Messenger: The Story of Jean of Arc* was released by Sony-Columbia and French producer Gaumont. Also released that year was Ang Lee's *Ride with the Devil*, produced by

Universal and described in the *New York Times* as a "chilly epic."[12] Neither film was a major hit. As well as *Gladiator*, 2000 saw the release of Roland Emmerich's *The Patriot*, another Sony-Columbia production, with a negative cost of $110 million.[13] In 2001, Jerry Bruckheimer and Michael Bay's *Pearl Harbor* hit cinema screens (a Disney production with a negative cost of $140 million) as did *Captain Corelli's Mandolin* (directed by John Madden, funded by the Disney subsidiary Miramax, costing $57 million) and *Enemy at the Gates* (directed by Jean Jacques Arnaud, funded by a consortium of European producers as well as the U.S. production company Mandalay, affiliated to Universal, costing $68 million).[14] Clearly, this is still only a handful of films, but it includes projects budgeted far beyond the average negative cost of a major studio release at the time, which was $54.8 million in 2000 and $47.7 million in 2001 (see fig. 6.1). *The Patriot* cost more than double the average cost of a studio production in its year of release, and *Pearl Harbor* was almost three times more. Both were conceived of as exemplary high-risk/high-return blockbusters, and like all the epics that followed, they originated with powerful mainstream producers and distribution companies rather than highly motivated individuals working at the margins of the system.[15] The first real indicators that the epic film had returned to industrial 'favour' became visible with the production of a series of films that each reformulated elements from *Titanic* and *Saving Private Ryan* in both direct and indirect fashion.

The Patriot originated with the production company Centropolis, run by director Roland Emmerich and producer Dean Devlin, who had been responsible for 1998's *Godzilla* and the hits *Independence Day* (1996) and *Stargate* (1994). *The Patriot* was described in both the *New York Times* and the *New Yorker* as a "Revolutionary War epic" and in *Variety* as an "epic that has some emotional pull and isn't dull or stuffy."[16] Scriptwriter Robert Rodat, who had also written *Saving Private Ryan*, said of *The Patriot*, "I like writing big canvas movies, the essence of [which] has to be a big story. That's certainly what David Lean taught us."[17] This 'Lean-esque' epic starred Mel Gibson as Benjamin Martin, a skilled, initially unwilling hero, who decides to fight after a family member is killed by the English villain Tavington (Jason Isaacs), much like William Wallace in Gibson's *Braveheart*.

In 1998, Centropolis had seen their much-hyped, monster movie *Godzilla* panned by critics while Spielberg's World War II epic gained a greater share of revenues and critical admiration. In 2000, Centropolis returned with an expensive, sincere historical wartime epic of American history from the pen of *Saving Private Ryan*'s screenwriter. On the evidence of their other releases, invariably science fiction or disaster movies, one can safely say that *The Patriot* was a very unusual choice for Devlin and Emmerich. Although it originated with a screenwriter and star that had some commitment to epics, *The Patriot* had also been constructed to resemble prior observable production patterns. The resulting film made $113.3 million at the U.S. box office and $101.7 million overseas, more than enough for it to be classified a worthwhile investment.[18]

Fig. 6.1: MPAA Member Average Negative Costs

Year	Average Negative Cost Per Feature (USD in Millions)	% Change	Previous Period % change 2003 vs . . .
2003	$63.3	8.6%	–
2002	$58.8	23.3%	8.6%
2001	$47.7	(13.1%)	33.9%
2000	$54.8	6.5%	16.5%
1999	$51.5	97.7%	24%

Note: Due to changes in financial reporting regulations in the year 2000, abandoned project costs are no longer included in studio overhead, and as such are no longer part of negative costs.

Source: *U.S. Entertainment Industry: 2003 MPA Market Statistics* 19. Obtained via application to MPAA Online, http://www.mpaa.org/useconomicreview.

As well as the combat movies that extended *Saving Private Ryan*'s memorialising project, World War II was also the subject of 2001's *Pearl Harbor* and the literary adaptation *Captain Corelli's Mandolin*, both of which combined a wartime setting with a romantic narrative in the *Titanic* mould. *Pearl Harbor* was the only genuine high-budget attempt to appeal to the same audiences who had flocked to *Titanic*, and although it went on to become the seventh highest grossing film of 2001, with a $450.5-million worldwide box office take, it failed to achieve anything close to the $1.8-billion theatrical take of Cameron's film. Another attempt to recapture *Titanic*'s primarily female audience was Twentieth Century Fox's eastern epic *Anna and the King* (1999), which performed adequately but unremarkably at the box office (it took $39.3 million in the U.S. and $74.7 million overseas on a $75-million budget). These films fostered a sense that *Titanic* was a one-off event—a financial bonanza that the industry has been unable to recreate despite numerous relatively success-ful follow-ups.[19] Epics since *Titanic* have been more routine blockbusters both in terms of budget and performance, even when they have been designed to resemble Cameron's film.

Also in production in 2000 and 2001 was Martin Scorsese's *Gangs of New York* (2002), described in *Variety* as a "historical/political/romantic epic" and in the *New York Times* as "a brutal . . . epic of 19th-century criminality."[20] Scorsese had been planning the film, loosely based on Herbert Asbury's 'informal history' of the same name, for over twenty years.[21] It was produced by Miramax, a Disney subsidiary, and incurred a negative cost of $97 million (as fig. 6.1 indicates, $38 million over the average negative cost for 2002). Again, it is likely that the green light was dependent on the success of other epics, even if the project itself had been alive in Scorsese's mind for years. *Gangs of New York* made $181 million in worldwide box office receipts.[22]

The year 2002 also saw the release of Shekhar Kapur's *The Four Feathers*, based on the classic A. E. W. Mason novel, filmed most successfully by Alexander and Zoltan Korda in 1939. Kapur's version, produced by a consortium of independent financiers and distributed by Miramax and Paramount, was a critical and commercial failure that earned a paltry $18 million in the U.S. despite its $80-million budget.[23] Meanwhile, Universal's *K-19: The Widowmaker* (2002) was a submarine movie, thus part of a distinct subcycle of war movies, but the true historical story it depicted (of a failing Soviet sub) and the involvement of *National Geographic* as a producer and co-financier marked it as educational in a similar fashion to other epics.[24] The film's negative cost was $100 million, but it only grossed $35.2 million in the U.S. and $30.5 overseas, and thus can be regarded as a flop.[25]

Most of these films were not the most successful releases of any given year, nor was there a huge range of epics on release at the turn of the millennium. However, by 2000, epics were being consciously developed by the majors and included in production schedules. *Gladiator* came at a time when the studios were increasingly willing to weather the potential risks that making historical epics might incur. The success of the film encouraged a new bout of imitation and experimentation, but before the epics of 2003/2004 are addressed, it is necessary to explore another related phenomenon, the increasing centrality of hugely expensive, hugely popular fantasy epics, many of which owed a narrational and thematic debt to the biblical epics of the roadshow period.[26]

Like *Jaws* (1975), George Lucas's original *Star Wars* trilogy is often discussed as a harbinger of what was to happen to Hollywood movies in the 1980s.[27] Throughout this decade, the family story at the centre of *Star*

Wars, which spoke to and dramatised children's deepest fears and desires, became a touchstone for subsequent releases.[28] What was not immediately exploited were the epic dimensions of Lucas's fable. In earlier chapters I have identified the fantasy epic as a mediating vehicle for baby boomer filmmakers' epic impulses. For all the light sabres and space dogfights, the original three *Star Wars* films depicted the decline of a civilisation and the ultimate overthrow of a galaxy-spanning corrupt empire. This sort of epic narrative was only occasionally seen in other releases of the 1980s, and the few films that sought to overtly pursue this route, such as David Lynch's *Dune* (1984), fared badly.[29] However, in 1997 the *Star Wars* films were rereleased, with additional effects, over the course of one summer. This exhibition strategy, in which each film immediately followed the last on release, worked to stress the 'epicness' of the narrative. The original *Star Wars* films now appeared as one long, coherent epic story. The inclusion of new CGI vistas and cityscapes also made them look more like conventional historical epics.

The rerelease was followed by a second trilogy of prequels, which further emphasised the epic elements of the originals. At the centre of *The Phantom Menace* (1999), *Attack of the Clones* (2002) and *Revenge of the Sith* (2005) was the story of a liberal democratic republic in decline, falling into tyranny and despotism. Sequences of armies at war; thousand-strong councils in debate; endless vistas of Italianate cities, underwater cities, futuristic cities; various barren, aquatic, lush and volcanic landscapes, all teeming with CGI extras, abounded. The first film also concerns the discovery, in some desert backwater, of a prophesied messiah, the product of a virgin birth, who will "bring balance to the Force." At the centre of the narrative were the Jedi, warrior monks with supernatural powers. Subsequent films document both the undermining of a galaxy-wide democracy and the gradual corruption of this messiah, until eventually Anakin Skywalker (Hayden Christiansen) becomes the evil Darth Vader of the earlier trilogy.

The first two of these films made numerous references to the historical epics of the roadshow period. *The Phantom Menace* contains a futuristic chariot race that George Lucas claimed was a conscious homage to *Ben-Hur*, while *Attack of the Clones* features extended scenes in a Coliseum-type arena that closely resembles the ancient Roman settings of *Ben-Hur*, *Spartacus* (1960) and *Quo Vadis* (1951).[30] The broader narrative of a civilisation's decline and fall seems to be drawn from histories of ancient Rome and filmic accounts such as Anthony Mann's *The Fall of the Roman Empire* (1964). Meanwhile, the story of Anakin is a Christ allegory that, at least initially, recalled New Testament epics such as *The Greatest Story Ever Told* (1965). When George Lucas finally returned as a director, it seems that he also returned to the narrative preoccupations of the roadshow historical epic, like so many other baby boomers.

Also taking on increasingly epic dimensions was the Wachowski brothers' *Matrix* trilogy. *The Matrix* (1999) had been a dystopian, 'cyberpunk', science-fiction film, renowned for its innovative and spectacular action sequences. However, the two sequels, *The Matrix Reloaded* and *The Matrix Revolutions* (both 2003), came to look more like a futuristic Christian allegory than the edgy, iconoclastic original—and sweeping scenes of armies clashing in a blighted, postapocalyptic landscape quickly took precedence over the elegant kung-fu of the first film. At least one English critic saw in it "an echo of the old biblical epics of DeMille."[31] Most epic of all, however, was Peter Jackson's *Lord of the Rings* trilogy. Working in New Zealand, Jackson filmed all three volumes of J. R. R. Tolkien's fantasy novel in one epic shoot. A movie was then released every Christmas between 2001 and 2003. After opening with a genuinely epic battle sequence and a voice-over stressing the grave historical importance of a magical ring, the films told the story of a young hobbit's quest to destroy the ring. Eventually, this simple quest narrative came to encompass huge, amazingly staged and realised battles for the future of humankind. Jackson has said that he tried to treat Tolkien's story as if it had really happened in the millennia before recorded history rather than as a fantastic piece of whimsy.[32] Thus it could be claimed that he made his fantasy epic as if it were a historical epic. The 'Lord of the Rings Audience Research Project' has found that audiences and critics consistently defined the films as 'epics' rather than as fantasy or adventure movies—presumably because the focus on apocalyptic events at the heart of the films almost exactly meets the principle conceptual requirements of the genre.[33]

All of these fantasy and science-fiction epics were major hits, most of them grossing far more than the conventional epics of the period. At the time of this writing, the original *Star Wars* was the second highest grossing domestic release of all time, *The Phantom Menace* the fifth, *Lord of the Rings: The Return of the King* (2003) seventh, *Lord of the Rings: The Two Towers* (2002) eleventh, *Lord of the Rings: The Fellowship of the Ring* (2001) sixteenth and *The Matrix Reloaded* twenty-fourth.[34] In many ways, the increasingly epic elements incorporated into various fantasy-themed, family-adventure films demonstrated that 'epic' narratives had become a constituent part of mainstream cinema by the end of the 1990s.

Further proof arrived in 2000, when DreamWorks and Universal released *Gladiator*—easily the most nostalgic entry in the 1990s epic cycle.

2. *Gladiator* and Public Entertainment

Gladiator originated with the writer David Franzoni, who had previously worked on the Whoopi Goldberg vehicle *Jumpin' Jack Flash* (1986) and on a TV biopic of Harry Cohn, *Citizen Cohn* (1992). Franzoni also developed the script for *Amistad* (1997), which had been purchased by DreamWorks for Spielberg to direct. A three-picture deal with DreamWorks followed, and the next project that Franzoni pitched, directly to Spielberg, was *Gladiator*.[35] Franzoni's pitch must have taken place late in 1997. Precise dates are difficult to obtain, but it is likely that DreamWorks green-lighted *Gladiator* shortly before the release of *Titanic*, which is further proof that the studio was more interested in the prestige and cultural merit of epics than in pursuing trends purely for the sake of short-term profit. On hearing the pitch Spielberg apparently claimed that "this is the right time for this kind of film."[36] Franzoni then produced a first draft, inspired partly by a book about gladiators called *Those About to Die* by Daniel P. Maddix and partly by the story of Commodus as it appears in the *Augustan Histories*. This first draft, dated 4 April 1998, resembled the movie as it was produced in outline but also contained some substantial differences.[37] In this version the main character was named Narcissus, after the gladiator who had actually killed the emperor Commodus, and the story was more upbeat and even ironic in tone. For example, Franzoni's Narcissus is sponsored by the producers of a popular brand of olive oil (their slogan: "Narcissus would kill for a taste of Golden Pompeii Olive Oil"), and in the end he manages to escape from Rome with both his wife and his child in tow.

While Franzoni completed his script, DreamWorks began to organise financing. *Gladiator* was initially budgeted at $100 million and eventually came in at $103 million. As a way of minimising risk, DreamWorks and Universal Studios shared the negative costs (building on their preexisting distribution relationship). How much Universal actually contributed to the final budget has not been reported, but the studio handled overseas theatrical distribution, and the two companies split the proceeds fifty–fifty.[38] The murkiness of Hollywood's financial arrangements mean that it is difficult to know for sure exactly how the rest of the profits from the film were shared out. In their 2000 Annual Report to shareholders,

Vivendi, the conglomerate that owned Universal Pictures at the time, noted that they held television licensing rights to *Gladiator* in some markets, while *Variety* has reported that Universal owns the right to distribute DreamWorks titles on video and DVD.[39] Thus, in a complex fashion, the risk of producing *Gladiator* was shared by two major financier-distributors—a practice that has become increasingly prevalent amongst the majors in the 1990s. The high cost of epics in particular has meant that several significant entries in the cycle have been funded in this manner.[40] For example, *Braveheart* and *Titanic* were both Twentieth Century Fox/Paramount co-productions.

On a day-to-day level, *Gladiator* was overseen by two executive producers, Walter Parkes and Laurie MacDonald, and two line producers, Douglas Wick and Branko Lustig, who set about hiring 'above-the-line' talent to work on the film as well as assembling the crew, hiring equipment, leasing studio space and scouting overseas locations.[41] One of their most significant signings was the director Ridley Scott. Scott was renowned as a visually inventive director and had, in the past, fashioned hugely influential and acclaimed films such as *Alien* (1979), *Blade Runner* (1982) and *Thelma & Louise* (1991). However, few of these had been outstanding performers at the box office, despite his reputation. Since 1992, when his epic *1492: Conquest of Paradise* proved a critical and commercial failure, Scott's reputation had diminished, but DreamWorks remained keen to hire him—partly because the director seemed to embody the studio's mandate to work with creatively daring directors. As Douglas Wick put it, "The idea of Ridley Scott being a tour guide through second-century Rome was very exciting—that was a bus I wanted to get on."[42] Unlike many of the filmmakers discussed in previous chapters, Scott apparently felt no particularly deep attachment to the project. *Gladiator* was packaged by the studio, and Scott took creative control of the project long after it had been initiated.

With Scott on board, the producers began to assemble a cast. The role of Maximus was given to New Zealander Russell Crowe—not an unknown at the time but certainly not a star, either.[43] Crowe had a handful of memorable performances under his belt, most notably in *L.A. Confidential* (1997), and he was chosen for *Gladiator*, Douglas Wick claimed, because "it was crucial to find an actor who you could believe possessed the ferocity of this great warrior, but in whom you could also see a man of strong principle and character. Russell Crowe's name came up pretty fast."[44] Other cast members included veteran actors Richard Harris as Marcus Aurelius, Oliver Reed as Proximo and Derek Jacobi as the senator Gracchus. Ridley Scott's Rome, was, like William Wyler's and Cecil B. DeMille's, quickly populated by British actors. The remaining roles were filled by relative unknowns such as the Danish actress Connie Nielsen and the American actor Joaquin Phoenix.

As the cast was being assembled, and filming locations arranged in England, Malta and Morocco, the script underwent several revisions. Scott asked John Logan, who he had previously worked with when he produced the HBO TV movie *RKO 281* (1999), to rewrite Franzoni's first draft. Logan changed the name of the central character and added the murder of Maximus's family as well as Commodus's unhealthy interest in his sister and her son and a failed senatorial conspiracy against the emperor. When filming started, a third writer, Englishman William Nicholson, writer of the C. S. Lewis biopic *Shadowlands* (1993) and a series of epic fantasy novels for children, was brought on board to make day-to-day revisions.[45] Nicholson has said of his contribution, "When I came on board [Maximus] was just a killing machine. I changed the story so that he was acting out of love, not hate."[46] One can also assume that Ridley Scott also played a substantial role in shaping the story as the production process rolled on, and that supplementary revisions to the narrative were made during postproduction and editing. For example, the afterlife sequences were 'pick-ups' filmed while Ridley Scott was scouting locations for his next film. At the level of production, and therefore narrative content, *Gladiator* was a highly collaborative work, unlike the maverick epics of the early-to-mid-1990s.

Principal photography on *Gladiator* took five months, beginning in January 1999. Postproduction work, from editing and the inclusion of CGI effects, through the writing of the music by Hans Zimmer, to the planning of a marketing campaign and the creation and distribution of prints, took a further eleven months. The film opened on 5 May 2000, on 2,938 screens in the United States alone. It went on to make $187.7 million at the domestic box office and a further $248.3 million overseas.[47] Worldwide, *Gladiator* was the second highest grossing film of 2000 after John Woo's *Mission: Impossible II*. Its success was cemented in ancillary markets and led to the development of a third group of historical epics, examined shortly. A great deal of time and money was invested in *Gladiator*, despite the dire warnings appearing in *Variety*. At a thematic level, the film brought together elements from a range of earlier roadshow-era epics, in a manner that seemed to justify its production.

At the beginning of *Gladiator*, the general Maximus is charged by the then emperor Marcus Aurelius with the task of restoring the Roman republic. Aurelius is worried that the democratic ideals of Rome have been corrupted by despotism and thinks that his son, Commodus, does not have the strength or the will to set things right. He tells Maximus that "Commodus is not a moral man." When Commodus hears of the plan he kills his father, and then tries to kill Maximus—the only other person aware of Aurelius's last wishes. Maximus escapes, but his wife and child are killed by Commodus's guards. He is then captured by slave traders and sold to Proximo, a gladiator tycoon based in North Africa. Maximus's success in the provincial arena ensures that he is brought back to Rome and back into the emperor's orbit. There, his popularity as an entertainer prohibits Commodus from having him killed. A plan is formulated by various senators to depose Commodus and put Maximus back at the head of his army. It fails, and Maximus is finally forced to face Commodus in the arena. Despite a mortal wound delivered seconds before the fight begins, he kills Commodus, passes on Marcus Aurelius's orders and dies. We see him briefly in the afterlife, where he is reunited with his family. At the end of the film the Roman republic is reinstated, in defiance of the historical record.

As many reviewers noted, *Gladiator* cobbles together elements drawn from a number of iconic historical epics.[48] The story of gladiatorial training and rebellion was familiar from Stanley Kubrick's *Spartacus* (1960). A similarly disgraced hero's fight for vengeance in the arena could be seen in Wyler's *Ben-Hur* (1959), while the film is set in the same period as Anthony Mann's *The Fall of the Roman Empire* (1964) and features many of the same characters. The story it tells, of a dissolute emperor and the disillusioned general who opposes him, resembled Mervyn LeRoy's *Quo Vadis* (1951). Clearly, links to the epics of the roadshow period were far more overt in *Gladiator* than they had been in previous epics. The filmmakers seemed to foreground their attempts at imitation, thus emphasising that *Gladiator* was, in some ways, an epic *about* epics.

Furthermore, *Gladiator* has been interpreted in various ways. Monica C. Cyrino sees in it a parable of a contemporary America blinded to political truth by a violent yet pacifying mass media.[49] For Richard Rushton it is a critique of movie spectacle that consistently links CGI sequences to political fascism.[50] Geoff King has claimed that it is representative of a new form of spectacle, in which kinetic editing has overtaken use of the wide screen to make the film play better on TV.[51] Martin Fradley has demonstrated that Maximus's story, and the actions of star Russell Crowe at the 2001 Academy Awards, can be read as hysterical declarations of a crisis in white male identity.[52] Classics scholars have produced a collection of admirably diverse essays, many of which use the film as a way of discussing the period in which it is set.[53] None of these works examine the focus on entertainment (rather than spectacle or history) at the heart of *Gladiator*. Nevertheless, *Gladiator* seems focused on the politics of popular entertainment.

When *Gladiator* begins, the games have been absent from the circuses of Rome for a long time (just as epics had been absent from cinema screens for some time in the 1990s). The philosopher-emperor Marcus Aurelius had outlawed them, forcing promoters such as Proximo out into the provinces, but when Commodus assumes the throne he revives the games, telling his sister that, in the arena, "I will give the people a vision of Rome, and they'll love me for it." Later, the senator Gracchus says of Commodus's plans, "I think he knows what Rome is. Rome is the mob. He will conjure magic for them and they will be distracted. He'll take away their freedom, and still they'll roar. He will bring them death, and they will love him for it." Commodus uses the sport in the arena as a violent political distraction, and the adulation he craves is the adulation of a people driven wild by displays of senseless violence. Ironically, this brings Maximus into a position of real power. Unlike the other gladiators, Maximus has experience fighting real battles for meaningful political goals (in his eyes, spreading the democratic ideals of Rome, no matter how warped they may have become in the eternal city itself). In the scenes that follow, Maximus effectively uses the gladiatorial circus as a medium for social change. He offers viewers something more than mere diverting entertainment. Instead he is able to effectively convey a dissenting political opinion, and, at the film's climax, change the world, by ridding it of Commodus and enacting the orders of Marcus Aurelius.

The rise of despotism in ancient Rome has frequently been linked to the accompanying rise of violent blood sports in the empire's arenas. The ancient historian Juvenus wrote that, with the empire's decline, "the people that once bestowed commands, consulships, legions and all else, now meddles no more and longs for just two things—bread and circuses."[54] More recently, social commentators such as Salvador Ginler, whose work deploys conceptions of ideology and hegemony most famously employed by cultural critic Theodore Adorno, have used the term *bread and circuses*, and the sense of obfuscation it hints at, to discuss contemporary mass culture.[55] Adorno himself has argued that "[M]odern mass culture [is] a medium of undreamt of ideological control."[56] His conclusions are derived from the work of Marxist critic Antonio Gramsci.[57]

For such thinkers, the 'traditional' western values of intellectual rigour, rationalism, cultural integrity and even liberal democracy have been irreversibly compromised by a widely circulated, technologically produced 'mass culture' including movies and television, which all serve to blunt intellectual, spiritual and moral sensibilities.[58] For them, mass culture is the 'bread and circuses' of the modern age, a distraction that serves to reinforce and legitimise a corrupt status quo. *Gladiator* seems to consciously engage with this conception of culture. The film is focused on a ruler whose ultimate downfall is his heavy reliance on the distractions of the arena. It follows that *Gladiator* can be read as a defence of popular entertainment, especially epics. Critics of Hollywood have often dismissed epics as 'middlebrow', thus culturally insignificant, forms of expression.[59] *Gladiator* champions the middlebrow, the popular-yet-meaningful, as a vital medium of political and social expression. The film is certainly not a response to Adorno's work, nor to ideological critiques of Hollywood originating in academia, but it is a response to critical dismissal of the epic and the Hollywood action blockbuster more generally.

Gladiator's story is founded on the assumption that thrilling entertainment has the capacity to deaden an audience's sense of lived reality. When Commodus first returns from the northern frontier he is unpopular with the masses. He passes through streets lined with crowds, but when he finally meets the awaiting senators, he says, "Thanks for the 'loyal subjects'. I trust they were not too expensive." In fact, several close-up shots show us jeering, angry onlookers rather than fanatical devotees. Commodus immediately sets about scheming to dissolve the Senate, motivated by fantasies of benevolent paternalistic rule rooted in his own unhappy childhood, much like the Pharaoh Rameses in *The Prince of Egypt*, another epic of family dysfunction. His plans to earn the love of the mob in the arena are both a heartfelt expression of his own inadequacy and a calculated sleight of hand designed to mask his real political intentions. While they watch the games, Commodus removes liberty and agency from the people. His plans are thwarted because the entertainments he relies on can also be used by others to provide more than mere meaningless thrills. In Maximus's hands, the mass entertainment of the arena offers an opportunity for change that the political system does not. Increasingly, his staged fights are shaped by the ideological battles taking place offstage and can be read as political statements in themselves.

After arriving in Rome, the first gladiatorial contest that Maximus participates in is itself a kind of historical epic. As Maximus and a posse of other gladiators are ushered into the arenas, the tribune calls out,

Today we reach back to hallowed antiquity to bring you a recreation of the second fall of mighty Carthage! On the barren plain of Zama, there stood the invincible armies of the barbarian Hannibal. Ferocious mercenaries and warriors from all brute nations, bent on merciless destruction, conquest. Your emperor is pleased to give you, the barbarian horde!

As the "Legionnaires of Scipio Africanus" file in, Maximus begins issuing orders. He and his colleagues are actors in a bloody display of Roman might, masked in the language of defence and victimhood, and the ensuing battle is intended to demonstrate the might of Rome, and by association, the might of the emperor, the man who is 'pleased to give' both the barbarians and the legionnaires up to the crowd.[60] What follows is a subversion of both actual history (in an echo of *Gladiator* itself) and of Commodus's plans. The gladiators literally and symbolically defeat the forces of the empire. As the barbarians triumph, Maximus shows the people of Rome that the empire and the emperor are not inviolate. More important, Maximus gains 'creative control' of the arena. By winning, he dictates the meaning of the entertainment, which becomes, at its simplest, 'Might does not equal right.' This first victory also sets Maximus on a course that will lead him to face Commodus in the arena. Every one of his subsequent triumphs is a symbolic defeat for the emperor. Eventually, the only way that Commodus can win is by playing Maximus at his own game. Throughout the film, the political power of entertainment increases exponentially until it becomes the medium of Commodus's demise. Unlike his father, Commodus dies in public, under the glare of the mob, and his death takes on a political meaning much like the other staged fights that Maximus had dominated. Despotism will not stand.

Although *Gladiator* recognises that entertainment can bedazzle, the film eventually argues that certain forms of mainstream entertainment can also play a profoundly *positive* role in the lives of viewers, when correctly used. Such assumptions are integral to the historical epic, as has been seen throughout this book. Filmmakers have traditionally used the epic to make grandiose, sweeping statements about history, humanity and belief. In the arena, Maximus offers up similarly meaningful and affecting entertainments (some of them with a historical 'setting') intended to challenge and enlighten the viewer. Thus, Maximus's position in the arena can be read as equivalent to the position of the epic filmmaker in the Hollywood system.[61] In at least one interview, writer David Franzoni chose to compare his characters to recognisable Hollywood figures and said, "Promoter Proximo is a sort of Mike Ovitz, and Commodus is a sort of Ted Turner. And Maximus is the hero we all wish ourselves to be: the guy who can rise above the mess that is modern society."[62] The resulting film shows an idealistic, politically motivated entertainer bending the confines of his chosen medium in an attempt to affect the lives of audiences. The same impulse has been integral to the epics of the 1990s.

Gladiator clearly equates the success of Maximus's political agenda with his popularity and stresses that culturally resonant entertainments only have value if they are seen. Thus, the film seemed to justify its existence in allegory. In making such a clear return to the narrational and iconographic terrain of the roadshow cycle (in a more overt fashion than any preceding epic), *Gladiator* seemed to argue that historical epics were desperately needed in contemporary film culture, despite perceived economic risks attached to the form. Furthermore, external attempts to classify epics as unstable investments were becoming increasingly untenable. *Gladiator*, it turned out, performed so exceptionally in the theatrical 'tournament' that it inspired a host of epic imitators.

Because *Gladiator*'s cinematic antecedents were so transparently nostalgic, its effect was much more straightforward than many of the films discussed previously. When studios began to green-light related projects, they sought out historical epics, rather than war films, or romances, or westerns with epic qualities. As *Variety* put it in 2002, "The $458-million global B.O. [box-office gross] for DreamWorks-Universal's *Gladiator* encouraged studio brass to dust off toga pics stuck in development hell; now 18 months later, the scripts have been written and the talent deals are in place."[63] *Gladiator* therefore ensured the consolidation of prior trends.[64] On the one hand, there followed an increase in the production of historical epics with ancient-world settings, such as *Troy*, *Alexander* and even *The Passion of the Christ*. On the other hand there emerged a series of related epics from the people involved with *Gladiator*.

The next project from original screenwriter David Franzoni, a man with two historical epics behind him, was the Jerry Bruckheimer production *King Arthur*. This version of the Arthurian legend was a supposedly 'accurate' account, which linked the story of Arthur to the decline of the Roman Empire as an international power in the fourth century—turning the traditionally medieval story of Arthur into an ancient-world epic. Sequences of Roman centurions battling woad-daubed pagan warriors on a distant northern frontier closely resembled the opening scenes of *Gladiator*, as did the story of a disillusioned Roman soldier who comes to fight against the forces of the empire. *Gladiator*'s other writer, John

Logan, went on to write *The Last Samurai* (2003) for Edward Zwick. In 2001, Logan was then commissioned to pen a biopic of Abraham Lincoln for DreamWorks.[65] At the same time, DreamWorks SKG's head of film production, Walter Parkes, who worked on *Gladiator*, was hoping to direct a Logan script set during World War II, described by *Variety* as being "in the spirit of *Bridge on the River Kwai*."[66] Director Ridley Scott went on to make a variety of films but returned to the epic with *Kingdom of Heaven*, a $150-million medieval epic set during the crusades, released in 2005. Star Russell Crowe has also returned to the genre in Peter Weir's *Master and Commander: The Far Side of the World* (2003).

Given the image of epics as perilous investments, how can we explain why so many were made in the late 1990s and early 2000s? The answer lies in the changing structure of the film industry. Despite what commentators looking to the lessons of Hollywood's past might say, the production of epics made more economic sense in the millennial marketplace than ever before. To understand this, one has to look beyond Arthur DeVany's 'tournament' and examine how Hollywood movies make their money today.

3. The Epic in the Film Marketplace

In the 1980s and early 1990s, the majors all underwent a series of mergers and restructurings, which transformed them into cohesive multimedia corporations.[67] They became better positioned to take advantage of ancillary revenues such as television and video and better able to generate so-called 'synergies' between media products. As Stephen Prince puts it, during the 1980s:

> The film industry and its product underwent a substantial and far-reaching transformation whose implications were still being worked out over a decade later. As a result of these transformations, Hollywood ceased operating as a film industry, and film stopped being its primary product. Instead of making films, the industry shifted to the production of filmed entertainment, a quite different enterprise that encompassed production and distribution of entertainment in a variety of markets and media.[68]

Key amongst these markets was home video. At the end of the 1970s, video emerged alongside various forms of TV licensing as a new stage on the ladder of ancillary revenue streams. The majors quickly penetrated the market, both as suppliers and distributors.[69] Their investments paid off. In 1981, 3.1 million prerecorded videocassettes were sold; by 1989, this had risen to 207.5 million, without taking video rentals into account.[70] The rapid expansion of the market meant that successful cinema releases now had a vastly extended opportunity for recoupment, while unsuccessful films had a second chance to find an audience. As David A. Cook has noted, "[T]he modern era of super-blockbuster films" was reinforced by "looming video competition, once predicted to inhibit this trend, as feature films rapidly became the basic programming content of both home video and cable."[71]

It has been estimated that today a successful film will make around three-quarters of its total revenue in ancillary markets such as video, pay cable licensing, TV licensing and DVD sales.[72] Thus, theatrical grosses only provide an indicator of the total amount that a film can earn for its distributors. Nevertheless, the theatrical market remains important, because success in ancillary markets is dependent on success at the theatrical box office.[73] A hit at the cinema is usually a hit in all markets, while a flop often remains a flop.

Fig. 6.2: DVD Statistics

Year	DVD Players Shipped to Dealers (thousands)	Installed Consumer Base (thousands)	Average DVD Player Price (USD)	DVD Units Shipped to to Dealers (millions)[1]	Titles Available on DVD[2]
1999	4,100	4,800	$275	98	5,000
2000	8,499	14,700	$204	182	8,500
2001	12,706	31,400	$153	364	13,000
2002	17,090	56,500	$140	685	20,000
2003	21,674	90,187	$122	1,023	29,000

1. Includes Sell-Through and Retail DVD.
2. Titles available on DVD include Movies and Music Videos.

Source: CEA, Digital Entertainment Group, reprinted *2003 MPA Market Statistics* 32.

for general DVD statistics). That year, 99.9 million DVDs were sold to dealers in the U.S. alone (see fig. 6.3 for sales information). A paltry 8.6 million of these were to rental companies such as Blockbuster. By comparison, in 1999, 647.2 million videocassettes were sold, 86.2 of them to the rental market. Over the next five years, the DVD format exploded in popularity. In 2002, 1.1 billion DVDs were sold in the U.S. (110.9 million to the rental sector). The average price of a DVD player had dropped to $122, and 29,000 titles were available in the format. Although the videocassette market had declined considerably as a result, it had not vanished entirely. In 2003, 293.6 million cassettes were sold. These figures indicate that the emergence of DVD as an exhibition format radically increased the size of the subsequent run market.

In 1999, combined DVD and videocassette sales were 746.1 million units. By 2003, this figure had soared to 1.4 billion units. The market doubled and continues to grow. Furthermore, the majors make more profit from the sale of DVDs than they do from the sale of cinema tickets and from the sale of home video.[74] The format is particularly cheap to manufacture and distribute. So, as Joel W. Finler puts it, "[T]he DVD market has provided the film studios with a large new source of income at minimum cost, and allows them to exploit their back catalogues more than ever before."[75] Although the majors have been far from stable over the last few years, many of them seeing their share price fall drastically after making unwise investments during the 'dot-com' boom, the rapidly expanding DVD market has acted as a bulwark against lasting financial problems.

Gladiator performed exceptionally well on DVD. According to Janet Wasko, it was the film that "opened Hollywood's eyes to the DVD goldmine."[76] Although it was only the second highest grossing film of 2000, on DVD it outsold the highest grossing, *Mission: Impossible II,* by a considerable margin.[77] DreamWorks astutely released the DVD version of the film several weeks before the VHS.[78] It went on to become the best-selling DVD of the year, selling over five million units in the U.S. alone.[79] Prior to this, the highest selling DVD of all time had been James Cameron's *Titanic.*[80] Both *Gladiator* and *Titanic* have since been eclipsed, but epics continue to perform disproportionately well on the format. *Variety* reported of another epic, "[A]lthough it never quite reached the $200-million mark at the box office, *Pearl Harbor* will almost certainly get there on home video after generating an estimated $130 million in consumer spending in a record-setting first week of release."[81] As Wasko notes, "*Pearl Harbor*'s first-day release on DVD supposedly attracted $65.7 million compared to an opening weekend box office of $59.1 million."[82] *Pearl Harbor,* the seventh highest grossing theatrical release of the year, became the number two highest grossing DVD after DreamWorks SKG's *Shrek* (which had been the third highest grossing theatrical release). In 2004, *Gladiator* and *Pearl Harbor* remained the joint sixteenth highest grossing sell-through DVDs of all time, despite the many thousands of DVDs released in the years following their initial run.[83]

The sales figures in figure 6.2 indicate that consumers are more willing to purchase DVDs than to rent them, much to the delight of the majors, who make more money from this market.[84] Historical epics were consistently amongst the highest selling of all retail DVDs in the early 2000s (alongside family films, as with video). On DVD epics often outsold films that had been more popular at the theatrical box office, which may be because epics appeal to demographic groups that would not usually go to the cinema, such as older people.[85] In response to this trend, *USA Today* argued that the musical biopic *Ray* (2004) was "one of a growing number of dramas that performed better on DVD than they did in theatres, primarily because they appeal to older movie fans."[86] According to the article, DVD has been particularly successful with older viewers, and film types that appeal to an older demographic tended to perform disproportionately well in the format. One could also speculate that the type of dramatic, nostalgic stories told in epics and the kinds of cinematic experience they offer is one that consumers have been particularly keen to recreate in the home, despite the limitations that home viewing imposes on spectacle.

It must be stressed that the relationship between DVD and the theatrical market differs considerably from the video sales and rental market of the 1990s, before the DVD format was introduced. When it was released on video in 1991, *Dances with Wolves* failed to enter the top ten lists of video sales or rentals in the United States, according to Billboard charts reported in *People* magazine.[87] Costner's film had been the third highest grossing theatrical release of 1990, after *Home Alone* and *Ghost*, but the most successful video release of 1990 was *Pretty Woman*, actually the fourth highest grossing theatrical release of the year. The sales list was heavily biased towards family films, especially Disney movies, both contemporary (*The Little Mermaid*) and 'classic' (*The Jungle Book*), as well as *Teenage Mutant Ninja Turtles: The Movie* (1990). The rental chart looks a little different, with fewer family films and more action adventures such as *The Hunt for Red October* and *Total Recall*, but again, *Dances with Wolves* failed to feature.[88] The split between retail and rental markets in 1990 is representative of broader trends across the decade. Family films tended to sell well (as did soft-core pornography, filmed concerts and workout videos), while more 'mature' films topped the rental charts. Of course, MPAA (Motion Picture Association of America) statistics suggest that the retail market was much larger than the rental market, but these trends hold true. In 1996, when *Braveheart* was released on video, the film topped the rental chart but failed to appear in the top ten retail sales chart. Alternatively, in 1998, *Titanic* was the tenth highest grossing retail release, failed to appear on the rental chart at all, but was the highest selling DVD. Taken together these trends offer compelling evidence that the above average performance of epics on the retail DVD format is a new phenomenon.

Ultimately, the size of the DVD market, and the exceptional performance of historical epics within it, has rendered perceptions of risk previously attached to the form increasingly inaccurate. In the case of epics, theatrical revenues are often surpassed on DVD, which has proven a far more profitable exhibition format. Even epics that perform modestly at the box office can become major hits in the DVD market. Furthermore, older epics seem to do equally well on DVD. Since 2000, roadshow epics such as *Spartacus* and *Lawrence of Arabia* have been released in sumptuous extended formats to considerably success, as have *Schindler's List*, *Dances with Wolves* and other more recent epics. It may be that the calculated opulence of DVD packaging, both as a physical item and as a media experience replete with all manner of 'extras,' is a successful expression of the scale and prestige integral to the epic—and the format is capable of expressing the close parallels between production values and cultural import that distinguish epics in a manner that other formats cannot muster. It is not excessive to claim that the enormous expansion of the DVD market at the end of the 1990s cemented the revival of the epic. Of course, many other film cycles have benefited from this shift, but the impact on preexisting attitudes towards epics cannot be underestimated.

Equally significant has been the overseas theatrical market, another area that became more important to Hollywood in the 1980s. According to Tino Balio:

> The growth of the overseas market during the 1980s resulted from the upgrading of motion picture cinemas, the emancipation of state-controlled broadcasting, the spread of cable and satellite services, and the pent-up demand for entertainment of all types. At one time theatrical revenues constituted nearly all of the foreign revenues of American film companies, but by 1989 they accounted for little more than a quarter. The major sources of revenue overseas

for Hollywood product became home video, theatrical exhibition and television, in that order.[89]

Of course, the overseas market had been vital to the American film industry during the roadshow period, when runaway productions and internationally resonant epics had been among Hollywood's most successful productions and the phenomenon Balio documents was a reorientation rather than an unprecedented shift. Nevertheless, the trend is pertinent because historical epics tend to gross more overseas than domestically. This is especially true of epics with an international (i.e., non-American) setting. For instance, 58.9 percent of *Gladiator*'s theatrical gross was made overseas. *Gladiator* was one of only three films in the top ten of 2000 to make more in this market than at home. (The others were *Mission: Impossible II* and Disney's *Dinosaur*, the first of which proved a long-standing rule that Tom Cruise films play well overseas, especially in Japan, while the latter was a sort of animated pre-historical epic aimed at children.)[90] Of the films already discussed in this thesis, *Dances with Wolves* made 56.6 percent of its gross overseas, *Schindler's List* 69.7 percent, *Saving Private Ryan* 54.9 percent, *Titanic* 67.3 percent and *Braveheart* 64 percent. More recently, we can see a similar breakdown in the grosses of *The Last Samurai*, which made 66.1 percent of its $455-million worldwide gross in overseas markets (much of it in Japan, again).[91] *Troy* made an astonishing 73.3 percent of its $497.4-million gross overseas.[92] Effectively, *Troy* performed unremarkably in the domestic market but was a major hit overseas. *King Arthur* made a total of $158 million at the box office, 67.2 percent of which came from overseas.[93]

If we compare the top 100 highest grossing movies of all time in the U.S. to overseas figures, we see that Hollywood's historical epics occupy consistently higher positions in the latter chart. *Titanic* is the still the highest grossing film in either market (it earned $1.2 billion overseas, and $600 million in the U.S.).[94] The other contemporary epics featured in the U.S. list rank far lower: *Saving Private Ryan* is forty-seventh, *Gone with the Wind* fifty-seventh, *Pearl Harbor* at fifty-eighth, *Gladiator* sixty-second and *Dances with Wolves* sixty-fifth.[95] Alternatively, in the overseas box office top 100, *Troy* is twenty-first, *The Last Samurai* twenty-fourth, *Gladiator* forty-seventh, *Pearl Harbor* fifty-first, *Dances with Wolves* fifty-seventh, *Schindler's List* sixty-seventh and *Gone with the Wind* ninety-first.[96] The only exception is *The Passion of the Christ*, which ranks ninth in the U.S., where it grossed $370.2 million, and sixty-third overseas, where it grossed $235 million. This atypical skew towards the American market is linked to the film's specifically American religious appeal, discussed in the next chapter, despite the use of subtitles and the apparently 'international' story it depicts. The atypicality of this one release aside, the figures offer compelling evidence that epics are more likely to connect with an international audience than many other Hollywood releases. Epics are not the only cycle to do this, but it is a constant feature of their reception.

Expansions of the DVD market and increased overseas revenues have turned epics from fiscal risks into particularly astute and viable investments. More and more epics are being produced that perform far better in these markets than at the domestic box office. In an article on *The Last Samurai*, *Variety* reported that "even though domestic box office is likely to fall far short of matching production costs all is not lost . . . a pic like 'Samurai' is just the kind of title that should perform especially well in the homevid and DVD."[97] The article concluded:

> For years the rule of thumb has seen pics break even when domestic b.o. [box office grosses] matched production costs, with foreign grosses equating to exhibitors' split. Ancillary [revenue] from homevid and TV distribution was viewed as compensating for marketing costs. But the enormous popularity of DVD is changing the profitability equation. Many pics can fall short theatricality and still turn a profit thanks to the DVD phenomenon.[98]

It is telling that *Variety* used *The Last Samurai* to illustrate their argument. In the case of high-cost epics, U.S. theatrical grosses are increasingly losing their position as an indicator of future or ancillary performance. At the U.S. box office epics often look like relatively routine blockbusters. Most perform adequately, and while some are hits, some also are flops. In ancillary markets the same films can garner far higher returns. So, the film market today is very different from the film market of the roadshow period and also from the marketplace of the 1980s and early 1990s. It is no coincidence that epics have reached their highest visibility in concert with the firm establishment of the DVD market. In fact, this market, and the overseas theatrical box office, formed the economic foundation against which one can chart the revival of the American film epic. It is often, and accurately, claimed that ancillary markets are hit-driven, that films that perform well at the box office also perform well on video and DVD. However, there are nuances of financial performance in these markets with which such a generalisation fails to adequately engage. Certain film types are favoured in certain ancillary markets in a manner that can have a profound effect on subsequent theatrical releases.

Conclusion

At the end of *Gladiator*, Juba (Djimon Hounsou) goes to the spot where his friend Maximus died. He pushes two small effigies of Maximus's wife and son into the bloodstained dirt and says, "Now we are free, I will see you again. But not yet." He then walks away, and the camera pans upward, through streams of dawn light that slant through the shutters of the darkened coliseum, until the city of Rome appears, pink in the morning light. The ethereal score rises to a crescendo in a moment filled with optimism and uncertainty. Juba is stepping out into a new world, unlike anything he has known before, and, in truth, quite unlike anything that actually existed at the time.[99] In this world he is free, democracy is restored, Maximus has triumphed and taken his place in the afterlife. As the audience leaves the auditorium, or switches off their DVD player, a similar shift in the fortunes of the historical epic has occurred. The cycle has reached maturity and solidity.

Since 2000, historical epics have no longer been the sole province of cinematic visionaries. They might be exceptional in terms of budget and production resources, less ubiquitous than superhero films or romantic comedies, but epics are now a regular part of Hollywood's production schedules. The majors have a strong financial incentive to green-light them. In fact, the financial incentives attached to epics have never been stronger. Chapter 2 argued that, at the beginning of the 1970s, the film marketplace became incapable of supporting historical epics. This event has shaped industrial attitudes to the form ever since. Prior to its release, some in the industry began referring to *Dances with Wolves* as 'Kevin's Gate,' suggesting that Costner's epic western might share the same ignominious fate as Michael Cimino's disastrously unsuccessful *Heaven's Gate*.[100] Spielberg and Universal assumed *Schindler's List* would be a commercial failure, *Titanic* was deemed an colossal risk, and even *Gladiator* was viewed as hazardous, potential 'box-office poison.' However, such views no longer reflect the reality of the film marketplace, which today does more than support these films. It *encourages* them. Although production of epic films has diminished since 2004, it is no longer feasible to claim that historical epic films are perilous investments by any means.

As a result, the likelihood that something leftfield would emerge from the epic tradition, something truly visionary and unique, has diminished. The narrational and thematic confines of the epic are beginning to seem increasingly fixed. Empires will fall. Heroes will rise. Suicidal acts of commitment will abound. Who would have expected, then, that the most maverick and controversial historical epic ever made would appear in 2004? The film drew battle lines across Hollywood. It divided the whole nation. It bucked all trends. Most important, it attempted to do more than edify its audience. It wanted to *convert*. With the revival of the epic established, the final chapter will try to understand *The Passion of the Christ*.

Notes

1. Arthur DeVany, *Hollywood Economics: How Extreme Uncertainty Shapes the Film Industry* (London: Routledge, 2004), 7.

2. Dade Hayes, "Pricey, dicey pix," *Variety* 5 May 2000, unpaginated, obtained from Variety Online, http://www.variety.com/article/VR1117781275.

3. Marc Graser, "H'w'd's New Toga Party," *Variety* 1 Sept. 2002, unpaginated, obtained from Variety Online, http://www.variety.com/article/VR1117872109.

4. Peter Bart, "Tribute or Tribulation," *Variety* 17 Apr. 2000, 58.

5. Todd McCarthy, rev. of *Gladiator*, *Variety* 24 Apr. 2000, unpaginated clipping, obtained from NYPL, and Mark Morris, rev. of *Gladiator*, *Observer* 23 Apr. 2000, Screen, 3.

6. Christopher Noxon, "The Roman Empire Rises Again," *Los Angeles Times* 23 Apr. 2000, Calendar, 3.

7. DreamWorks Pictures, *Gladiator* press kit, NYPL, 1.

8. McCarthy, unpaginated.

9. Rick Altman, *Film/Genre* (London: BFI, 1999), 46.

10. Steve Neale, *Genre and Hollywood* (London: Routledge, 2000), 43.

11. Alan Lovell and Gianluca Sergi, *Making Films in Contemporary Hollywood* (London: Hodder Arnold, 2005), 116.

12. Steven Holden, "Far From Gettysburg, A Heartland Torn Apart," *New York Times* 24 Nov. 1999, 14.

13. Financial data obtained from Box Office Mojo, http://www.boxofficemojo.com/movies/?id=thepatriot.htm.

14. Unless otherwise noted, all financial data in this paragraph is taken from Box Office Mojo, http://www.boxofficemojo.com/movies.

15. See Julian Stringer, "Introduction," to Julian Stringer, ed., *Movie Blockbusters* (London: Routledge, 2003), 1–14.

16. Elvis Mitchell, "A Gentle Farmer Who's Good at Violence," *New York Times* 28 Jun. 2000, unpaginated, obtained from http://movies2.nytimes.com/mem.movies/review.htm; David Denby, "No Limit," *New Yorker* 3 Jul. 2000, 87; and Todd McCarthy, rev. of *The Patriot*, *Variety* 16 Jun. 2000, unpaginated clipping obtained from 'The Patriot' clippings file, NYPL.

17. Robert Rodat, quoted in Rick Lyman, "At the movies," *New York Times* 23 Jun. 2000, E8.

18. Financial data obtained from Box Office Mojo, http://www.boxofficemojo.com/movies/?id=thepatriot.htm.

19. Financial data for *Anna and the King* from the Internet Movie Database, http://www.uk.imdb.com/title /tt0166485/business.

20. Todd McCarthy, rev. of *Gangs of New York*, *Variety* 5 Dec. 2002, unpaginated, obtained from http://www.variety.com/VR1117919499, and A. O. Scott, "To Feel a City Seethe," *New York Times* 20 Dec. 2002, unpaginated, obtained from http://movies2.nytimes.com/mem. movies/review.htm.

21. Herbert Asbury, *The Gangs of New York: An Informal History of the Underworld* (1927; London: Arrow, 2002).

22. Financial data, including budget, obtained from Box Office Mojo, http://www.boxofficemojo.com/movies/?id=gangsofnewyork.htm.

23. Financial data obtained from the Internet Movie Database, http://www.uk.imdb.com/title/ tt0240510/business.

24. Indeed, *National Geographic* presented the film in these terms. See Anon., "Major Stars Shine for NGS," *National Geographic* (Aug. 2002), article in preliminary, unpaginated section of magazine.

25. Financial data obtained from the Internet Movie Database, http://www.uk.imdb.com/title/tt0267626/business.

26. The discussion of the fantasy epic that follows is the result of conversations with Peter Krämer, and many of the points made here can be attributed to him and are likely to feature in Krämer's forthcoming work on 1980s and 1990s Hollywood, *The Big Picture*.

27. Peter Krämer "'The Best Disney Film Disney Never Made': Children's Films and the Family Audience in American Cinema since the 1960s," in Steve Neale and Murray Smith, eds., *Contemporary Hollywood Cinema* (London: Routledge, 1998), 185–200.

28. This point is best made in Peter Krämer, "'It's aimed at kids—the kid in everybody,': George Lucas, *Star Wars* and children's entertainment," in Yvonne Tasker, ed., *Action and Adventure Cinema* (London: Routledge, 2004), 358–370.

29. *Dune* grossed $30.9 million at the domestic box office. Financial data obtained from Box Office Mojo, http://www.boxofficemojo.com/movies/?id=dune.htm.

30. See Lucas's comments on the DVD commentary of *The Phantom Menace*.

31. Tom Shone, *Hollywood Blockbusters, or, How I Learned to Stop Worrying and Love the Summer* (London: Simon and Schuster, 2004), 305.

32. His comments can be found on the writers' and director's commentary, *Lord of the Rings: The Fellowship of the Ring* (Peter Jackson, 2001), Special Edition DVD release.

33. Findings reported at the panel on the 'Lord of the Rings Audience Research Project,' at the Society for Cinema and Media Studies Conference, University College London, May 2005.

34. Financial data obtained from the Internet Movie Database, http://www.uk.imdb.com/ boxoffice/alltimegross.

35. See John Soriano, "WGA.org's Exclusive Interview with David Franzoni," Writer's Guild of America Web site, http://www.wga.org/craft/interviews/franzoni2001.html.

36. Quote attributed to Steven Spielberg by David Franzoni, quoted in Lewis Beale, "The Roman Empire Strikes Back," *Daily News, New York* 30 Apr. 2000, Showtime, 3.

37. The brief summary of Franzoni's script which follows, and discussion of John Logan's draft, is all derived from Jon Solomon, "*Gladiator* from Screenplay to Screen," in Martin M. Winkler, ed., *Gladiator: Film and History* (London: Blackwell, 2004), 1–16.

38. Andrew Hindes, "U suits up for D'Works *Gladiator*," *Variety* 13 Nov. 1998, unpaginated, obtained from http://www.variety.com/article/VR1117488480.

39. *Vivendi-Universal 2000 Annual Report*, 17. Obtained from http://www.vivendi-universal.com/vu/en/files/2000annualreport.pdf.

40. Joel W. Finler argues that the increased returns available in ancillary markets make such arrangements more financially worthwhile than they had been in previous years. See Joel W. Finler, *The Hollywood Story* 3rd ed. (London: Wallflower, 2003), 7.

41. Branko Lustig was a producer on *Schindler's List* and a Plaszow camp survivor. David Franzoni was also given a producer credit on the film, and, by his own account, he played an occasionally active role in the production process.

42. Douglas Wick, quoted in Christopher Noxon, "The Roman Empire Rises Again," *Los Angeles Times* 23 Apr. 2000, Calendar, 3.

43. See Michael Fleming and Andrew Hindes, "Crowe girding for *Gladiator*," *Variety* 11 Sept. 1998, unpaginated, obtained from http://www.variety.com/article/VR111740307.

44. Douglas Wick, quoted in the *Gladiator* press kit, NYPL, 2.

45. Thus Nicholson's involvement with *Gladiator* mirrors Christopher Fry's involvement with *Ben-Hur*.

46. Mark Lawson interviews William Nicholson, *Front Row*, BBC Radio 4, broadcast 26 Apr. 2005.

47. Financial data obtained from Box Office Mojo, http://www.boxofficemojo.com/movies/?id=gladiator.htm.

48. See, for example, Todd McCarthy's review for *Variety*, cited above, and Godfrey Cheshire, rev. of *Gladiator*, *New York Press* 3 May 2000, 32.

49. Monica C. Cyrino, "Gladiator and Contemporary American Society," in Winkler, 124–149.

50. Richard Rushton, "Narrative and Spectacle in *Gladiator*," *Cineaction* 56, 2000, 35–43.

51. Geoff King, *New Hollywood Cinema: An Introduction* (London: I.B. Tauris, 2002), 240–247.

52. Martin Fradley, "Maximus Melodramaticus: Masculinity, masochism and white male paranoia in contemporary Hollywood cinema," in Tasker, 235–251.

53. Many examples can be found in Sandra T. Joshel, Margaret Malamud and Donald T. McGuire Jr., eds., *Imperial Projections: Ancient Rome in Modern Popular Culture* (Baltimore: John Hopkins University Press, 2001).

54. Juvenal, quoted in Patrick Brantlinger, *Bread and Circuses: Theories of Mass Culture as Social Decay* (Ithaca, NY: Cornell University Press, 1983), 22. The term refers to the fact that, in the Roman circus, bread was traditionally thrown to the crowd before the games began.

55. See Salvador Ginler's claim, "Of all the contributions made by Roman thought and imagery to what would later become the mass society outlook, probably the most important was the belief that the multitude must be fed bread and cheap entertainment if it was to be kept quiet, submissive and loyal to the powers that be" (Ginler, quoted in Brantlinger, 22–23). This vision of culture is thoroughly surveyed in Brantlinger's book.

56. Theodor W. Adorno, *The Culture Industry: Selected Essays on Mass Culture* (London: Routledge, 1991), 138.

57. See the entry on 'Hegemony,' in Julian Wolfreys, *Critical Keywords in Literary and Cultural Theory* (New York: Palgrave-Macmillan, 2004), 81–88.

58. Brantlinger, 249–277.

59. For more on the critique of epics as 'middlebrow', and thus culturally denigrated, see Mark Jancovich, "Dwight MacDonald and the Historical Epic," in Tasker, 84–99.

60. Martin Fradley argues that a near hysterical white male 'victimhood' runs throughout the film, in Fradley, 245.

61. Related interpretations that view the film as a metaphor for Hollywood are Rushton, 35–43 and Morris, 3.

62. David Franzoni, quoted in Soriano, unpaginated.

63. Marc Graser, "H'w'd's new toga party," *Variety* 1 Sept. 2002, unpaginated, obtained from http://www.variety.com/article/VR1117872109.

64. For more industry discussion of this trend, see Stephen Galloway, "Big Pictures: Sword and sandals films are back in style," *Hollywood Reporter* 1 Oct. 2002, 18–20, and Michael Fleming, "Hits offer up new H'wood history lesson," *Variety* 19 Apr. 2001, 30.

65. Michael Fleming, "DreamWorks logs Logan as Lincoln Scribe," *Variety* 5 Dec. 2001, unpaginated, obtained from http://www.variety.com/article/VR111785625.

66. Fleming, unpaginated.

67. For more details on this period and process, see Thomas Schatz, "The Return of the Hollywood Studio System," in Erik Barnouw et al., *Conglomerates and the Media* (New York: The New Press, 1997), 73–106.

68. Stephen Prince, *A New Pot of Gold: Hollywood under the Electronic Rainbow, 1980–1989* (Berkeley: University of California Press, 2000), xi.

69. A comprehensive overview of video and Hollywood can be found in Fredrick Wasser, *Veni, Vedi, Video: The Hollywood Empire and the VCR* (Austin: University of Texas Press, 2001).

70. Prince, 95.

71. David O. Cook, *Lost Illusions: American Cinema in the Shadow of Watergate and Vietnam 1970–1979* (Berkeley: University of California Press, 2000), 65.

72. Douglas Gomery, "The Hollywood Blockbuster: Industrial Analysis and Practice," in Stringer, 78.

73. Ibid., 77.

74. Janet Wasko, *How Hollywood Works* (London: Sage, 2003), 133.

75. Finler, 7.

76. Wasko, 134.

77. See figures reported in Scott Hetttrick and Enrique Rivero, "D'Works to bow colossal *Gladiator* DVD," *Variety* 19 Sept. 2000, unpaginated, obtained from http://www.variety.com/article/VR1117786593.

78. See Hettrick and Rivero, unpaginated.

79. Figures reported in Scott Hettrick and Jennifer Netherby, "*Pearl* harbors top sales," *Variety* 10 Dec. 2001, unpaginated, obtained from http://www.variety.com/article/VR1117857020.

80. Hetrick and Netherby, unpaginated.

81. Ibid.

82. Wasko, 134.

83. Anon., "Top 25 DVD Sellers of All Time," *Video Store Magazine* 20 Jun. 2004, 32.

84. Wasko, 133.

85. Wasko notes that the success of *Gladiator* on DVD "pointed to young men as the major purchasers," but no data to support this assertion is cited, and thus it is not clear if this observation is anecdotal or based on direct research. See Wasko, 134.

86. Thomas K. Arnold, "Older Audience Pass on Theatres," *USA Today* 4 Jul. 2005, unpaginated, obtained from http://www.usatoday.com/life/movies/news/2005-07-04-dvd-older-viewers_x.htm.

87. *The 2001 People Entertainment Almanac* (New York: Cader, 2000), 110–112.

88. Again, the source for this data, and all that follows, is *The 2001 People Entertainment Almanac*, 110–112.

89. Tino Balio, "'A major presence in all of the world's important markets,' The globalisation of Hollywood in the 1990s," in Steve Neale and Murray Smith, eds., *Contemporary Hollywood Cinema* (London: Routledge, 1998), 59–60.

90. Financial data obtained from Box Office Mojo, http://www.boxofficemojo.com/movies/?id=gladiator.htm.

91. All financial data used in this section is available on Box Office Mojo and can be easily accessed via http://www.boxofficemojo.com/movies.htm.

92. Financial data obtained from Box Office Mojo, http://www.boxofficemojo.com/movies/?id=troy.htm.

93. Financial data obtained from Box Office Mojo, http://www.boxofficemojo.com/movies/?id=kingarthur.htm.

94. Financial data obtained from Box Office Mojo, http://www.boxofficemojo.com/movies/?id=titanic.htm.

95. Chart data obtained from the Internet Movie Database, http://www.uk.imdb.com/boxoffice/alltimegross?region=non-us.

96. Chart data from the Internet Movie Database, http://www.uk.imdb.com/boxoffice/alltimegross.

97. Carl DiOrio, "B.O. doesn't tell Samurai Tale," 18 Jan. 2004, unpaginated, obtained from http://www.variety.com/article/VR1117898592.

98. DiOrio, unpaginated.

99. One might usefully extend this observation to note how these scenes appear to resolve the Marxian debate about mass culture present in the film. Fredric Jameson has argued that mass cultural works often contain a 'utopian charge' fulfilling unconscious cultural desire for social liberation. See Fredric Jameson, *Signatures of the Visible* (New York: Routledge, 1992), 1.

100. Mike Medavoy and Josh Young, *You're Only As Good As Your Next One: 100 Great Films, 100 Good Films, and 100 for Which I Should Be Shot* (New York: Atria, 2002), 160.

chapter looks to the roots of such responses and attempts to understand why this highly unusual epic was made, and why it was interpreted in this way.

So far, most scholarly discussion of *The Passion* has tended to focus on the film's appeal to extreme conservative Christian groups. The contrast between negative reviews and the film's sometimes rapturous popular reception seemed to indicate that the United States was becoming increasingly divided along political and religious lines. *The Passion* acted as a lightning rod for political comment, highlighting preexisting debates about the role of religion, politics and entertainment in American life (briefly discussed in chapter 2). However, this chapter seeks to offer a more measured account of the film and its success. In the 2000 census, over 159.5 million adult Americans identified themselves as Christian, out of a total adult population of 207.9 million.[7] One can therefore assume that the vast majority of movie viewers in the USA are likely to consider themselves Christians. A 2006 survey suggests that over 90 percent of Americans profess some belief in God, but only a handful identified themselves with what might be called 'extremist' positions.[8] Thus, only 5 percent of Americans professed to be atheists, and 15 percent claimed to be evangelicals, while a majority of 47 percent identified themselves using the somewhat vague label of 'Bible believing.'[9] This massive Christian demographic is clearly not particularly unified in terms of denomination, commitment or opinion, but it does indicate that Christianity is an important part of life for many Americans and an important factor in *The Passion*'s success. However, the ways that Hollywood movies, including epics, engage and speak to Christians is rarely discussed, despite the fact that the historical epic has traditionally made overt appeals to Christians. This final chapter looks beyond the production imperatives that have led to the revival of the epic to examine how Mel Gibson's film reengages with biblical stories that appear to have been jettisoned from the contemporary epic cycle, despite their strong presence in the roadshow cycle.

As we have seen, epic films with biblical settings were amongst the biggest hits of the roadshow era. *Samson and Delilah*, which effectively started the cycle in 1949, had its origins in the Old Testament, as did DeMille's 1956 *The Ten Commandments*. Other major epic hits of the 1950s like *Quo Vadis* (1951), *The Robe* (1953) and *Ben-Hur* (1959) used fictional narratives to illustrate events of the New Testament. In the 1960s, highly budgeted biblical epics such as George Stevens's *The Greatest Story Ever Told* (1965), Nicholas Ray's *King of Kings* (1961) and John Huston's *The Bible: In The Beginning* (1966) continued to be released, although their profitability declined. With the wider decline of the roadshow epic cycle, mainstream Hollywood movies increasingly tended to avoid overt engagement with the founding myths of Judeo-Christian belief. In 1996, social commentators Powers, Rothman and Rothman noted that "moviemakers since 1965 have largely ignored traditional religious themes . . . the veritable parade of epic biblical films—such as those of Cecil B. DeMille—has disappeared, never to return."[10] As we have seen, Peter Krämer has disagreed and argued that oblique forms of spirituality continued to figure strongly in fantasy and science fiction films throughout the 1970s and 1980s. The fantasy epic cycle that moved to prominence in the 1990s was chief amongst these, as the last chapter noted. However, films with overtly biblical, especially New Testament, settings have almost entirely vanished from mainstream production trends. The most obvious exception was Martin Scorsese's *The Last Temptation of Christ* (1988). Despite a welter of media interest, Scorsese's film only grossed $8.4 million on theatrical release, in a year when the highest grossing film, Barry Levinson's *Rain Man* (1988), took $171.2 million.[11] Of course, the box office performance of Scorsese's film was sufficient for a minority interest art movie, but it offered little assurance that the biblical epic held any great popular appeal.

In particular, the final dream sequence of Scorsese's film, which showed Christ having sex with, and marrying, Mary Magdalene, generated enormous controversy.[12] The scene so offended a number of Christian groups in America that some theatres showing the film, and the offices of the distributor, Universal, were picketed by outraged believers—precisely the audience who might have made the film a success.[13] If anything, *The Last Temptation of Christ* seemed to offer the majors a compelling reason to *avoid* the production of biblical epics at all costs. By contrast, *The Passion* emerged at a time when ancient-world epics were commonplace, as the previous chapter has demonstrated, and although it also generated enormous controversy, it was hugely profitable. Very few generic terms were used in reports about the film's production, in its marketing (as the first section of this chapter will show) and in reviews. Nevertheless, *The Passion* can clearly be understood as part of the epic cycle in terms of setting, theme and narrative structure, even if it was highly unusual in terms of style, content and appeal.

Indeed, Heather Hendershot has identified a healthy market for "Christian films [which] are usually distributed exclusively through alternative means, shown in churches or sold in Christian bookstores. These films rarely make a blip on the secular culture's radar screens, but they are widely known among born-agains."[14] However, Hollywood has tended to ignore the Christian market, and the only other successful and genuinely mainstream cinematic biblical epic produced since *The Bible: In the Beginning* in 1966 had been DreamWorks SKG's *The Prince of Egypt* in 1998. Unlike Mel Gibson, DreamWorks sought to stress the inclusive, uncontroversial nature of its film, which began with an intertitle stating, "The filmmakers have tried to remain faithful to a story that is a cornerstone of religious belief for Christians, Jews and Muslims," thus inviting interfaith interpretations. As chapter 5 demonstrated, DreamWorks SKG's biblical epic was a hit, but it was by no means a standout success when compared to breakthrough epics such as *Saving Private Ryan*, *Titanic* or *Gladiator*.

Consequently, *The Passion* was the first film in a long time that suggested that contemporary audiences might be willing to engage with explicitly religious epics to the same degree as in the roadshow period—hence my focus on the spiritual elements of the film and its reception. Rather than claiming that its success was entirely attributable to the increasing political power of an amorphous and 'fundamentalist' religious right, this chapter asks: How did *The Passion* engage a broad swath of Christian viewers, many of whom must have been moderate in their opinions, and what did it offer them?[15] The first section examines the marketing of the film, while the second looks at the narrative of *The Passion* in more detail. These two sections show that the film was presented as a transformative spiritual experience that many ordinary Christians could identify with, and that the extreme violence at its heart served to confirm the power of this experience. Conceptions of religious ritual are used to explain Christian responses to the film. The conclusion then examines the ways that the ritualistic elements of Gibson's film drew upon preexisting features of the contemporary epic cycle.

1. Presenting *The Passion*

The Passion's origins as a film project stretch back to 2002, but Mel Gibson's obsession with the Passion has deeper roots, as he repeatedly explained in interviews given during the marketing of the film. Gibson told Diane Sawyer, on an *ABC News* special, that, when he had made his name in films such as Richard Donner's *Lethal Weapon 2*, the third highest grossing domestic release of 1989, he had also been an alcoholic and frequently considered committing suicide.[16] In 1992, while Gibson was contemplating the final hours of Jesus Christ's life, he claimed, "I fell to my knees and God saved me. The wounds of Jesus healed my wounds."[17] Gibson quit drinking, his suicidal urges diminished, and he began attending church regularly after a long period of absence. Like many addicts, Gibson's reformation was far from permanent; in 2006, he fell spectacularly off the wagon and was arrested for drunk driving in Malibu. Nevertheless, in almost every interview he gave before this moment, Gibson made clear that this phase of the Christian story, the so-called Passion (a term derived from the Latin *passus* meaning 'having suffered'), was, for him, intrinsically powerful. It had literally altered him and the trajectory of his life.

Later, Gibson told Peter J. Boyer of the *New Yorker* that he felt as if he was being encouraged, by divine forces, to film the Passion. He explained, "You get signals. Signs. 'Signal graces,' they're called."[18] According to Boyer, one of these signal graces (which had apparently taken many forms) had been Gibson's repeated encounters with writings and artefacts associated with Anne Catherine Emmerich. Emmerich was a stigmatic, illiterate nun who had lived in Westphalia during the nineteenth century and who had experienced a series of visions of Christ's final hours. These had been transcribed by the German Romantic poet Clemens Brentano and released in book form in 1824, shortly after Emmerich's death. Gibson acquired a copy of the Brentano book as part of a bulk buy from a nunnery that was closing down. One day, he has said, he was reaching for another book and Brentano's fell onto his desk. He proceeded to read and was fascinated by Emmerich's visions.

During the filming of the aptly titled *Signs* (2002), Gibson had gone to buy some antique church furniture from a secondhand store in Philadelphia. While he was paying, the dealer had given him a small piece of cloth, which was apparently part of Anne Catherine Emmerich's habit. In this way, and others, Gibson got the feeling that God was trying to tell him something. By placing this particular story of the film's origins in the public domain, Gibson suggested that the film was a devotional gesture directly inspired by God, thus providing committed Christians with an incentive to attend and suggesting a framework for viewing. In the accounts, the making of the film was presented as Gibson's divinely inspired 'duty,' which in turn suggested that devout viewers also had a similar 'duty' to see the film.

Thus inspired, Gibson began working on a script with screenwriter Benedict Fitzgerald in 2002. On completion the script was translated into Latin, Aramaic and Hebrew, because Gibson claimed he wanted the film to appear as 'authentic' as possible. To this end, Gibson also claimed that he had hoped, at least initially, to release *The Passion* (as it was then called) without subtitles, which may have been one reason why none of the major distributors were willing to provide funding, including Twentieth Century Fox, with whom Gibson's production company, Icon, had a 'first look' deal.[19] Ultimately, Gibson put up the $30-million production budget himself, and Icon produced the film on its own.[20] Eventually, it was released by the independent distributor Newmarket, which had previously found success with *Donnie Darko* (2001), *Y Tu Mamá También* (2001) and *My Big Fat Greek Wedding* (2002).[21]

Filming began in Italy in late 2002, and Gibson has claimed that throughout the shoot he was increasingly aware of the film's divinely inspired power. As he put it, "The Holy Ghost was working through me on this film, and I was just directing traffic."[22] Every morning the cast and crew attended a Latin Mass, and Gibson claimed that several atheists and Muslims had been converted to Christianity on the set.[23] Thus, Gibson repeatedly suggested that, from the moment of its inception, *The Passion* was imbued, perhaps by God, with some transformative spiritual power. Ruminating on the events of the Passion had transformed Gibson. Making *The Passion* had transformed others. What effect, Gibson asked, might it have on audiences?

However, even during production the film began to generate controversy. On 9 March 2003, the *New York Times* published an article that revealed some previously unknown facts about Gibson.[24] It explained that Gibson followed the 'schismatic' or 'traditionalist' branch of Catholicism, which rejects liberalising reforms introduced in the 1960s by the Second Vatican Council.[25] In Gibson's church Mass was said in Latin, the priest faced the altar and salvation was only available to Catholics. Writer Christopher Noxon discussed the strictness of Gibson's faith before examining Gibson's father, Hutton, a schismatic in his eighties who holds some extremely right-wing, conspiratorial, anti-Semitic beliefs. Noxon expressed concern that Gibson's forthcoming film might reflect these beliefs. After reading Noxon's piece, a group of alarmed Catholic and Jewish scholars independently formed what they described as an 'ad-hoc advisory group' and contacted Icon offering their services.[26] They hoped to find out what Gibson was doing and to make him aware of the potential controversy attached to depictions of the Passion.

Throughout western history, passion plays (staged recreations of Christ's final days or hours) have been thought to amplify anti-Semitic feeling by blaming the death of Christ on Jewish, rather than Roman, tormentors.[27] Consequently, in 1988, the U.S. National Conference of

Catholic Bishops issued strict guidelines as to how this aspect of Christ's story could be depicted.[28] Filmmakers were particularly encouraged not to combine different Gospels. However, Gibson did not accept the authority of the U.S. bishops, and Icon refused to provide the ad-hoc scholars with a script, who nevertheless obtained one via clandestine means and sent a lengthy report suggesting corrections and changes to Icon in May 2003.[29] Icon still refused to deal with the scholars, and many apparently worrying elements were kept in the film. At this moment, *The Passion* began to generate news headlines across the world.[30]

Shortly after receiving the scholars' report, Icon initiated a unique marketing campaign. The company contacted various Christian marketing companies, including Outreach, Inc. in California, as well as Christian PR guru A. Larry Ross—who had also worked with DreamWorks on *The Prince of Egypt*. Together they designed a marketing campaign that specifically responded to the criticisms made in the ad-hoc report.[31] Gibson was sent out into the field, bypassing conventional media altogether, visiting Catholics and Protestants alike, stressing that *The Passion* was not the work of a sectarian extremist. His talks invariably took the form of confessionals that simultaneously presented, and promoted, *The Passion* as the devotional gesture of a devout believer. Journalist Peter J. Boyer accompanied Gibson on many of these visits and wrote, "[A]t each he was received with an enthusiasm that seemed to reach beyond the movie itself, to a deeply felt disaffection from the secular world; now an icon of that world was on their side."[32]

The film was shown to Christian leaders across the USA, including the Protestant preacher Billy Graham, and even to the Pope. Graham said afterwards, "Every time I preach or speak about the cross, the things I saw on the screen will be on my heart and mind."[33] It was initially reported that the Pope had said of *The Passion*, "It is as it was," but the Vatican quickly acted to quell these rumours and told the press that although the Pope and the Vatican approved of the movie, the leader of the faith had made no specific comments about it.[34] Along with Gibson's testimonials, such 'official endorsements' stressed the spiritual resonance of the film and acted as further encouragement for regional church staff, of all denominations, to promote the movie when they returned to their own churches. *The Passion*, Gibson suggested, was a major evangelising opportunity. To this end, Icon encouraged preachers to screen DVD trailers for the film, and sold door hangers, postcards and booklets for churches via their Web site.[35] Such material was aimed at generating interest amongst established congregation members, but, Icon stressed, it was also supposed to link local churches to *The Passion* in the minds of any spiritually uncommitted viewers who may have found the film inspirational.[36] Icon sought to spark a form of 'spiritual synergy', whereby *The Passion* and churches reached out to apostate America together in a manner that further stressed Gibson's moral commitment and presented the film as a powerful spiritual experience, imbued with the potential to convert, to evangelise, to *change* its audience.

Furthermore, at his testimonials, Gibson claimed that with *The Passion* he had sought to be faithful to the Gospels and to produce a textually accurate vision of events. Accusations of anti-Semitism were, Gibson claimed, veiled attacks on the Bible itself, made by an atheistic, 'liberal-humanist' media. Presumably many of the pastors, priests and preachers at these preliminary screenings, who had spent their lives meditating on the events of the Passion, agreed. (Alternatively, for the ad-hoc group and many others, the film did seem to attribute responsibility for Christ's murder to Jewish authorities, presented Jewish observers as bloodthirsty, and repeatedly associated the Jewish characters with evil and Satanism.) However, whatever his personal prejudices, Gibson was able to downplay such complaints by positioning his film as a defiant statement in what has come to be known in the United States as the 'culture wars.'

The origins of the 'culture wars' can be traced back to the turn of the twentieth century, but the term gained real cultural significance in the 1960s, when the widely reported liberalisation of attitudes amongst certain sectors of the population was countered by the equally rapid rise of combative conservatism.[37] Social historian Sara Diamond has described the conservative groups that emerged at this time as "the New Right"; an increasingly unified coalition of evangelical Christians, political conservatives and socially minded "neoconservatives."[38] Collectively, these groups came to constitute a "new cultural axis," in the words of James Davison Hunter, committed to maintaining older, orthodox values (particularly those outlined by religious doctrines). They regarded these values as integral to American society, in the face of a widespread liberalisation of attitudes toward sexual relations, family structures, patriotism and other issues.[39] For such groups the media constituted a key battleground, partly because those who work in the arts and media have tended to take a relatively liberal stance on social issues, and partly because conservative thinkers quickly recognised that the media plays a key role in disseminating popular values and attitudes.[40]

During a television address in 1968, Richard Nixon had described his supporters as a "silent majority" of social and political conservatives, opposed to Lyndon Johnson's 'Great Society.'[41] The New Right quickly came to categorise themselves in similar terms. They claimed to stand for an underrepresented majority of the American population, whose views rarely featured in the mainstream media, thus Jerry Falwell and Paul Weyrich chose to call the lobbying group they founded in 1979 'the Moral Majority.' Despite the shadow cast on American conservatism by the Watergate scandal in the 1970s, the power of right-wing religious lobbying groups has grown steadily over the previous forty years. Their objections to the values represented in the mainstream media seemed to crystallise in 1992, the year that Gibson had his much-vaunted epiphany.[42] That year, movie critic Michael Medved published his controversial best seller *Hollywood vs. America: Popular Culture and the War on Traditional Values*, in which he claimed, "Tens of millions of Americans now see the entertainment industry as an all-powerful enemy, an alien force that assaults our most cherished values and corrupts our children."[43] As we saw in chapter 2, Medved quoted statistics suggesting that a large proportion of Americans, regardless of faith or ethnicity, shared his opinions, and did, indeed, constitute a 'majority.'[44] These included Republican vice president Dan Quayle, who in 1992 made a widely reported speech attacking the popular television show *Murphy Brown*. Quayle denounced the show's title character, played by Candice Bergen, for having a child out of wedlock and went on to argue that the American media increasingly reflected the debased values of an unrepresentative 'cultural elite.'

According to William D. Romanowski, "Quayle created a mythical 'Us versus Them,' the 'Us' being the silent majority of middle Americans pitted against film and television producers, artists, journalists and academics, those 'left-wing, out-of-step, valueless Democrats.'"[45] Quayle's speech prompted media comment across America. The *Los Angeles Times* ran a cover story asking, 'Is Hollywood Ruining America?' the mainstream National Council of Churches issued a statement claiming, "We deplore the increasing glorification of violence and sexual violence in the visual media," and in 1993, a coalition of Southern Baptists accused the nation's television networks of contributing to "the moral breakdown in our society."[46] Although these groups represented specific, usually Christian, interests, it must be stressed that the 'culture wars' were and are not an insignificant matter of dispute between minority Christian groups, politicians and entertainers. As James Davison Hunter argues, "To frame the contemporary culture war in this way ignores the central role played by a wide range of cultural actors on both sides who are neither fundamentalists on the one hand, nor secular activists on the other."[47] Furthermore, Hunter observes that the culture wars "frequently seem abstract to people only until a part of their own lives intersects an issue of the culture war. . . . All of a sudden what had long been confined to the abstract becomes very real."[48] Although activists only constitute a small minority of the population, many Americans have some investment in the issues under discussion.

Arguably, Mel Gibson's career is, in many ways, eminently representative of a personal investment in the culture wars. In *Hollywood vs. America* Michael Medved reserved some of his strongest criticism for the *Lethal Weapon* movies that had made Mel Gibson a star. He described Gibson's character, the suicidal cop Martin Riggs, as "a repellent role model . . . [a] brooding, disturbed, unpredictable head case [and] an insulting treatment of Vietnam veterans."[49] Medved also was highly critical of the graphic violence in *Lethal Weapon* and the ironic, often comedic context in which it occurred.[50] Medved argued that, by starring in the *Lethal Weapon* movies, Mel Gibson was representative of the worst amoral excesses of the film industry. It is unclear whether or not Gibson was directly influenced by Medved's comments, but the pair certainly seemed to have been influenced by similar currents of popular discourse.[51] Thus, in 1992, Gibson had his moment of spiritual transformation. Although afterwards he continued to make action films of all types, including more *Lethal Weapon* movies, Gibson also began directing and taking roles in other sorts of cinematic projects. At this point we can see the first traces of the impulse that led to *The Passion*.

Gibson's directorial debut was *The Man Without a Face* (1993), a relatively low-budget, character piece in which he also starred as a disfigured recluse. Like many of Gibson's later films, *The Man Without a Face* dealt with issues of guilt, shame and social rejection. It was critically well regarded but only modestly successful in financial terms.[52] Then, in 1995, Gibson produced, directed and starred in *Braveheart*, the twelfth-century historical epic that cost $72 million, made $75.6 million in domestic receipts and $134.8 million overseas, and won Best Director and Best Picture Oscars.[53] *Braveheart* told the story of man who stands up for (very contemporary notions of) liberty in the face of ruthless historical despotism. The film climaxed with scenes of sacrificial torture and murder that spoke of a burgeoning preoccupation with the Passion and clearly anticipated Gibson's later work.

Over the next few years, Gibson also starred in *The Patriot* (2000) and *We Were Soldiers* (2002), epics that each dealt with the legacy of past atrocities in different ways. In *The Patriot*, Gibson played a retired scout struggling to compensate for his violent, amoral youth, when he fought on the 'wrong side' of the Franco-Indian War, by fighting on the 'right side' during the War of Independence. As Mark Glancy has shown, this film, like *The Passion*, was adopted by conservative commentators in America, who viewed it as a welcome attack on liberal values and a defiant statement on gun control.[54] Alternatively, *We Were Soldiers* was a Vietnam movie that painted the beginnings of the conflict as necessary and triumphant, in contrast to the guilt-ridden histories of Oliver Stone and Francis Ford Coppola. *We Were Soldiers* may have been viewed by Gibson as a partial apology or corrective for the damaged character of Martin Riggs, but both films are also representative of the sort of ethical journey that Gibson himself was on. This was made even more explicit by his decision to star in *Signs,* where he played a disenchanted preacher rediscovering his faith through a violent encounter with alien invaders. The end of the film showed a 'born again' Gibson straightening his dog-collar and striding out into a future of religious certainty. Gibson's next film would be *The Passion*.

At the testimonial marketing events organised by Icon, Gibson clearly sought to position his film as a vital viewing experiences for those on the conservative side of the culture wars. However, the culture wars also formed an essential backdrop that allowed Gibson to present his movie career as a familiar story of sin, guilt and ultimate salvation. This narrative of personal redemption was the chief subject of Gibson's testimonials, and it ultimately served to stress the profound transformative power of Gibson's film. Mel Gibson came to his church meetings a transformed man. Meditating on the Passion had changed him from a member of the despised liberal 'cultural elite' into a warrior for disaffected Christians. He was, in essence, a defector in the culture wars, someone who had moved from the 'wrong side' of amoral liberalism (as conservatives may have seen it) to the 'right side' of committed, conservative Christianity. Furthermore, at his preview screenings Gibson invited the assembled Christians to see themselves as a community under siege and presented his movie as a unifying faith experience.[55] Impassioned defences of the film were also featured on Christian Web sites, often sponsored by Icon, which encouraged Internet users to register their support for Gibson and his movie and to drum up interest amongst acquaintances.[56] Some churches were also encouraged to reserve cinemas for their congregations, thus adding to box office demand. Gibson presented *The Passion* as more than just an opportunity for audiences to register their religious solidarity. It was supposed to be a potent evangelical tool, and

Gibson's life, even the trajectory of his career as a star, spoke profoundly of this.

The positive responses of Billy Graham, other religious leaders, and Dr. James Dobson of Focus on the Family, who described *The Passion* as "the most heart-wrenching, powerful portrayal of Christ's suffering I have ever seen," seem to have been matched by Christian audiences. A survey of almost 6,000 Christian viewers reported that "75% of respondents said that viewing *The Passion* had helped them to grow spiritually, 80% indicated that it had given them a better understanding of God's love for all human beings, 73% said that it strengthened their faith and 74% said that it helped them draw closer to God."[57] For these viewers the film was far more than entertainment; it was an innately powerful experience. The next section examines the film itself and attempts to account for such responses.

The Passion went on to gross $125.2 million on its first five days on release, the highest 'weekend' domestic receipts ever taken at that time, and it went on to gross over $370 million.[58] If one divides this figure by the average ticket price in 2004 (approximately $6.50, according to the MPAA), it appears that approximately 55–60 million tickets for *The Passion* were sold. The figures suggest that the film successfully reached far more viewers than a small minority of midwestern conservative evangelical Christians or Catholics. Anecdotal evidence indicates that the film was extremely popular with urban Latin American audiences (invariably communities with strong Catholic traditions). According to Newmarket head Bob Berney, the film's highest cinema grosses came from theatres in Latino districts of New York City.[59] Meanwhile, the audience survey indicates that many white protestant Americans were also attracted to the film. In fact, the above figures indicate that over one-fifth of the American population may have gone to see the movie. Arguably then, *The Passion* had successfully connected with relatively mainstream Christian viewers in America—the majority of moderate, 'Bible-believing' Americans— many of whom found it genuinely moving. The next section examines the film itself and asks: What might the violent narrative of *The Passion* have offered a diverse Christian audience?

2. The Power of *The Passion*

For non-Christians the events depicted in *The Passion* can be difficult to comprehend, particularly because very little contextual information about the life or teachings of Christ is given. For Christians, of course, the meaning of such events would have been immediately accessible, but it would not have been uniform. Although there is agreement amongst Christians on some general issues (that, for example, Christ 'died for our sins'), there are also major divergences in interpreting the relevance and significance of the crucifixion. Nevertheless, the Christian church has emphasised three readings of the crucifixion throughout its history, which are not mutually exclusive, but which are often ranked in terms of importance by Christians, including Mel Gibson.[60]

The first Christian view of the Passion is sometimes known as the 'Christus Victor' account. It suggests that, through his death and resurrection, Christ triumphed over sin, death and Satan. The crucifixion is the moment where an Old Testament god wins out over the devil. A second key theological interpretation is known as the 'substitutionary' view. This account proposes that in the moment of the Passion, Jesus offered satisfaction for the sins of all humanity, past and present. Effectively, he took the punishment due to all sinners and, because he was the son of God, he redeemed everyone. This view is at the theological core of *The Passion*. When Gibson said, "The wounds of Jesus healed my wounds," he was suggesting that Christ's death on the cross had allowed his own salvation. For Gibson, the letting of Christ's blood was an inherently powerful moment, which is arguably why he chose to emphasise it on screen. Finally, a third theological view, sometimes called the 'subjective' interpretation, is also visible in the film. In this reading Christ's death on the cross is primarily proof of God's love, and Christ's sacrifice is the ultimate demonstration of the Christian character. Although Gibson does emphasise Christ's and God's love for humanity, his obsessive focus on blood and torment is arguably an attempt to revise more liberal interpretations by emphasising the violent aspects of the Passion story. The crucifixion was, for Gibson, more than just an exemplary moment of divine love. It was a potent historical event with ramifications for all human history. Hence the introductory title, taken from the Old Testament book of Isaiah: "He was wounded for our transgressions, crushed for our iniquities; by his wounds we are healed."[61] As we shall see, Gibson's film was designed to reflect the 'power of the Passion.'

The Passion begins in the garden of Gethsemane, on the night before Jesus Christ (James Caviezel) is crucified. Jesus stands in the garden and prays. After a few moments, an androgynous black-clad figure steps out of the undergrowth and begins to taunt him. The figure asks, "Do you really believe that one man can bear the full burden of sin? No one man can carry this burden, I tell you." It quickly becomes apparent that the figure is supposed to be Satan. This incident is drawn from the writings of Anne Catherine Emmerich rather than the Bible. Indeed, it has been argued that as much as 80 percent of Gibson's film is a dramatisation of Emmerich's transcribed visions.[62] These features include Satan's appearances and the focus on the two Marys (Jesus's mother and Mary Magdalen) as principal observers. Gibson's depiction of Satan as being either female or of unclear gender has also been viewed by some scholars as evidence of his misogyny and homophobia (the character is in fact played by a woman, Rosalinda Celentano).[63] Gibson claimed that he wanted to make the devil "alluring, attractive. It looks almost good—but not quite."[64]

Although there is a long Catholic tradition of placing Satan in the Christ story, embodied in Emmerich's work, the appearance of Satan in this film seems to contradict Gibson's attempts to produce a textually accurate account and could presumably deter non-Catholic viewers. If Satan's appearances are not congruent with the Gospels, one must ask why the character appears at all. In fact, the inclusion of Satan appears to be a piece of metaphysical scene setting. The physical appearance of Satan is evidence that Jesus is *not* delusional, and that important metaphysical events are in play. Jesus may have occasional doubts (about his purpose, not his divine parentage), but the audience is assured that *The Passion* will not be a relativistic account. The spiritual significance of the Passion is immediately established as *real*.[65] Effectively, the audience is placed within a coherent spiritual world, where God and the devil are in conflict, thus encouraging interpretation along the 'Christus Victor' lines. The final scene of Satan howling in a barren wasteland at the moment of Jesus's death bears this out.

After taunting Jesus, Satan vanishes, and Jesus undergoes the first of many violent encounters with the authorities. A group of temple guards arrive in the garden to arrest him. In the ensuing scuffle one has his ear severed by the disciple Peter (Francesco De Vito). Jesus picks it up and, with one very quiet miracle, puts it back on. Again this establishes the certainty of his divinity, but it is also one of the ways that Gibson shows the essentially loving nature of Christ—he is willing to heal his enemy, even as he awaits capture and torture. Nevertheless, Jesus is beaten by the guards and taken to the temple, where he is condemned as a blasphemer.[66]

Meanwhile, his mother, Mary (Maia Morgenstern), and her companion Mary Magdalen (Monica Belucci) head to the temple. Throughout the film, the two Marys stand on the periphery of events, observing the suffering of Christ, and the narrative is frequently mediated through them. The film repeatedly cuts away from scenes of torture to show the mother Mary's chastened, shocked response, providing viewers with a more sympathetic point of identification than the otherwise bloodthirsty crowd. Again, this focus on the maternal female observer is drawn from the writings of Anne Catherine Emmerich and longstanding Catholic traditions rather than from the Gospels themselves.[67] However, Mary's position as a concerned viewer, with a personal investment in events, seems to closely mirror the position of Christians watching at the beginning of the twenty-first century.

After his first trial, Christ is beaten (again) and taken to the Roman court, where the governor Pilate (Hristo Naumov Shopov) can find no fault with him. He is passed on to Herod (Luca De Dominicis), the local king, who also dismisses the charges against him. However, the Jewish high priest Caiphas (Mattia Sbragia) repeatedly threatens that if Pilate does not kill Jesus, he will precipitate a riot.[68] In these sequences, accusations of anti-Semitism hold the most weight. Throughout the film, the Romans are depicted as sympathetic proto-Christians, even as they torture Christ, while the Jewish crowd, and High Priest Caiphas, repeatedly call for Jesus' death. Such scenes certainly appear incontrovertibly anti-Semitic, but the broad popular success of the film seems to suggest that many ordinary, moderate Christians did not necessarily interpret them entirely in this way, presumably because they remain relatively faithful to accounts offered in the New Testament, even if Vatican II's prohibitions are violated.

A number of 'historical Jesus' scholars have sought to account for the apparent anti-Semitism of certain Gospels by arguing that the New Testament was created at a moment when the newly established Christian faith was seeking to distance itself from older forms of Judaism and stress links to Rome.[69] By the same token, for many contemporary Christians we can assume that the Bible is a vital repository of myth, which can be analysed and discussed but which ultimately offers profound truths. Furthermore, there is a sizable minority of fundamentalists who believe the New Testament to be documentary truth.[70] Whatever their individual understanding of the Bible might be, few Christians could claim that Gibson's was an account of the Passion that was not recognisably drawn from the New Testament, which may well explain why many readily accepted the film and often repudiated well-justified accusations of anti-Semitism.[71] Effectively, the problems with *The Passion* derived from problematic elements of the Bible itself. It must also be noted that all forms of Christian doctrine stress the culpability of individual sinners, and a sense of what might be termed 'observer guilt' clearly pervades *The Passion*. For many Christian viewers, questions of anti-Semitism were probably far less important than questions of personal responsibility. As we shall see, many viewers seemed to identify closely with Christ's tormentors even when the film appeared to demonise them. The mob of onlookers who surround Christ throughout *The Passion* may well be supposed to stand in for cinemagoers, and many viewers may well have understood their role in these terms.[72]

Eventually, Pilate decides to whip Jesus, and at this point the relentless violence of the film really begins. Jesus is scourged for twenty minutes, has a crown of thorns forced onto his head, and is then taken for crucifixion (at Caiphas's insistence). Unsure of what else to do, Pilate literally washes his hands of the affair, and Caiphas accepts responsibility, in one of the film's most controversial scenes. This is the so-called 'blood libel' that the ad-hoc scholars' report was particularly unhappy with. In the Gospel of Matthew, Caiaphas (as he is usually named) says at this moment, "His blood be on us and on our children." Christian anti-Semites have interpreted this to mean that the Jews are eternally responsible for the death of Christ. These words were included in the first cut of Gibson's film but were later removed (although it has been noted by several reviewers that the statement is still audible, and that Gibson had merely removed the subtitles).[73] However, although this moment has clear anti-Semitic overtones, it is drawn directly from the Gospel of Matthew.

Then, Jesus shoulders the cross and walks for half an hour through the city streets, falling numerous times, until he reaches the hill at Calvary, where he is nailed to his cross and dies. In flashback we see occasional glimpses of the Last Supper, the Sermon on the Mount and Jesus's early life, but ultimately the audience is presented with far more images of Christ's suffering in the present than of his ministry in the past. For an hour, the film offers up a protracted vision of one human being's physical agony, which begs the question: why? If Gibson believed that the most important aspect of the Christian story is the crucifixion—the moment when Christ took on the punishment for our sins—why did he show the violence inflicted on his body *before* that moment in such detail? And why might audiences find this spiritually uplifting? The answer, I would like to propose, is that the excessive violence of the film is an attempt to make this punishment seem 'real' in the lives of the viewers, in a manner which accounts for the emotional power that many Christians felt was an intrinsic part of the viewing experience.

Although Gibson and Christian audiences were angered by reviews that described the film as pornographic, the comparison is useful. As Linda Williams puts it, pornography makes "an almost visceral appeal to the body" not entirely dissimilar from "thrillers, weepies and low comedies," which also seek "to elicit 'automatic' bodily reactions."[74] *The Passion* performs a related function. It seeks to inspire an immediate, traumatic response. The violence in *The Passion* is almost too much to bear, because it appears too real and occurs too often. Critic Susan Thistlewaite described the number of children taken to see *The Passion* by devout Christian parents as a form of child abuse.[75] The idea that the film abuses its audience is also useful. Even viewers who praised the film talked about the experience of watching it as an act of endurance, a difficult, unpleasant experience, which was nevertheless rewarding in spiritual terms.[76] Gibson had produced a film that was mentally painful to watch. The movie critic and Catholic Mark Kermode described the film as "an accomplished test of cinematic endurance . . . that attempts to trample the audience underfoot while keeping their eyes turned ever heaven-wards."[77] In a special issue of the theological journal *Crosscurrents*, Björn Krondorfer noted that "I would describe my viewing experience as aesthetic and spiritual distress over having been exposed to prolonged scenes of graphic violence."[78] By emphasising the agony of Christ's final hours, Gibson effectively forced viewers to undergo an agony of their own, an agony of watching. Christians who believed that Christ was punished for their sins were afforded an extremely diluted punishment of their own, which was the source of the film's unusual power to edify *and* appall.

After Christ dies, his body is taken down from the cross and given to Mary, who suddenly looks into the camera and directly at the audience. Audience surveys quote at least one respondent who viewed this as a moment of accusation:

Then it hit me . . . my God . . . she is looking at me . . . accusing me??? I wanted to shout out 'I didn't do anything. It wasn't me. It wasn't my fault!' At that point it was like my soul was naked to the world and God saw all the sin I denied and hid and I realised it was my fault, and He did die for me. I could handle no more. I suspect feelings like these may be one reason people hated this movie. They don't want to accept the fact that we are all sinners who share in the responsibility for Christ's death.[79]

The viewer's reaction provides a very good illustration of the reaction that Gibson had set out to achieve. The respondent apparently felt that he or she had undergone a profoundly affecting spiritual experience, a view apparently shared by many other Christian audience members. The audience survey reported that "a significant number of Christian viewers considered *The Passion* to be a deeply personal and devotional experience rather than an intellectual exercise or mere entertainment."[80] To classify a cinematic experience of this nature we have to look seriously at the spiritual dimensions of the film. Far from being passive entertainment, *The Passion* offered Christians an engaging participatory experience that ultimately bears comparison to religious ritual.

According to the theologian John Lyden, religious rituals such as communion "make the religious realm visible in the world in a way that myth cannot."[81] Lyden argues that all religions provide adherents with a mythic vision of an ordered spiritual universe, in which their individual lives have a greater meaning. This ideal spiritual world is described in myths, legends and holy books, but religious ritual serves to turn such mythic visions of the universe into a concrete feature in the lives of adherents. Rituals are moments when the spiritual and the ordinary intersect, and by acting out rituals such as communion, Christians are actively engaging with the ideal spiritual world of Christianity. During communion, Christians respond to Christ's order, "Do this in memory of me" and thus enter into dialogue with their saviour. In the same way, confession is for Catholics a moment when the mysteries of Christianity become an active part of ordinary life. Sins are passed from the sinner to God. As Lyden puts it, ritual "is the 'doing' of religion, as critical to religious life as the beliefs and ideas expressed in mythology or theology. Essentially, each religion must be performed to become meaningful."[82]

The violent events of *The Passion* may not initially appear to be facets of an 'ideal' world. However, Christ's actions clearly present a vision of selfless Christian sacrifice, which embodies Christ and God's unconditional love for humanity, in accordance with the 'subjective' interpretation of the Passion. The film also provides a vision of God's triumph over Satan, in accordance with the 'Christus Victor' view. Finally, the scenes showing Christ's revival in the tomb demonstrate the ultimate reward of devotional Christianity in action. The resurrection of the body is assured, along with the vital 'substitutionary' interpretation of the Passion. Thus the film offers a direct connection to the events of the Passion and the principle ideals of the faith. These are made to seem physiologically *real* for viewers through the invocation of an agony that links to Christ's agony. In this way Gibson's film sought to make the spiritual world of Christianity accessible in a manner akin to ritual. He created an experience in which audiences were invited to suffer alongside Christ, thus gaining a more intimate understanding of the sacrifice he made. The film offered Christians of all denominations and levels of commitment a near physical and spiritual connection to their saviour.

In the final scenes, the ritual is concluded when the agony of Christ is explicitly linked to the more limited forms of agony offered to viewers. Gibson cuts from Mary cradling her son's body to the interior of Christ's tomb, and the audience is allowed to experience the resurrection from Christ's perspective. The door of the tomb is opened, and light floods in, revealing a suddenly vacated shroud. Then a resurrected Christ steps into view. The audience has missed seeing the central miracle of Christianity occur on screen by seconds. Christ has returned from the dead, and in the process his body has been remade, and all his wounds are gone, with one vital exception. When he stands we see the mark of the crucifixion on his palm. He appears contemplative, and when the uplifting, triumphal music reaches a climax, he strides purposefully into the light of day. At this point, the credits roll.

The scene carefully places viewers back alongside Christ and demands that onlookers reflect on their own agony just as Christ reflects on the purpose of his suffering. Viewers have been asked to experience a ritual of pain, complicity and guilt, but are, finally, offered redemption. Thus, cinemagoers are effectively 'forgiven' by being brought close to Christ and back into the fold of Christian salvation, in a manner that seems to link Christ's departure from his tomb to the audience's departure from the cinema. Christ bears the scars of his most significant spiritual endeavour, the crucifixion, but he is also renewed. In similar fashion viewers must now leave the darkened auditorium and return to their ordinary lives, albeit with a new, more intimate appreciation of what Christ 'did for them.' After seeing the film, one American viewer declared that "[We] should all see *The Passion* every year for the rest of our lives—lest we forget."[83] Arguably, this individual spoke for many viewers who had found the cinematic ritual offered in the film profoundly affecting. By expressing a desire to annually repeat the experience of watching the film, this one viewer seemed to suggest that *The Passion* had the potential to enter into the same field of association as other annual religious rituals.[84] Gibson and Icon evidently agreed, and a slightly edited version of *The Passion* was rereleased on a limited number of screens in Easter 2005.[85]

Conclusion

The Passion sets out to affect audiences by traumatising them with extended scenes of visceral suffering. Towards the end, onlookers in the movie theatre are identified as guilty observers, but the conclusion proffers forgiveness and redemption. Christ's sacrifice is authenticated, and in the process a transformative emotional experience is offered to viewers. Although other contemporary epics have been less overtly religious in terms of theme and setting, several have offered similar experiences. As we have seen, many contemporary epics have attempted to inspire feelings of 'indebtedness' or commemorative fervour in audiences. The epic film's defining feature, a narrative reconstruction of 'important' historical events, is often tied to a broader social agenda, a desire to change opinion and society. But do the other epics of the 1990s cycle also operate in the same 'ritualistic fashion' as Gibson's film? Could this be a new feature of the genre?

Key scenes in *Saving Private Ryan* are clearly designed to emphasise the brutal, shocking violence of warfare. Like the violence in *The Passion*, the opening scenes of mass killing on Omaha Beach are deeply disturbing, and were, as we have seen, viewed by critics as unprecedented in their realism and viscerality. Michael Hammond has argued that the sequence has the "intended affect of approximating war neurosis."[86] For Hammond, the violence of *Saving Private Ryan* is designed to instill in viewers a sense of shell shock, which links the experience of watching Spielberg's film to the real experiences of World War II veterans. Furthermore, the film is centred around a defining example of benevolent sacrifice. The greatest generation, represented onscreen by Miller and his men, are shown to be exemplars of ideal human virtue. Miller rescues Ryan but lays down his own life in the process. Viewers (represented onscreen by Ryan's family) are asked to leave the auditorium feeling that they, like Ryan, owe a great debt to the greatest generation, and that they should try and live up to the model of virtue presented in the film.

Schindler's List seeks to make the horrors of the Holocaust real for viewers in a related fashion. Sara R. Horowitz reports hearing an audience member saying, "Now I know it really happened" after watching the film.[87] In many shocking scenes, Spielberg focuses on the callous violence of the Nazis. Repeatedly, audiences are forced to watch Jews of all ages being murdered on a whim by Amon Goeth and his men. At the same time, the film offers a model of self-sacrificing benevolence in the form of Oskar Schindler, and in the climatic moments Schindler breaks down, realising just how much more he could have sacrificed to save a few more lives. The scene stresses Schindler's innate goodness, and also the guilt of those who have failed to act. It asks audiences to live up to the ideals that Schindler stands for, by bringing a proactive, interventionist attitude to the issues of the day. The film could therefore be said to offer a transformative experience through exposure to the Holocaust.

Although *Titanic* was more obviously designed to function as entertainment, the sinking of the ship is depicted in meticulous, exacting detail, and Rose's narrative is explicitly calculated to convey a sense of emotional reality. Viewers ultimately learn that Jack, the love of her life, sacrificed himself so that Rose might live. She tells her assembled listeners, "He saved me in all the ways a person can be saved." Jack is another ideal paradigm of self-sacrificing goodness, and the violent, spectacular destruction of the ship is carefully contrasted with the example of moral benevolence he sets. John C. Lyden claims that the popular success of *Titanic* was the result of its "'religious' power . . . to convey catharsis, hope, empathy and the value of independence to its audience."[88] In the conclusion, Rose is reunited with Jack in a scene that might be a dream, or a vision of the afterlife. It is made clear that Jack 'lives on' in Rose's memory, and the recollection of his sacrifice was a form of public remembrance for Rose.

The end of *Schindler's List* performs a similar function. Actors and their real-life counterparts are shown laying stones on the real Oskar Schindler's grave in the present, a long-standing Jewish tradition. Similar scenes of posthumous commemoration feature in the final scenes of *Saving Private Ryan*, which concludes in the veterans' cemetery. In each case, those who sacrificed themselves are shown to have a life beyond death, both as memories and as models of human virtue. As a result, their actions continue to resonate in the present and continue to require commemoration.

Each of these epics offers a powerful emotional experience. They all seek to make the past seem both visually and emotionally real, and they all depict ideal acts of human goodness. Whether or not they can also be described as rituals is unclear. Overt religious elements are not emphasised in any of these films, although they may be present in the background. *Schindler's List* opens with the Seder ritual, key scenes of *Saving Private Ryan* occur in a derelict church, and *Titanic* appears to conclude with a vision of the afterlife. Furthermore, none are biblical epics in the manner of *The Passion*, with an obvious religious significance. However, it should not be assumed that ritualistic religious power is intrinsic to the biblical epic, either. *The Prince of Egypt* tells a powerful story, but it is not a transformative emotional experience. Further work would be needed to establish how viewers responded to the biblical epics of the roadshow period, but there is little evidence to suggest that they were met with the tears and shock that greeted the films discussed above, including *The Passion*. Finally, not all contemporary epics offer such emotionally affecting visions of the past, although many try.

Ultimately, *The Passion* can be described as a ritual because the emotional experience it offers is located in a clear religious framework. The film was presented and received as an act of Christian devotion, and the transformative experience it offered was prescribed by preexisting interpretations of the crucifixion. However, *The Passion* builds on features that are present in other key historical epics of the contemporary period. Many of these films seek to provide an intellectual *and* emotional engagement with the past. Throughout this book, we have seen that epics invariably offer educational and edifying experiences. Filmmakers and audiences have been attracted to the epic film because it is overtly serious in ways that other film types are not. However, *The Passion* emphasises that epics also often have a great emotional power. It appears that the most artistically and financially successful epics are those that make the past seem 'emotionally real.'

In earlier chapters I sought to explain why the epic has been revived, but in this chapter I have hopefully suggested one model for understanding how the epic can affect viewers. Traditionally, epics seek to be bigger in all ways than other releases. The ritual elements of *The Passion* speak of the ambition at the core of the Hollywood historical epic. Gibson profoundly believed that his film could change lives. Like all epics, *The Passion* sought to be more than entertainment.

Notes

1. David Denby, "Nailed," *New Yorker* 1 Mar. 2004, 84 and 86.

2. Kenneth Turan, "A Narrow Vision and Staggering Violence," *Los Angeles Times* 24 Feb. 2004, Calendar, A1.

3. A. O. Scott, "Good and Evil Locked in Violent Showdown," *New York Times* 25 Feb. 2004, E1.

4. See, for example, Christopher Hitchens, "Schlock, Yes; Awe, No; Fascism, Probably," *Slate.com* 27 Feb. 2004, available at http://www.slate.msn.com/id/2096323, and John Dominic Crossan, "Hymn to a Savage God," in Kathleen E. Corley and Robert L. Webb, eds., *Jesus and Mel Gibson's The Passion of the Christ* (New York: Continuum, 2004), 8–27.

5. Financial data obtained from Box Office Mojo, http://www.boxofficemojo.com/movies/?id=passionofthechrist.htm; all-time chart obtained from the Internet Movie Database, http://www.uk.imdb.com/boxoffice/alltimegross.

6. See audiences responses in Robert H. Woods, Michael C. Jindra and Jason D. Baker, "The Audience Responds to *The Passion of the Christ*," in S. Brent Plate, ed., *Re-Viewing The Passion: Mel Gibson's Film and Its Critics* (New York: Palgrave-Macmillan, 2004), 170–171.

7. U.S. Census Bureau, *Statistical Abstract of the United States 2000*. Obtained via download from http://www.census.org.

8. Anon., "In the world of good and evil," *Economist* 16 Sept. 2006, 58.

9. Ibid.

10. Stephen Powers, David J. Rothman and Stanley Rothman, *Hollywood's America: Social and Political Themes in Motion Pictures* (Boulder, CO: Westview, 1996), 120.

11. Financial data obtained from Box Office Mojo, <http://www.boxofficemojo.com/movies/?id=lasttemptationofchrist.htm>.

12. See Robert Riley, *Film, Faith and Cultural Conflict: The Case of Martin Scorsese's The Last Temptation of Christ* (Westport, CT: Praeger, 2003); and Charles Lyons, *The New Censors: Movies and the Culture Wars* (Philadelphia: Temple University Press, 1997), 146–182.

13. Ibid., 24–33.

14. Heather Hendershot, "Waiting for the End of the World: Christian Apocalyptic Media at the Turn of the Millennium," in Jon Lewis, ed., *The End of Cinema as We Know It: American Film in the Nineties* (New York: New York University Press, 2001), 336.

15. Clearly there were other viewers, and certainly some would have been attracted entirely by the media furore surrounding the film.

16. Diane Sawyer's interview with Gibson was shown on "From Pain to Passion: A Prime-Time Event," *ABC News* 16 Feb. 2004.

17. Mel Gibson, quoted in Deborah Caldwell, "Selling Passion," in Jon Meacham et al., *Perspectives on* The Passion of the Christ (New York: Miramax, 2004), 216.

18. Gibson is quoted as saying this in Philip J. Boyer, "The Jesus War," *New Yorker* 15 Sept. 2003, 70. This and Deborah Caldwell's article are arguably the two most useful studies of the film for those interested in its production and marketing.

19. Icon was founded by Gibson in 1989, before his self-styled 'epiphany'. Nevertheless, both the name and logo of the company (a glowing medieval icon featuring the Virgin Mary) were designed to reflect Gibson's religious beliefs.

20. This was not a particularly unusual strategy for Icon, which had been successful enough in the past to fund certain projects independently. Indeed, the mission statement on their Web site claims, "Unlike many other independents, Icon internally funds most of its development and packaging cost, allowing it to retain creative control of its projects through production," available via http://www.iconmovies.us.

21. For details on the relationship between Icon and Newmarket, and more discussion of Newmarket's releases, see Lynn Hirschberg, "The Hard Sell," *Sunday Telegraph* 22 Jan. 2005, 49–51.

22. Mel Gibson, quoted in Gary Younge, "Bloodthirsty or a Classic?" *The Guardian* 4 Aug. 2004, 16.

23. Caldwell, 216.

24. Christopher Noxon, "Is the Pope Catholic Enough?" *New York Times Magazine* 9 Mar. 2003, 60.

25. The Second Vatican Ecumenical Council was held intermittently between 1962 and 1965. For details of the wide-ranging changes in the faith that it brought about see Timothy Walch, *Catholicism in America* (Malabar, FL: Robert E. Kreiger, 1989), 89–92.

26. This account of the ad-hoc scholars group, Gibson's reaction and subsequent media furore is all taken from Boyer's article in the *New Yorker*. The full report can be found in Mary C. Boys et al., "Ad Hoc Scholars Report," in Meacham et al., 225–254.

27. Much has been written on this aspect of the film. See Marvin Perry and Frederick M. Schweitzer, "The Medieval Passion Play Revisited," in Plate, 3–20.

28. Full details of the Vatican's prohibitions can be found in Boys et al., 225–254.

29. See Boys et al., 225–254.

30. See Pamela McClintock, "Passion is a news sensation," *Variety* 13 Apr. 2004, unpaginated, obtained from http://www.variety.com/article/VR1117903140.

31. This account of the film's marketing is all drawn from Caldwell, 211–224.

32. Boyer, 68.

33. Billy Graham, quoted in Robert K. Johnston, "*The Passion* as Dynamic Icon: A Theological Perspective," in Plate, 58.

34. See Anon., "Passion gets pass from Pope," *Variety* 18 Dec. 2003, unpaginated, obtained from http://www.variety.com/article/VR1117897281.

35. For details of this material, and its intended function, see Caldwell, 220.

36. Ibid.

37. James Davison Hunter, *Culture Wars: The Struggle to Define America* (New York: Basic, 1991), 67–108. For a detailed study of popular opinion during the 1960s, see William G. Mayer, *The Changing American Mind: How and Why American Public Opinion Changed between 1960 and 1988* (Ann Arbor: University of Michigan Press, 1993), and, for a specific account of attitudes during the late 1960s, see Daniel Yankelovich, *The New Morality: A Profile of American Youth in the 1970s* (New York: McGraw-Hill, 1974), 3–11.

38. Sara Diamond, *Roads to Dominion: Right Wing Movements and Political Power in the United States* (New York: Guildford, 1995), 109–204.

39. Hunter, 90.

40. In this way, critiques of the media that originate on the extreme right often bear close comparison to leftist critiques of ideology and mass culture. See Joanne Hollows, "Mass Culture Theory and Political Economy," in Joanne Hollows and Mark Jancovich, eds., *Approaches to Popular Film* (Manchester: Manchester University Press, 1995), 33.

41. Quoted in Thomas Frank, *What's the Matter with America? The Resistible Rise of the American Right* (London: Secker and Warburg, 2004), 2.

42. For a detailed overview of the emergence and deployment of the term 'culture wars,' see Lyons (1997), 1–25.

43. Michael Medved, *Hollywood vs. America: Popular Culture and the War on Traditional Values* (New York: HarperCollins, 1992), 3.

44. Similar work has been carried out in Powers, Rothman and Rothman (1996).

45. William D. Romanowski, *Pop Culture Wars: Religion and the Role of Entertainment in American Life* (Downer's Grove, IL: Intervarsity, 1996), 15.

46. All sources quoted in Romanowski, 16.

47. Hunter, 48.

48. Ibid., xi.

49. Medved, 210 and 229.

50. Ibid., 187.

51. Medved even observes that Gibson was an acquaintance whose apparently devout private life was at odds with the film roles that Medved criticised. See Medved, 229.

52. The film grossed $24.8 million domestically, see Box Office Mojo, http://www. boxofficemojo. com/movies/?id=manwithoutaface.htm.

53. Financial data obtained from Box Office Mojo, http://www.boxofficemojo.com/ movies/?id=braveheart.htm.

54. Mark Glancy, "The War of Independence in Feature Films: *The Patriot* (2000) and the 'Special Relationship' between Hollywood and Britain," *Historical Journal of Film, Radio and Television* 25, no. 4 (Oct. 2005), 533–534.

55. Caldwell, 215.

56. Such as http://www.supportmelgibson.com and http://www.seethepassion.com.

57. Woods, Jindra and Baker, 170.

58. Carl DiOrio, "Passion breaks B.O. mark," *Variety* 2 Mar. 2004, unpaginated, obtained from http://www.variety.com/ article/VR1117901039.

59. See Hirschberg, 49.

60. This entire paragraph is drawn, and sometimes paraphrased, from Robert K. Johnston, 60–65.

61. I use the somewhat controversial term 'Old Testament' rather than 'Hebrew Bible' simply because it is part of the common Christian lingua franca—which, of course, reveals the extent to which the linguistic 'norms' of Christianity include troubling dismissals of Judaism as a matter of orthodoxy.

62. The 80 percent claim comes from John Dominic Crossan, "Hymn to a Savage God," in Corley and Webb, 12. Crossan's article is perhaps the best of the critiques produced by 'historical Jesus' scholars, and provides a comprehensive exploration of what the reliance on Emmerich means for the film.

63. See Gaye W. Ortiz, "'Passion'-ate Women: The Female Presence in *The Passion of the Christ*," in Plate, 115–117.

64. Mel Gibson, quoted in Mark Allen Powel, "Satan and the Demons," in Corley and Webb, 73.

65. Of course, the presence of Satan can have exactly the opposite effect on nonbelievers.

66. Jon Meacham, "Who Really Killed Jesus?" in Meacham et al., 7.

67. Ortiz, 117–119.

68. It is unclear why Gibson uses the spelling 'Caiphas', rather than the more usual 'Caiaphas', in the film's subtitles.

69. See E. P. Saunders, *The Historical Figure of Jesus* (New York: Penguin, 1995), 16–22, as well as Mark Allen Powell, *Jesus as a Figure in History: How Modern Historians View the Man from Galilee* (Louisville, KY: Westminster John Knox, 1998).

70. For a detailed historical overview of the various Christian groups in America, from fundamentalists to liberal Episcopalians, see Steve Bruce, *Pray TV: Televangelism in America* (London: Routledge, 1990), 1–70.

71. See, for example, the many accounts defending the film by moderate theological scholars, which have appeared in academic journals and collections since 2004, such as the work of Robert K. Johnston, cited above.

72. I do not mean to excuse or refute anti-Semitism content in the film, only to suggest an alternate understanding of the film's meaning to audiences who genuinely seemed not to understand the complaint.

73. For an account of the history of the 'blood libel' see Marvin Perry and Frederick M. Schweitzer, "The Medieval Passion Play Revisited," in Plate, 4–5. For an account of Gibson's response, see Boyer, 67.

74. Linda Williams, *Hardcore: Power, Pleasure and the 'Frenzy of the Visible'* (London: Pandora, 1990), 5. Williams goes on to explain that these reactions "may seem like reflexes, but they are all culturally mediated." In effect, my own analysis of *The Passion* is an attempt to understand how and why such mediations occur within this particular film.

75. Susan Thistlewaite, "Mel Makes a War Movie," in Meacham et al., 144–145.

76. One survey of various Christian 'advisory Web sites' that rate and discuss the 'ethical content' of movies quoted a typical respondent who said, "The beatings and torture are very savage. . . . [A]t the very least parents should see this film before deciding whether to allow their children to attend. The rest of us, however, should all see *The Passion* every year for the rest of our lives." Anonymous respondent, quoted in Neal King, "Truth at Last: Evangelical Communities Embrace *The Passion of the Christ*," in Plate, 157.

77. Mark Kermode, rev. of *The Passion of the Christ*, *Sight and Sound* Apr. 2004, 63.

78. Björn Krondorfer, "Mel Gibson's Alter Ego: A Passion for Violence," *Crosscurrents* 54, no. 1 (Spring 2004), 20.

79. Woods, Jindra and Baker, 171.

80. Ibid.

81. John C. Lyden, *Film as Religion: Myths, Morals and Rituals* (New York: New York University Press, 2003), 79.

82. Ibid., 80.

83. Anonymous viewer, quoted in King, 157.

84. This reading can also be applied to the annual Easter telecast of *The Ten Commandments*, a less obviously ritualistic film in terms of structure, which nevertheless seems to have taken on ritual trappings in its life as a religious televisual experience. See Sumiko Higashi, "Antimodernism As Historical Representation in a Consumer Culture: Cecil B. DeMille's *The Ten Commandments*, 1923, 1956, 1993" in Vivian Sobchack, ed., *The Persistence of History: Cinema, Television and the Modern Event* (New York: Routledge, 1996), 107.

85. *The Passion Recut* had eight minutes of violence removed and was sold as a more 'family-friendly' although no less affecting, experience than the original. See details at Icon's Web site http://www.iconmovies.us.

86. Michael Hammond, "*Saving Private Ryan*'s 'Special Affect,'" ["Effect"? pls confirm] in Yvonne Tasker, ed., *Action and Adventure Cinema* (London: Routledge, 2004), 163.

87. Sara R Horowitz, "The Cinematic Triangulation of Jewish American Identity: Israel, America and the Holocaust," in Hilene Flanzbaum, ed., *The Americanization of the Holocaust* (Baltimore: John Hopkins University Press, 1999), 119.

88. Lyden, 178. Like many of Lyden's analyses, he is too vague in the application of his sterling theoretical work.

Conclusion:
The Epic in the Age of Shock and Awe

At the beginning of this book, I looked at the production of James Cameron's *Titanic* (1997) and asked three questions. The answers to these questions allow us to effectively plot the trajectory of the historical epic in American film culture since the end of the roadshow period. First I asked: Why were audiences ready to embrace an apparently 'old-fashioned' historical epic? The answer seems to be that although new generations have emerged, and the media environment has radically altered since the late 1960s, audiences have never really stopped seeking out historical epics. At the end of the roadshow era, epics became unprofitable as a result of overproduction rather than in response to a turnaround in audience tastes. Throughout the 1970s and 1980s, roadshow epics and historical epic miniseries thrived on television, providing new generations of film viewers with access to the epic. Furthermore, Cameron's film was not the first historical epic with close links to the roadshow period to be released in the 1990s. For viewers, *Titanic* was merely the latest in a series of occasional 'maverick epics,' many of which had been highly successful in America and overseas, even if the trade press did not recognise the popularity of the epic at the time of its release. Put simply, audiences of all ages were accustomed to historical epics as a production category and had been exposed to an increasing number at cinemas since the release of *Dances with Wolves* (1990).

Second I asked: Why was James Cameron so keen to produce a historical epic? Cameron was a baby boomer, and, like many members of his generation, the historical epic film had been presented to him when he was a young boy as the most educational, meaningful and resonant form of mainstream cinema that Hollywood had to offer. The historical epic came to occupy this privileged position in response to a complex series of shifts in creative lassitude, policy and industrial organisation after World War II, as we saw in chapter 1. By the late 1990s, Cameron was one of the most powerful and highly regarded mainstream filmmakers in contemporary Hollywood. With this maturity came a desire to tell meaningful stories about the past, which is not to say that Cameron's previous films had been in any way meaningless, but the epic has traditionally offered overt forms of historical comment, in contrast to the oblique resonances provided by other types of mainstream movie.

Cameron wanted to produce a serious film about the sinking of the *Titanic*, and his experiences as a baby boomer biased him towards the epic as a form of expression. In part, he may have hoped that *Titanic* would consolidate his legacy as a serious filmmaker, but he also clearly believed that contemporary audiences would benefit from an 'old-fashioned' historical epic, just as Cameron had benefited from similar movies in his youth. The narrational focus on young people in love was clearly designed to resonate with younger viewers, and Cameron's epic can clearly be perceived as an attempt to reconstitute the epic for a new generation.[1] This desire united many of the baby boomer filmmakers who unwittingly collaborated to bring about the revival of the epic in the 1990s. Ultimately, many filmmakers' fascination with the epic has been a product of their formative cinematic experiences.

Third, why was Twentieth Century Fox willing to fund *Titanic*? The film's $200-million budget may have been unprecedented, but it was representative of an increasing industrial willingness to fund historical epics in the mid-to-late 1990s. Prior maverick epics such as *Dances with Wolves*, *Schindler's List* (1993), *Forrest Gump* (1994) and *Braveheart* (1995) had been both critically and commercially successful. Cameron's film could therefore be perceived as a worthwhile investment. Fox was taking a risk, but it was a gamble that made sense if evaluated in the light of prior successful trends. Concerns expressed in the trade press were part of an industrial debate over whether or not Fox's gamble would pay off. When it did, a new stage in the revival of the epic was achieved.

After the release of *Titanic*, many more epics were put into production. None achieved the same degree of financial success at the theatrical box office, but the market had changed in subtle but substantial ways to ensure the longer term commercial viability of the genre. The widespread adoption of DVD technology, and the burgeoning importance of the overseas exhibition market, ensured the consolidation of the historical epic cycle. Fox's decision to green-light *Titanic* can retrospectively be understood as a wise investment. The extraordinary theatrical success of the film suggested that there was a massive, untapped market for epics. Arguably, DVD technology has made this market more accessible, thus diminishing the risk of overproduction that stymied the roadshow cycle.

This book has explained why contemporary filmmakers have been drawn back to the historical epic in the 1990s, and how the epic has become a regular feature of contemporary production schedules as a result. I hope my study has demonstrated that it is misleading to perceive mainstream Hollywood productions as purely driven by financial imperatives. After all, many filmmakers sought to produce epics in defiance of perceived industrial logic. The genre was never revived simply because it could make money. By the same token, epics are not frivolous spectacles designed to pacify or placate an undemanding public, nor is their meaning only accessible through critical conceptions of a collective public unconscious (although such readings are eminently valuable). Since the late 1940s, Hollywood filmmakers have used the epic film to examine the past, make sense of the present and debate the influence that historical events have had on contemporary society. This has remained a constituent feature of the genre even as the current cycle seemed to decline in popularity. In different ways, *Master and Commander: The Far Side of the World* (2003—hereafter *Master and Commander*), *King Arthur* (2004), *Alexander* (2004) and *Kingdom of Heaven* (2005) all offered visions of the past that addressed, with varying degrees of allegorical subtlety and success, the defining geopolitical events of the day. For epics released after 11 September 2001, the chief topic for debate could only be the '9/11' terrorist attacks in New York and America's subsequent 'war on terror.' Perhaps unsurprisingly, this most recent group of epics focused quite directly on the politics of empire and historical clashes between East and West.

Imperial ambitions have always been a key subject for historical epic films.[2] Many of the roadshow-era epics used either the ancient Roman empire or the nineteenth-century British empire as a narrational terrain where America's role in the twentieth century could be safely explored in allegory. Often, as Melani McAlister has argued, such films favourably contrasted America's "benevolent supremacy" during the Cold War with the active interventionist policies of older empires.[3] A similar preoccupation with the politics of empire can be seen at some level in many of the films discussed in this book. *Dances with Wolves* documents the subjugation and destruction of native cultures when white colonialists begin to penetrate the American West. Like almost all World War II films, *Schindler's List* and *Saving Private Ryan* occur against the backdrop of

Allied attempts to resist and avert German imperial ambitions. *Braveheart* told the story of Scottish natives combating the early English empire, while *The Prince of Egypt* depicted the trials of the Hebrews under imperial Egyptian rule. Although James Cameron's *Titanic* was not directly concerned with empire, the film nevertheless seemed to relate the sinking of the *Titanic* to the decline of nineteenth-century European empires in favour of American cultural dominance in the twentieth century.[4]

Like the roadshow epics on which it was based, *Gladiator* included some quite overt rumination on the morality of empire and democracy. However, without the Cold War frame that informed so many epics in the 1950s, *Gladiator's* political commentary never went beyond a fairly simplistic philosophical level (democracy = good/dictatorship = bad, freedom = good/empire = bad). By contrast, the epics made to capitalise on *Gladiator's* success were produced and released during a period of far greater political turmoil than any prior entries in the 1990s cycle. As we all know, the events of September 11th, 2001 gave way to wars in Afghanistan and Iraq, which have in turn ushered in an ever-worsening climate of international ill will, distrust and opposition. Suddenly, historical films about imperial warfare and invasion took on a degree of immediacy and significance that earlier epics could not match.

Consequently, the *New York Times* was keen to perceive Peter Weir's adaptation of Patrick O'Brian's seafaring novels, *Master and Commander* and *The Far Side of the World*, as a burning contemporary allegory. A. O. Scott noted, "It is tempting to read some contemporary geopolitical relevance into this film, which appears at a moment when some of the major English-speaking nations are joined in a military alliance against foes we sometimes need to be reminded are not French."[5] Interestingly, Scott's review clearly viewed the British ship as an allegorical surrogate for contemporary America, and he concluded, "It makes you wish Napoleon were still around, so we—that is, I mean, the British Empire—could beat him all over again."[6] Alternatively, Christopher Hitchens decried the film's adaptation for failing to provide a more rigorous intellectual debate about the morality of colonial wars, past and present.[7] The novel on which *Master and Commander* (Patrick O'Brian's *The Far Side of the World*) was principally based had been set during the War of 1812, and the story concerned an ongoing pursuit and battle with an American frigate. By contrast, Weir's film relocated the action to the Napoleonic Wars, which had pitted the putative American navy against the British. Presumably, the change was made to ensure that the film was more accessible to the American market, but it also helped to suggest British/American unity, and opposition to France, at a time when similar alliances were being forged over the war in Iraq. Furthermore, *Master and Commander* (in keeping with O'Brian's novels) presented the British Empire in relatively unproblematic terms—as a site of adventure and conflict but not as a philosophical or moral idea to be probed in the manner of many other epics. The French Empire, ruled by the despotic Napoleon, was assumed to be a malign force, but the British Empire was essentially benign.

Master and Commander was not the only film to present the history of empire as a relevant framework through which contemporary affairs could be understood. *King Arthur* transformed the medieval story of Arthur and his knights into a Dark Ages epic, which examined the impact of a declining Roman Empire in backwaters such as northern Britain. In the film, Roman characters are presented as imperial aggressors, and Arthur (Clive Owen) was reimagined as a Roman general with an initially firm commitment to Rome's civilising mission. However, when Arthur is exposed to the depths of Roman violence and corruption he decides to switch sides, joining the British resistance and going on to fight a successful guerrilla war against both Roman interests and 'Nazi-esque' Anglo-Saxon invaders. Thus, *King Arthur* eventually championed the rights of native peoples to resist non-native invaders, although it also seemed to suggest that it was appropriate for foreigners to assist in struggles of resistance, as long as they went home afterwards. Thus the film could be said to both critique and support similar forms of military action in the present. Nevertheless, it is significant that both *Master and Commander* and *King Arthur* presented their allegorical narratives quite directly in terms of empire. Throughout the twentieth century, it was extremely uncommon for ordinary Americans to perceive their country as an imperial power.[8] Since the events of September 11 and the invasion of Iraq, however, this relatively benign view of the USA's global role has been challenged by a number of prominent leftist thinkers stridently seeking to classify American foreign policy as aggressively imperialistic. While the opinions of the general population remain unclear, the allegorical preoccupation with empire visible in many post-2001 epic films sometimes seems to unquestioningly link current American military activities to actions of colonial aggressors in the past—thus taking sides in a highly partisan debate.

Such sentiments have been particularly visible in films depicting earlier examples of western military intervention in the Middle East, released in 2004/2005. Director Ridley Scott described *Kingdom of Heaven* as a highly relevant story that "should be very useful today . . .

in our post-9/11 world."[9] In the film, Orlando Bloom plays Balian, an iterant blacksmith turned knight, whose involvement with the Crusades gradually leads him to take control of Jerusalem on the eve of a climactic battle with Arab forces. Balian defends the city, but then brokers a truce with Arab forces and departs, leaving Jerusalem in Arab hands. His decision is quite clearly coded as a just and noble act, and the film even suggests that European scheming and aggression is directly responsible for radicalising the native Arabs. The film climaxes with an older Balian watching a new group of crusaders heading into the region to embark on yet another hopeless military escapade. Thus, *Kingdom of Heaven* incontrovertibly seems to suggest that western intervention in the Middle East is a grave error, in a manner that must be understood in relation to the current war in Iraq. Oliver Stone's *Alexander* tells the story of a conqueror whose imperial ambitions are not matched by his ability to maintain order amongst the people he subjugates. Repeatedly, Alexander (played by Colin Farrell) talks of liberating the people he invades; repeatedly, his men question the wisdom of an endless colonial war in a manner that seems to link Alexander's hubris to George W. Bush's attempts to 'liberate' the same peoples of Afghanistan and Iraq over 2,000 years later.

We should not assume that this recent subcycle of epics are entirely coherent or profound critiques of American foreign policy. Most are loosely critical of 'interventionism' in a general sense, but they also all seem to justify the ideals behind military action, even if the action itself is presented as pointless or malign. Nevertheless, even suggesting that the current war in Iraq, or the 'war on terror,' has parallels in the history of empire can be a politically partisan act. As ever, these epic films seek to wow audiences with spectacles of the past, but they can be also be understood as attempts to interpret the past and make sense of the present on the largest possible screen, with the greatest possible production resources. The current cycle of epics may have entered its terminal phases, but the genre continues to exist as a powerful and alluring idea, and, as many, many epics tell us, ideas are hard to kill.

Notes

1. For evidence of young people's responses to *Titanic*, see Dierdre Dolan, "New York's Streetwise Adolescents Drowning in their *Titanic* Tears," *New York Observer* 23 Feb. 1998, 12.

2. Brian Taves has argued that the focus on empire in a range of historical swashbucklers and adventure films works to dramatise the founding philosophies of American

identity. Clearly many epics perform a related function. See Brian Taves, *The Romance of Adventure: The Genre of Historical Adventure Movies* (Jackson: University Press of Mississippi, 1993), 223.

3. Melani McAlister, *Epic Encounters: Culture, Media and U.S. Interests in the Middle East* (Berkeley: University of California Press, 2001), 46.

4. A reading of the film made all the more obvious in the early script drafts quoted in the introduction.

5. A. O. Scott, "Master of the Sea (and the French)," *New York Times* 14 Nov. 2003, unpaginated, obtained from http://movies2.nytimes.com/mem/movies/review. html?title1=MASTER.

6. Ibid.

7. Christopher Hitchens, "Empire Falls," *Slate.com* 14 Nov. 2003, http://slate.msn. com/id/2091249.

8. Richard Crockatt, *America Embattled: September 11, Anti-Americanism and the Global Order* (London: Routledge, 2003), 24.

9. Ridley Scott, "When Worlds Collide," *Guardian* 29 Apr. 2005, Friday Review, 7.

Bibliography

1. Books, Articles and Reports

Adorno, Theodor W. *The Culture Industry: Selected Essays on Mass Culture.* London: Routledge, 1991.

Altman, Rick. *Film/Genre.* London: BFI, 1999.

Anderson, Christopher. *Hollywood TV: The Studio System in the Fifties.* Austin: University of Texas Press, 1994.

Andrew, Geoff. "Indian Bravery." *Time Out* 9 Jan. 1991.

Andrews, Lynn. *Medicine Woman.* New York: Harper and Row, 1981.

Anonymous. "Biblical Film Cycle Hits New High; 12 Upcoming." *Variety* 17 June 1953.

Anonymous. "DeMille Remake Recalls Silent Era; UA New Policy Set." Screen Section, *Los Angeles Times* 1 June 1952.

Anonmous. "Film Shorts." *Hollywood Reporter* 31 Jan. 1992.

Anonymous. "Major Stars Shine for NGS." *National Geographic* Aug. 2002.

Anonymous. "Passion gets pass from Pope." *Variety* 18 Dec. 2003.

Anonymous. "Prince Gets the Royal Treatment." *The Daily News, New York,* 13 Dec. 1998.

Anonymous. Review of *Lonesome Dove. Variety* 15 Feb. 1989.

Anonymous. "Spielberg Tells a Powerful Holocaust Tale." *Houston Chronicle* 15 Dec. 1994.

Anonymous. "Spielberg's War." *New York Times* 28 Jul. 1998.

Anonymous. "The Teachings of Chairman Jeff." *Variety* 24 Sept. 1990.

Anonymous. *U.S. Entertainment Industry: 2003 MPA Market Statistics,* obtained via application to http://www.mpaa.org/useconomicreview.

Ansen, David. Review of *Dances with Wolves*. *Newsweek* 19 Nov. 1990.

———. Review of *Saving Private Ryan*. *Newsweek* 13 Jul. 1998.

———. Review of *Schindler's List*. *Newsweek* 20 Dec. 1993.

Archerd, Army. "Just For Variety." *Variety* 23 Jul. 1998.

Arnold, Thomas K. "Older Audience Pass on Theatres." *USA Today* 4 Jul. 2005.

Arroyo, Jose, ed. *Action/Spectacle Cinema: A Sight and Sound Reader*. London: BFI, 2000.

Asbury, Herbert. *The Gangs of New York: An Informal History of the Underworld*. London: Arrow, 2002 (orig. pub. 1927).

Babington, Bruce, and Peter William Evans. *Biblical Epics: Sacred Narrative in the Hollywood Cinema*. Manchester: Manchester University Press, 1993.

Bach, Steven. *Final Cut: Dreams and Disaster in the Making of Heaven's Gate*. New York: Morrow, 1985.

Balio, Tino. *Grand Design: Hollywood as a Modern Business Enterprise, 1930–1939*. Berkeley: University of California Press, 1995.

Balio, Tino, ed. *The American Movie Industry*, rev. ed. Madison: University of Wisconsin Press, 1976.

———. "'A major presence in all of the world's important markets,' The globalisation of Hollywood in the 1990s," in Neale and Smith, 58–73.

———. "Hollywood Production Trends in the Era of Globalisation, 1990–99," in Neale (2002), 165–184.

———. "Retrenchment, Reappraisal and Reorganisation, 1948-" in Tino Balio, ed., *The American Movie Industry*, rev. ed. Madison: University of Wisconsin Press, 1985.

———. *United Artists: The Company Built by the Stars*. Madison: University of Wisconsin Press, 1976.

Ballard, J. G. *Empire of the Sun*. London: Flamingo, 1994.

Barker, Martin. *From* Antz *to* Titanic: *Reinventing Film Analysis*. London: Pluto, 2000.

Barnouw, Erik et al. *Conglomerates and the Media*. New York: The New Press, 1997.

Bart, Peter. *The Gross: The Hits, the Flops—The Summer that Ate Hollywood*. New York: St. Martin's Griffin, 2000.

———. "Tribute or Tribulation." *Variety* 17 Apr. 2000.

Baxter, John. *Steven Spielberg: The Unauthorised Biography*. London: HarperCollins, 1996.

Bayles, Martha. Review of *Lonesome Dove*. *Wall Street Journal* 6 Feb. 1989.

Beale, Lewis. "The Roman Empire Strikes Back." *Daily News, New York* 30 Apr. 2000.

Belton, John. *Widescreen Cinema*. Cambridge, MA: Harvard University Press, 1992.

Benson, Sheila. Review of *Dances with Wolves*. *Los Angeles Times* 9 Nov. 1990.

Bernard, Jami. Review of *Dances with Wolves*. *New York Post* 9 Nov. 1990.

Bernardoni, James. *The New Hollywood: What the Movies Did with the New Freedoms of the Seventies*. Jefferson, NC: McFarland, 1991.

Biskind, Peter. *Easy Riders, Raging Bulls: How the Sex, Drugs and Rock 'n' Roll Generation Saved Hollywood*. New York: Simon and Schuster, 1998.

Blake, Michael. *Dances with Wolves*. London: Penguin, 1991.

Bordwell, David. *Making Meaning*. Cambridge, MA: Harvard University Press, 1989.

——, with Janet Staiger and Kristin Thompson. *The Classical Hollywood Cinema: Film Style and Mode of Production to 1960*. London: Routledge, 1985.

Boyer, Philip J. "The Jesus War." *New Yorker* 15 Sept. 2003.

Boys, Mary C. et al. "Ad Hoc Scholars Report," in Meacham et al., 225–254.

Brantlinger, Patrick. *Bread and Circuses: Theories of Mass Culture as Social Decay*. Ithaca, NY: Cornell University Press, 1983.

Brodie, John. "Braveheart resurrects the epic." *Variety* 26 Mar. 1996.

——. "Oscar win vindicates kilt trip." *Variety* 1 Apr. 1996.

Brogan, Hugh. *The Penguin History of the USA*, 2nd ed. London: Penguin, 1999.

Brokaw, Tom. *The Greatest Generation*. New York: Delta, 1998.

——. *The Greatest Generation Speaks: Letters and Reflections*. New York: Delta, 2001.

Browne, Nick, ed. *Refiguring American Film Genres: History and Theory*. Berkeley: University of California Press, 1998.

Browning, Christopher R. *Nazi Policy, Jewish Workers, German Killers*. Cambridge: Cambridge University Press, 2000.

——. *The Origins of the Final Solution: The Evolution of Nazi Jewish Policy 1939–1942*. London: William Heineman, 2004.

Brownlow, Kevin. *David Lean, A Biography*. London: Richard Cohen, 1996.

Bruckheiner, Jerry. *Pearl Harbor: The Movie and Its Moment*. London: Boxtree, 2001.

Buckland, Warren. "The Role of the Auteur in the Age of the Blockbuster: Steven Spielberg and DreamWorks," in Julian Stringer, ed., *Movie Blockbusters*. London: Routledge, 2003.

Burleigh, Michael. *The Third Reich: A New History*. London: Pan Macmillan, 2000.

Caddies, Kelvin. *Kevin Costner: Prince of Hollywood*, rev. ed. London: Plexus, 1995.

Caldwell, Christopher. "Spielberg at War." *Commentary* 106, no. 4 (Oct. 1998): 48–52.

Caldwell, Deborah. "Selling Passion," in Meacham, 211–224.

Cameron, James. *Titanic: James Cameron's Illustrated Screenplay.* New York: HarperPerennial, 1997.

Cameron, Kenneth M. *America on Film: Hollywood and American History.* New York: Continuum, 1997.

Canby, Vincent. "For DeMille, Moses' Egypt really was America." *New York Times* 25 Mar. 1984.

———. "Saving a Nation's Pride of Being." *New York Times* 10 Aug. 1998.

Carnes, Mark C., ed. *Past Imperfect: History According to the Movies.* New York: Henry Holt, 1990.

Carter, Bill. "A Mini-Series Teaches ABC Hard Lessons." *New York Times* 8 May 1989.

Cartmell, D., ed. *Retrovisions: Reinventing the Past in Films and Fiction.* Sterling, VA: Pluto Press, 2001.

Castillo, Edward D. "Dances with Wolves." *Film Quarterly* 44 (1991): 14–22.

Caton, Steven S. *Lawrence of Arabia: A Film's Anthropology.* Berkeley: University of California Press, 1999.

Caulfield, Deborah. "And Other Relationships." *Los Angeles Times* 7 Mar. 1983.

Cawelti, John. *The Six-Gun Mystique.* Bowling Green, OH: Bowling Green University Press, 1971.

Chafe, William. *The Unfinished Journey,* 5th ed. Oxford: Oxford University Press 2003.

Cheshire, Godfrey. Review of *Gladiator, New York Press* 3 May 2000.

Cohen, Lizabeth. *A Consumer's Republic: The Politics of Mass Consumption in Postwar America.* London: Vintage, 2004.

Collins, Jim. "Genericity in the Nineties: Eclectic Irony and the New Sincerity" in Jim Collins, Hilary Radner and Ava Preacher Collins, eds. *Film Theory Goes to the Movies,* 242–264. London: Routledge, 1993.

Conant, Michael. *Antitrust in the Motion Picture Industry.* New York: Arno, 1978.

Cook, David O. *Lost Illusions: American Cinema in the Shadow of Watergate and Vietnam 1970–1979.* Berkeley: University of California Press, 2000.

Corley, Kathleen E., and Robert L. Webb. *Jesus and Mel Gibson's The Passion of the Christ.* New York: Continuum, 2004.

Costner, Kevin, Michael Blake and Jim Wilson. *Dances with Wolves: The Illustrated Story of the Epic Film.* New York: Newmarket, 1990.

Cox, Dan. "Dream Schemes, Pricey new studio ready to roll out first pix." *Variety* 18 Sept. 1997.

Coyne, Michael. *The Crowded Prairie: American National Identity in the Hollywood Western.* London: I.B. Tauris, 1997.

Creeber, Glen. *Serial Television: Big Drama on the Small Screen*. London: BFI, 2004.

Crockatt, Richard. *America Embattled: September 11, Anti-Americanism and the Global Order*. London: Routledge, 2003.

Crossan, John Dominic. "Hymn to a Savage God," in Corley and Webb, 8–27.

Crowther, Bosley. Review of *The Ten Commandments*. *New York Times* 9 Nov. 1956.

Cunningham, Philip. "Much will be required of the person entrusted with much: Assembling a Passion drama from the four gospels," in Meacham et al., 49–64.

Custen, George F. *Bio/Pics: How Hollywood Constructed Public History*. New Brunswick, NJ: Rutgers University Press, 1992.

Cyrino, Monica C. "*Gladiator* and Contemporary American Society," in Winkler (2004), 124–149.

Dale, Martin. *The Movie Game: The Film Business in Britain Europe and America*. London and New York: Cassell, 1997.

Davies, Natalie Zemon. *Slaves on Screen: Film and Historical Vision*. Cambridge, MA: Harvard University Press, 2000.

Davies, Serena. "Filmmakers on Film." *Daily Telegraph* 10 Jul. 2004.

Deloria, Philip J. *Playing Indian*. New Haven and London: Yale University Press, 1998.

DeMille, Cecil B., and Donald Hayne. *The Autobiography of Cecil B. DeMille*. London: W.H. Allen, 1960.

Denby, David. Review of *Dances with Wolves*. *New York* 19 Nov. 1990.

———. "Heroic Proportions." *New York* 27 Jul. 1998.

———. "Nailed." *New Yorker* 1 Mar. 2004.

———. "No Limit." *New Yorker* 3 Jul. 2000.

———. Review of *Schindler's List*. *New York* 13 Dec. 1993.

DeVany, Arthur. *Hollywood Economics: How Extreme Uncertainty Shapes the Film Industry*. London: Routledge, 2004.

Diamond, Sara. *Roads to Dominion: Right Wing Movements and Political Power in the United States*. New York: Guildford, 1995.

DiGiacomo, Frank. "Steven Ambrose Saves Spielberg's Butt." *New York Observer* 13 Jul. 1998.

DiOrio, Carl. "B.O. doesn't tell Samurai Tale." *Variety* 18 Jan. 2004.

———. "Passion breaks B.O. mark." *Variety* 2 Mar. 2004.

Dixon, Wheeler Winston, ed. *Film Genre 2000: New Critical Essays*. Albany: State University of New York Press, 2000.

———. "Twenty-Five Reasons Why It's All Over," in Lewis, 356–366.

Doherty, Thomas. "Saving Private Ryan." *Cineaste* 24, no. 1 (Winter 1998).

Doneson, Judith E. "The Image Lingers: The Feminisation of the Jew in *Schindler's List*," in Loshitzky, 140–152.

Dreyer, Rod. Review of *Saving Private Ryan*. *New York Post* 24 Jul. 1998.

———. "What 'Ryan' Teaches." *New York Post* 11 Jan. 1999.

Duke, Paul F. "D'Works: What Lies Beneath?" *Variety* 24 Jul. 2000.

Dunne, John Gregory. "Virtual Patriotism." *New Yorker* 16 Nov. 1998.

Ebert, Roger. Review of *Dances with Wolves*. *Chicago Sun-Times* 9 Nov. 1990.

Ehrenhaus, Peter. "Why We Fought: Holocaust Memory in Spielberg's *Saving Private Ryan*." *Critical Studies in Media Communication* 18, no. 3 (Sept. 2001): 321–337.

Eisner, Michael D., and Tony Schwartz. *Work in Progress*. London: Penguin Books, 1999.

Eldridge, David. *Hollywood's History Films*. London: I.B. Tauris, 2006.

Eller, Claudia. "Will *List* Speak for Itself?" *Los Angeles Times* 22 Nov. 1993.

Elley, Derek. *The Epic Film: Myth and History*. London: Routledge and Kegan Paul, 1984.

Elsaesser, Thomas. "The Blockbuster: Everything Connects but Not Everything Goes," in Lewis, 11–22.

———. "Subject Positions, Speaking Positions: From Holocaust, Our Hitler and Heimat to Shoah and Schindler's List," in Sobchack (1996), 145–186.

Elson, Jon. "Can *Saving Private Ryan* Save DreamWorks?" *New York Post*, 13 Jul. 1998.

Evans, Greg. "Orion creates epic pitch for *Dances with Wolves*." *Variety* 5 Nov. 1990.

Fabrikant, Geraldine, and Rick Lyman. "Dreaming in Tighter Focus." *The New York Times* 25 Sept. 2000.

Fensch, Thomas, ed. *Oskar Schindler and His List*. Forest Dale, VT: Paul S. Eriksson, 1995.

Field, Sid. *Four Screenplays: Studies in the American Screenplay*. New York: Dell, 1994.

Finler, Joel W. *The Hollywood Story*, 3rd ed. London: Wallflower, 2003.

Fleming, Charles. *High Concept: Don Simpson and the Hollywood Culture of Excess*. London: Bloomsbury, 1998.

Fleming, Michael. "DreamWorks logs Logan as Lincoln Scribe." *Variety* 5 Dec. 2001.

———. "Fantastic Voyage." *Movieline* Dec. 1997.

———. "Hits offer up new H'wood history lesson." *Variety* 19 Apr. 2001.

Fleming, Michael, and Andrew Hindes. "Crowe girding for *Gladiator*." *Variety* 11 Sept. 1998.

———. and Claude Brodesser. "U ready to explore 'Clark and Lewis' pic." *Variety* 10 Sept. 2004.

Foucault, Michel. *Discipline and Punish: The Birth of the Prison.* New York: Vintage, 1979.

Fradley, Martin. "Maximus Melodramaticus: Masculinity, masochism and white male paranoia in contemporary Hollywood cinema," in Tasker, 235–251.

Frank, Thomas. *What's the Matter with America? The Resistible Rise of the American Right.* London: Secker and Warburg, 2004.

Fraser, George MacDonald. *The Hollywood History of the World: From* One Million Years B.C. *to* Apocalypse Now. New York: Beech Tree Books, 1988.

Friedman, Lester D. *The Jewish Image in American Film.* Secaucus, NJ: Citadel, 1987.

Friedman, Lester D., and Brent Notbohm, eds. *Steven Spielberg: Interviews.* Jackson: University Press of Mississippi, 2000.

Gabbard, Krin. "Saving Private Ryan Too Late," in Lewis, 131–140.

Galloway, Stephen. "Big Pictures: Sword and sandals films are back in style." *Hollywood Reporter* 1 Oct. 2002.

Glancy, Mark. "The War of Independence in Feature Films: *The Patriot* (2000) and the 'Special Relationship' between Hollywood and Britain," in *Historical Journal of Film, Radio, and Television* 25, no. 4 (Oct. 2005).

Goldhagen, Daniel Jonah. *Hitler's Willing Executioners: Ordinary Germans and the Holocaust.* London: Abacus, 1997.

Goldsmith, Jill, and Carl DiOrio. "Mike Slipped a Mickey." *Variety* 4 Mar. 2004.

Gomery, Douglas. *Film History: Theory and Practice.* New York: Knopf, 1985.

———. "The Hollywood Blockbuster: Industrial Analysis and Practice," in Stringer, 72–83.

———. *Shared Pleasures: A History of Movie Presentation in the United States.* London: BFI, 1992.

Goodridge, Mike. "Selling Private Ryan." *Screen International* 24 Jul. 1998.

Graser, Marc. "H'w'd's New Toga Party." *Variety* 1 Sept. 2002.

Grindon, Leger. *Shadows on the Past: Studies in the Historical Fiction Film.* Philadelphia, PA: Temple University Press, 1994.

Gritten, David. "Grim. Black and White . . . Spielberg?" *Los Angeles Times,* Calendar, 9 May 1993.

Gross, Larry. "Big and Loud," in Arroyo, 3–8.

Grover, Ron. *The Disney Touch: Disney, ABC and the Quest for the World's Greatest Media Empire,* rev. ed. New York: McGraw-Hill, 1997.

Guider, Elizabeth. "Mel passionate about pic's positive message." *Variety* 25 Feb. 2004.

Gunbel, Andrew. "How Spielberg's D-Day hit movie was secretly hyped." *Independent on Sunday* 2 Aug. 1998.

Gutman, Roy. "Like Auschwitz." *Newsday* 21 July 1992.

Gutman, Yisrael. "The Response of Polish Jewry to the Final Solution," in David Cesarani, ed., *The Final Solution: Origins and Implementation*, 151–158. London: Routledge, 1994.

Haley, Alex. *Roots*. London: Hutchinson, 1977.

Hall, Sheldon. *Hard Ticket Giants: Hollywood Blockbusters in the Widescreen Era*. Ph.D. dissertation, University of East Anglia, 2000.

———. "*How the West Was Won*: History, Spectacle and the American Mountains," in Ian Cameron and Douglas Pye, eds., *The Book of Westerns*, 255–261. New York: Continuum, 1996.

———. "Tall Revenue Features: The Genealogy of the Modern Blockbuster," in Neale (2002), 11–26.

Hamilton, Neil A. *Atlas of the Baby Boom Generation: A Cultural History of Postwar America*. New York: Macmillan, 2000.

Hammond, Michael. "*Saving Private Ryan*'s 'Special Affect," in Tasker, 153–166.

———. "Some Smothering Dreams: The Combat Film in Contemporary Hollywood," in Neale (2002), 62–76.

Hasian, Jr., Marouf. "Nostalgic Longings, Memories of the Good War, and Cinematic representations in *Saving Private Ryan*." *Critical Studies in Media Communication* 18, no. 3 (Sept. 2001): 338–358.

Hayes, Dade. "Pricey, dicey pix." *Variety* 5 May 2000.

———. "So how does the Dream Work?" *Variety* 10 Jul. 2002.

———. "Super-Size *Pearl* pushes time limit." *Variety* 4 Jun. 2001.

Heard, Christopher. *Dreaming Aloud: The Life and Films of James Cameron*, rev. ed. Ontario: Doubleday, 1998.

Higashi, Sumiko. "Antimodernism as Historical Representation in a Consumer Culture: Cecil B DeMille's *The Ten Commandments*, 1923, 1956, 1993," in Sobchack (1996), 92–112.

———. *Cecil B. DeMille: A Guide to References and Resources*. Boston, MA: G.K. Hall, 1985.

Higgins, Bill. "Ryan Leaves Them Speechless." *Los Angeles Times*, 23 Jul. 1998.

Higson, Andrew. *English Heritage, English Cinema: Costume Drama Since 1980*. Oxford: Oxford University Press, 2003.

Hindes, Andrew. "'Private Ryan' Saving Grace." *Variety* 20 Jul. 1998.

———. "Studio Report Card 1998: DreamWorks." *Variety* 12 Jan. 1999.

———. "U suits up for D'Works Gladiator." *Variety* 13 Nov. 1998.

Hindes, Andrew, and Dan Cox. "Antz Colony Cranks It Up." *Variety*, 19 Oct. 1998.

Hirsch, Foster. *The Hollywood Epic*. South Brunswick, NJ: Barnes, 1978.

Hirschberg, Lynn. "The Hard Sell." *Sunday Telegraph* 22 Jan. 2005.

Hitchens, Christopher. "Schlock, Yes; Awe, No; Fascism, Probably." *Slate.com* 27 Feb. 2004, http://www.slate.msn.com/id/2096323.

Hoberman, J. *The Dream Life: Movies, Media and the Mythology of the Sixties.* New York: New Press, 2003.

———. Review of *Dances with Wolves. Village Voice* 20 Nov. 1990.

———. Review of *Forrest Gump. Village Voice* 12 Jul. 1994.

———. Review of *The Prince of Egypt. Village Voice* 22 Dec. 1998.

———. Review of *Schindler's List. Village Voice* 21 Dec. 1993.

Hoberman, J., et al. "Schindler's List: Myth, Movie and Memory." *Village Voice* 29 Mar. 1994.

Holden, Steven. "Far From Gettysburg, A Heartland Torn Apart." *New York Times* 24 Nov. 1999.

Hopp, Glenn. *Videohound's Epics: Giants of the Big Screen.* Detroit, MI: Visible Ink, 1999.

Horowitz, Sara R. "The Cinematic Triangulation of Jewish American Identity: Israel, American and the Holocaust," in Hilene Flanzbaum, ed., *The Americanization of the Holocaust*, 142–168. Baltimore, MD: Johns Hopkins University Press, 1999.

Howe, Neil, and William Strauss. *Millennials Rising: The Next Great Generation.* New York: Vintage, 2000.

Huhndorf, Shari M. *Going Native: Indians in the American Cultural Imagination.* Ithaca, NY, and London: Cornell University Press, 2001.

Hunt, Leon. "What Are Big Boys Made of? *Spartacus, El Cid* and the Male Epic," in Pat Kirkham and Janet Thumin, eds., *You Tarzan: Masculinity, Movies and Men*, 65–83. London: Lawrence and Wishart, 1993.

Jameson, Fredric. *Postmodernism, The Cultural Language of Late Capitalism.* Durham, NC: Duke University Press, 1990.

———. *Signatures of the Visible.* New York: Routledge, 1992.

Jancovich, Mark. "Dwight MacDonald and the Historical Epic," in Tasker, 84–99.

———. "Genre and the Audience: Genre Classifications and Cultural Distinctions in the Mediation of *The Silence of the Lambs*," in Melvin Stokes and Richard Maltby, eds., *Hollywood Spectatorship: Changing Perceptions of Cinema Audiences.* London: BFI, 2001, 33–45.

Johnson, Dirk. "Spiritual Seekers Borrow Indian Ways." *New York Times*, 27 Dec. 1993.

Jonston, Robert K. "*The Passion* as Dynamic Icon: A Theological Perspective," in Plate, 55–70.

Jowett, Garth. *Film: The Democratic Art.* Boston: Little Brown, 1976.

Kael, Pauline. "What's wrong with filmmakers." *Chicago Sun-Times* 13 March 1977.

Kasdan, Margo, and Susan Tavernetti. "Native Americans in a Revisionist Western," in Peter C. Rollins and John E. O'Connor, eds., *Hollywood's Indian: The Portrayal of the Native American in Film*, 121–136. Lexington: University Press of Kentucky, 1998.

Kauffman, Stanley. "War; and More." *The New Republic* 17 Aug. 1998.

Keane, Stephen. *Disaster Movies: The Cinema of Catastrophe*. London: Wallflower, 2001.

Keith, Todd. *Kevin Costner: The Unauthorised Biography*. London: Ikonprint, 1991.

Keller, James. "Masculinity and Marginality in *Rob Roy* and *Braveheart*." *Journal of Popular Film and Television* 24, no. 4 (Winter 1997): 146–154.

Keneally, Thomas. *Schindler's Ark*. London: Hodder and Stoughton, 1982.

Kermode, Mark. Review of *The Passion of the Christ. Sight and Sound* Apr. 2004.

King, Geoff. *New Hollywood Cinema: An Introduction*. London: I.B. Tauris, 2002.

———. *Spectacular Narratives: Hollywood in the Age of the Blockbuster*. London and New York: I.B. Tauris, 2000.

King, Neal. "Truth at Last: Evangelical Communities Embrace *The Passion of the Christ*," in Plate, 151–162.

King, Tom. *David Geffen: A Biography of New Hollywood*. London: Random House, 2000.

Klein, Herbert S. *A Population History of the United States*. Cambridge: Cambridge University Press, 2004.

Kodat, Catherine Gunther. "Saving Private Property: Steven Spielberg's American DreamWorks," in *Representations* 71 (Summer 2000): 77–105.

Kolker, Robert. *A Cinema of Loneliness: Penn, Stone, Kubrick, Scorsese, Spielberg, Altman*, 3rd ed. Oxford: Oxford University Press, 2003.

Krämer, Peter. "'The Best Disney Film Disney Never Made': Children's Films and the Family Audience in American Cinema Since the 1960s," in Neale (2002), 185–200.

———. "'It's aimed at kids—the kid in everybody': George Lucas, *Star Wars* and children's entertainment," in Tasker, 358–370.

———. *The New Hollywood: From* Bonnie and Clyde *to* Star Wars. London: Wallflower, 2005.

———. "Post Classical Hollywood" in John Hill and Pamela Church Gibson, *The Oxford Guide to Film Studies*, 289–309. Oxford: Oxford University Press, 1998.

———. "'Would you take your child to see this film?' The cultural and social work of the family adventure movie," in Neale and Smith, 294–311.

Krutnik, Frank. *In a Lonely Street: Film Noir, Genre and Masculinity*. London: Routledge, 1991.

Landy, Marcia. *Cinematic Uses of the Past*. Minneapolis: University of Minnesota Press, 1996.

———, ed. *The Historical Film: History and Memory in Media*. New Brunswick, NJ: Rutgers University Press, 2001.

Lev, Peter. *Transforming the Screen, 1950–1959*. New York: Scribner's, 2003.

———. *American Films of the' 70s: Conflicting Visions*. Austin: University of Texas Press, 2000.

Levy, Emanuel. *Oscar Fever: The History and Politics of the Academy Awards*. New York: Continuum, 2001.

Lewis, Jon, ed. *The End of Cinema as We Know It: American Film in the Nineties*. New York: New York University Press, 2001.

Litwak, Mark. *Reel Power: The Struggle for Influence and Success in the New Hollywood*. Los Angeles: Silman James, 1986.

Loshitzky, Yosefa. "National Rebirth as a Movie: Otto Preminger's *Exodus*." *National Identities* 4, no. 2 (2002): 119–131.

———, ed. *Spielberg's Holocaust: Critical Perspectives on Schindler's List*. Bloomington: Indiana University Press, 1997.

Lovell, Alan, and Gianluca Sergi. *Making Films in Contemporary Hollywood*. London: Hodder Arnold, 2005.

Lowry, Brian. Review of *Braveheart*. *Variety* 22 May 1995.

Lubin, David M. *Titanic*. London: BFI Publishing, 1999.

Lyden, John C. *Film as Religion: Myths, Morals and Rituals*. New York: New York University Press, 2003.

Lyman, Rick. "At the movies." *New York Times* 23 Jun. 2000.

———. "Into Summer With a Roar." *New York Times* 25 May 2001.

Lyons, Charles. *The New Censors: Movies and the Culture Wars*. Philadelphia: Temple University Press, 1997.

Madigan, Nick. "Studio Report Card 1997: DreamWorks." *Variety* 12 Jan. 1998.

Maeder, Edward, ed. *Hollywood and History: Costume Design in Film*. Los Angeles: Los Angeles County Museum, 1987.

Malone, M. S. Review of *Dances with Wolves*. *Christian Science Monitor*, 7 Dec. 1990.

Maltby, Richard. *Hollywood Cinema*, 2nd ed. Oxford: Blackwell, 2003.

———. "'Nobody Knows Everything': Post classical histriographies and consolidated entertainment," in Neale and Smith, 21–44.

Mancunovich, Diane J. *Birth Quake: The Baby Boom and Its Aftershocks*. Chicago: University of Chicago Press, 2002.

Marcus, Daniel. *Happy Days and Wonder Years: The Fifties and Sixties in Contemporary Cultural Politics*. New Brunswick, NJ: Rutgers University Press, 2004.

Marks, Clifford J., and Robert Torry. "'Herr Direktor': Biography and Autobiography in *Schindler's List*." *Biography* 23, no. 1 (Winter 2000): 49–70.

Marsh, Ed. *James Cameron's Titanic*. New York: HarperPerennial, 1997.

Maslin, Janet. "Target: Boomers and Their Babies." *New York Times* 24 Nov. 1991.

Masters, Kim. *The Keys to the Kingdom: How Michael Eisner lost his grip.* New York: HarperCollins, 2000.

Matthews, Jack. Review of *The Prince of Egypt. Newsday* 18 Dec. 1998.

———. Review of *Schindler's List. Newsday* 15 Dec. 1993.

Mayer, William G. *The Changing American Mind: How and Why American Public Opinion Changed between 1960 and 1988.* Ann Arbor: University of Michigan Press, 1993.

McAlister, Melani. *Epic Encounters: Culture, Media and U.S. Interests in the Middle East.* Berkeley: University of California Press, 2001.

McBride, Joseph. *Steven Spielberg: A Biography.* London: Faber and Faber, 1997.

McCarthy, Todd. Review of *Gangs of New York. Variety* 5 Dec. 2002.

———. Review of *Gladiator. Variety* 24 Apr. 2000.

———. Review of *The Patriot. Variety* 16 Jun. 2000.

———. Review of *Saving Private Ryan. Variety* 20 Jul. 1998.

———. Review of *Schindler's List.Variety* 13 Dec. 1993.

McClintock, Pamela. "Passion is a news sensation." *Variety* 13 Apr. 2004.

McDonald, William. "Long Delayed Lessons about Fathers at War." *New York Times* 26 Jul. 1998.

McGaa, Ed. *Rainbow Tribe: Ordinary People Journeying the Red Road.* San Francisco, CA: Harpercollins, 1992.

Meacham, Jon et al. *Perspectives on* The Passion of the Christ. New York: Miramax, 2004.

———. "Who Really Killed Jesus?" in Meacham et al., 1–16.

Medavoy, Mike, and Josh Young. *You're Only as Good as Your Next One: 100 Great Films, 100 Good Films and 100 for Which I Should Be Shot.* New York: Atria, 2002.

Medved, Michael. *Hollywood vs. America: Popular Culture and the War on Traditional Values.* New York: HarperCollins, 1992.

Miller, Douglas T., and Marion Novak. "The Precarious Prosperity of People's Capitalism," in Robert Griffith, ed., *Major Problems in American History Since 1945: Documents and Essays*, 213–226. Lexington, MA: D.C. Heath, 1992.

Mintz, Alan. *Popular Culture and the Shaping of Holocaust Memory in America.* Seattle: University of Washington Press, 2001.

Mitchell, Elvis. "A Gentle Farmer Who's Good at Violence." *New York Times* 28 Jun. 2000.

Monaco, Paul. *The Sixties: 1960–1969.* New York: Scribner's, 2001.

Morris, Mark. Review of *Gladiator. Observer* 23 Apr. 2000.

Mosley, Leonard. *Zanuck: The Rise and Fall of Hollywood's Last Tycoon*. London: Granada, 1984.

Musser, Charles. "The Travel Genre in 1903–1904: Moving Towards a Fictional Narrative," in Thomas Elsaesser, ed., *Early Cinema: Space, Frame, Narrative*. London: BFI, 1990.

Myles, Linda, and Michael Pye. *The Movie Brats: How the Film Generation Took Over Hollywood*. London: Faber and Faber, 1979.

Nadel, Alan. *Flatlining on the Field of Dreams: Cultural Narratives in the Films of President Reagan's America*. New Brunswick, NJ: Rutgers University Press, 1997.

———. "God's Law and the Wide Screen: *The Ten Commandments* as Cold War 'Epic.'" *PMLA* 108, no. 10 (1993).

Nagorski, Andrew. "Spielberg's Risk." *Newsweek* 24 May 1993.

Neale, Steve. *Genre*. London: BFI Publishing, 1980.

———. *Genre and Hollywood*. London: Routledge, 2000.

———. "Westerns and Gangster Films Since the 1970s," in Neale (2002), 27–47.

———, ed. *Genre and Contemporary Hollywood*. London: BFI, 2002.

Neale, Steve, and Murray Smith, eds. *Contemporary Hollywood Cinema*. London: Routledge, 1998.

Neve, Brian. *Film and Politics in America: A Social Tradition*. London: Routledge, 1992.

Novick, Peter. *The Holocaust and Collective Memory*. London: Bloomsbury, 1999.

Noxon, Christopher. "Is the Pope Catholic Enough?" *New York Times* 9 Mar. 2003.

———. "The Roman Empire Rises Again." *Los Angeles Times* 23 Apr. 2000.

O'Donoghue, K. S. "Memorial to WWII on Track." *Houston Chronicle* 1 Jul. 1999.

Ondaatje, Michael. *The English Patient*. London: Bloomsbury, 1992.

Ortiz, Gaye W. "'Passion'-ate Women: The Female Presence in *The Passion of the Christ*," in Plate, 109–120.

Palowski, Franciszek. *Witness: The Making of Schindler's List*, trans. Anna and Robert G. Ware. London: Orion, 1999.

Parisi, Paula. Titanic *and the Making of James Cameron*. London: Orion, 1999.

Parks, Walter, and Ridley Scott. *Gladiator: The Making of the Ridley Scott Epic*. London: Boxtree, 2000.

Pauly, Thoms H. "The Way to Salvation: The Hollywood Blockbuster of the 1950s." *Prospects: An Annual of American Cultural Studies* 5 (1980): 467–487.

People Magazine. *The 2001 People Entertainment Almanac*. New York: Cader, 2000.

Perlez, Jane. "Spielberg grapples with the Horror of the Holocaust." *New York Times* 13 Jun. 1993.

Perry, George. *Steven Spielberg: The Making of His Movies*. London: Orion, 1998.

Perry, Marvin, and Frederick M. Schweitzer. "The Medieval Passion Play Revisited," in Plate, 3–20.

Pizello, Stephen. "Five-Star General." *American Cinematographer* Aug. 1998.

Plate, S. Brent, ed. *Re-viewing The Passion: Mel Gibson's Film and Its Critics*. New York: Palgrave-Macmillan, 2004.

Powell, Mark Allen. *Jesus as a Figure in History: How Modern Historians View the Man from Galilee*. Louisville, KY: Westminster John Knox, 1998.

———. "Satan and the Demons," in Corley and Webb, 71–78.

Power, Samantha. *"A Problem From Hell." America in the Age of Genocide*. London: Flamingo, 2002.

Powers, Stephen, David J. Rothman and Stanley Rothman. *Hollywood's America: Social and Political Themes in Motion Pictures*. Boulder, CO: Westview, 1996.

Pratley, Gerald. *The Cinema of David Lean*. South Brunswick, NJ, and New York: A.S. Barnes, 1974.

Prince, Stephen. *A New Pot of Gold: Hollywood Under the Electronic Rainbow, 1980–1989*. Berkeley: University of California Press, 2000.

———. *Visions of Empire: Political Imagery in Contemporary American Film*. New York: Praeger, 1992.

Puttnam, Robert D. *Bowling Alone: The Collapse and Revival of American Community*. New York: Touchstone, 2000.

Rafferty, Terrence. "A Man of Transactions." *New Yorker* 20 Dec. 1993.

Rainer, Peter. "The Epic, an Endangered Species." *Los Angeles Times* 11 Mar. 1990.

Reardon, Barry D. "The Studio Distributor," in Jason E. Squire, ed., *The Movie Business Book*, 2nd ed. London: Fireside, 1992.

Redfield, James. *The Celestine Prophecies: An Adventure*. New York: Warner 1993.

Reed, Joseph W. *American Scenarios: The Uses of Film Genre*. Middletown, CT: Wesleyan University Press, 1989.

Riley, Robert. *Film, Faith and Cultural Conflict: The Case of Martin Scorsese's The Last Temptation of Christ*. Westport, CT: Praeger, 2003.

Roberts, Gillian. "Circulations of Taste: *Titanic*, the Oscars, and the middlebrow," in Stringer, 155–166.

Romanowski, William D. *Pop Culture Wars: Religion and the Role of Entertainment in American Life*. Downer's Grove, IL: Intervarsity, 1996.

Romney, Jonathan. Review of *Schindler's List*. *New Statesman and Society* 18 Feb. 1994.

Roof, Wade Clark. *A Generation of Seekers: The Spiritual Journeys of the Baby Boom Generation*. San Francisco: Harper, 1993.

Roquemore, Joseph H. *History Goes to the Movies*. New York: Doubleday, 1999.

Rosenfield, Paul. *The Club Rules: Power, Money, Sex and Fear; How It Works in Hollywood*. New York: Warner Books, 1992.

Rubin, Martin. *Thrillers*. Cambridge: Cambridge University Press, 1999.

Rushton, Richard. "Narrative and Spectacle in *Gladiator*." *Cineaction* 56 (2000): 35–43.

Russell, Louise B. *The Baby Boom Generation and the Economy*. Washington, D.C.: The Brookings Institution, 1982.

Russell, James. "Debts, Disasters and Mega-Musicals: The Decline of the Studio System," in Michael Hammond and Linda Ruth Williams, eds., *The Contemporary American Cinema Book*. London: McGraw-Hill, 2006.

Ryan, Tim. "Pearl of a Pre-Em." *Variety* 28 May 2001.

Sandler, Kevin S., and Gaylyn Studlar, eds. *Titanic: Anatomy of a Blockbuster*. New Brunswick, NJ, and London: Rutgers University Press, 1999.

Saunders, E. P. *The Historical Figure of Jesus*. New York: Penguin, 1995.

Schatz, Thomas. *Boom and Bust: The American Cinema in the 1940s*. New York: Scribner's, 1997.

———. *Hollywood Genres: Formulas, Filmmaking and the Studio System*. New York: Random House, 1981.

———. "The New Hollywood," reprinted in Stringer, 15–44.

———. "World War II and the War Film," in Nick Browne, ed., *Refiguring American Film Genres: History and Theory*. Berkeley: University of California Press, 1998.

Schiff, Steven. "Seriously Spielberg," in Friedman and Notbohm, 170–191.

Schuman, Howard, and Jacqueline Scott."Generations and Collective Memories." *American Sociological Review* 54 (June 1989): 359–381.

Scorsese, Martin, and Michael Henry Wilson. *A Personal Journey with Martin Scorsese Through American Movies*. London: Faber and Faber, 1997.

Scott, A. O. "Good and Evil Locked in Violent Showdown." *New York Times* 25 Feb. 2004.

———. "Master of the Sea (and the French)." *New York Times* 14 Nov. 2003.

———. "To Feel a City Seethe." *New York Times* 20 Dec. 2002.

Scott, Ian. "From Toscanini to Tennessee: Robert Risking, the OWI and the Construction of American Propaganda in World War II." *Journal of American Studies* 40, no. 2 (2006).

Scott, Ridley. "When Worlds Collide." *Guardian* 29 Apr. 2005.

Searles, Baird. *EPIC! History on the Big Screen*. New York: Abrams, 1990.

Shandler, Jeffrey. "Schindler's Discourse: America Discusses the Holocaust and Its Mediation, from NBC's miniseries to Spielberg's film," in Loshitzky, 153–170.

———. *While America Watches: Televising the Holocaust*. Oxford: Oxford University Press, 1999.

Sheen, Erica. "*The Ten Commandments* and *The Prince of Egypt*." *Polygraph* 12 (2000): 85–99.

Shone, Tom. *Blockbuster: How I Learned to Stop Worrying and Love the Summer.* London: Simon and Schuster, 2004.

Sklar, Robert. "'The Lost Audience': 1950s Spectatorship and Historical Reception Studies," in Melvyn Stokes and Richard Maltby, eds., *Identifying Hollywood's Audiences*, 81–91. London: BFI, 2000.

Smith, Gary A. *Epic Films: Cast, Credits and Commentary.* Jefferson, NC: McFarland, 1991.

Sobchack, Vivian. "Genre Film: Myth, Ritual and Sociodrama," in S. Thomas, ed., *Film/Culture: Explorations of Cinema in Its Social Context*, 147–167. Metuchen, NJ: Scarecrow Press, 1982.

———, ed. *The Persistence of History: Cinema, Television and the Modern Event.* New York: Routledge, 1996.

———. "'Surge and Splendor': A Phenomenology of the Hollywood Historical Epic," in Barry Keith Grant, ed., *Film Genre Reader*, 2nd ed., 280–307. Austin: University of Texas Press, 1995.

Solomon, Charles. *Prince of Egypt: A New Vision in Animation.* London: Thames and Hudson Ltd, 1998.

Solomon, Jon. *The Ancient World in the Cinema,* 2nd ed. New Haven, CT, and London: Yale University Press, 2001.

———. "*Gladiator* from Screenplay to Screen," in Winkler (2004), 1–15.

Soriano, John. "WGA.org's Exclusive Interview with David Franzoni." *Writer's Guild of America Web site*, http://www.wga.org/craft/interviews/franzoni2001.html.

Soukhanov, Anne, ed. *Encarta World English Dictionary.* London: Bloomsbury, 1999.

Spann, Susan. "Laughter at Film Brings Spielberg Visit." *New York Times* 13 April 1994.

Stark, Susan. "Spielberg Triumphs with his Forceful Epic of the Holocaust's Unlikely Hero." *Detroit News* 25 Dec. 1993.

Steinberg, Cobbet. *Film Facts.* New York: Facts on Film, 1980.

Stempel, Tom. *American Audiences on Movies and Moviegoing.* Lexington: University of Kentucky Press, 2001.

Sterrit, David. Review of *Schindler's List*. *Christian Science Monitor* 15 Dec. 1993.

Stringer, Julian, ed. *Movie Blockbusters.* London: Routledge, 2003.

Tasker, Yvonne, ed. *Action and Adventure Cinema.* London: Routledge, 2004.

Taubin, Amy. "War Torn." *Village Voice* 28 Jul. 1998.

Taves, Brian. *The Romance of Adventure: The Genre of Historical Adventure Movies.* Jackson: University Press of Mississippi, 1993.

Thistlewaite, Susan. "Mel Makes a War Movie," in Meacham et al., 127–146.

Thomson, David. *The New Biographical Dictionary of Film,* 4th ed. London: Little Brown, 2002.

——. "Presenting Enamelware." *Film Comment* Mar–Apr. 1994.

——. *Showman: The Life and Times of David O. Selznick.* New York: Knopf, 1992.

Toplin, Robert Brent. *Reel History: In Defense of Hollywood.* Lawrence: University Press of Kansas, 2001.

Tunison, Michael. "Spielberg at War." *Entertainment Today* 24 Jul. 1998.

Turan, Kenneth. "A Narrow Vision and Staggering Violence." *Los Angeles Times* 24 Feb. 2004.

——. Review of *The Prince of Egypt. Los Angeles Times* 18 Dec. 1998.

——. Review of *Saving Private Ryan. Los Angeles Times* 24 Jul. 1998.

——. Review of *Schindler's List. Los Angeles Times* 15 Dec. 1993.

Tzioumakis, Yannis. "Major Status, Independent Spirit." *New Review of Television Studies* 2, no. 1 (May 2004): 87–135.

U.S. Census Bureau, *Statistical Abstract of the United States 2003*, obtained via download from http://www.census.gov.

Usher, Shawn. Review of *Dances with Wolves. Daily Mail* 8 Feb. 1991.

Variety Staff. Review of *Braveheart. Variety* 19 May 1995.

——. Review of *Schindler's List. Variety* 20 Nov. 1993.

Vidal, Gore. *Screening History.* London: Abacus, 1993.

Vivendi-Universal 2000 Annual Report, obtained via download from http://www.vivendiuniversal.com/vu/en/files/2000annualreport.pdf.

Vogel, Harold J. *Entertainment Industry Economics.* Cambridge: Cambridge University Press, 1990.

Vogler, Christopher. *The Writer's Journey: Mythic Structure for Storytellers and Screenwriters,* 2nd ed. London: Boxtree Limited, 1996.

Walch, Timothy. *Catholicism in America.* Malabar, FL: Robert E. Kreiger, 1989.

Walker, John, ed. *Halliwells Film, Video and DVD Guide 2004.* London: Harpercollins, 2004.

Wasko, Janet. *Hollywood in the Information Age: Beyond the Silver Screen.* Cambridge: Polity Press, 1994.

——. *How Hollywood Works.* London: Sage, 2003.

Wasser, Fredrick. *Veni, Vedi, Video: The Hollywood Empire and the VCR.* Austin: University of Texas Press, 2001.

Weinraub, Bernard. "As problems delay *Titanic,* Hollywood sighs in relief." *New York Times* 29 May 1997.

——. "Moses and Rushes." *New York Times* 10 Apr. 1998.

——. "Steven Spielberg Faces the Holocaust." *New York Times* 12 Dec. 1993.

Westwell, Guy. *War Cinema: Hollywood on the Front Line.* London: Wallflower, 2006.

Williams, Linda. *Hardcore: Power, Pleasure and the 'Frenzy of the Visible.'* London: Pandora, 1990.

———. "Race, Melodrama and *The Birth of a Nation* (1915)" in Lee Grieveson and Peter Krämer, eds., *The Silent Cinema Reader.* London: Routledge, 2004.

Winkler, Martin M., ed. *Classical Myth and Culture in the Cinema.* New York and Oxford: Oxford University Press, 2001.

———, ed. *Gladiator: Film and History.* London: Blackwell, 2004.

———. 'The Roman Empire in American Cinema after 1945," in Sandra T. Joshel, Margaret Malamud and Donald T. McGuire Jr., eds., *Imperial Projections: Ancient Rome in Modern Popular Culture,* 50–76. Baltimore, MD: Johns Hopkins University Press, 2001.

Wolfreys, Julian. *Critical Keywords in Literary and Cultural Theory.* New York: Palgrave-Macmillan, 2004.

Wood, Michael. *America in the Movies, or, 'Santa Maria, It Had Slipped My Mind!'* London: Secker and Warburg, 1975.

Woods, Robert H., Michael C. Jindra and Jason D. Baker. "The Audience Responds to *The Passion of the Christ,*" in Plate, 163–180.

Wright, Will. *Sixguns and Society: A Structural Study of the Western.* Berkeley: University of California Press, 1975.

Wyatt, Justin. *High Concept: Movies and Marketing in Hollywood.* Austin: University of Texas Press, 1994.

Wyke, Maria. *Projecting the Past: Ancient Rome, Cinema and History.* London: Routledge, 1997.

Younge, Gary. "Bloodthirsty or a Classic?" *The Guardian* 4 Aug. 2004.

Zanuck, Darryl F. "Why Tora! Tora! Tora!?" *New York Times* 16 June 1969.

2. Press Kits and Unpublished Documents

Paramount Pictures, *Samson and Delilah* press kit (1949), BFIL.

Paramount Pictures, *The Ten Commandments* press kit (1956), BFIL.

MGM Pictures, *Ben-Hur* press kit (1959), BFIL.

Twentieth Century Fox Pictures, *Tora! Tora! Tora!* press kit (1970), BFIL.

Orion Pictures, *Dances with Wolves* press kit (1990), BFIL.

DreamWorks Pictures, *The Prince of Egypt* press kit (1998), AMPAS.

DreamWorks Pictures, *Gladiator* press kit (2000), PARC.

Breen, Joseph L. Letter to Luigi Laraschi, dated 29 Aug. 1954. 'The Ten Commandments' file, MPAA Collection, AMPAS.

Cameron, James. *Titanic* Screenplay—Working Copy (Undated), Paramount Script Collection, AMPAS.

Hopper, Hedda. Unpublished interview with Cecil B. DeMille, dated 10 Dec. 1957. 'Cecil B. DeMille' File, Hedda Hopper Collection, AMPAS.

Noerdlinger, Henry. Letter to Art Arthur, dated 8 Nov. 1956. The Henry S. Noerdlinger Collection, Folder 6, AMPAS.

"The Ten Commandments: A Tentative Script for LIMITED DISTRIBUTION" dated 1 May 1954. Paramount Script Collection, AMPAS.

Tunberg, Karl. 'Original' Screenplay for *Ben-Hur*, dated 20 July 1954. Turner-MGM Script Collection, AMPAS.

Wyler, William. Memo dated 30 Mar. 1960. The William Wyler Collection, Box 20, File 8, UCLA.

———. Transcribed interview. Ronald L. Davies Oral History Collection, File No. 175, AMPAS.

Zanuck, Darryl F. Telegram to Elmo Williams dated 24 Mar. 1969. The Elmo Williams Collection, file 157, AMPAS.

3. Documentaries on Television and Radio

"From Pain to Passion: A Prime-Time Event." *ABC News*, broadcast 16 Feb. 2004.

War Stories: Mark Cousins talks to Steven Spielberg. BBC2 Documentary, broadcast 13 Sept. 1998.

Mark Lawson interviews William Nicholson, *Front Row*, BBC Radio 4, broadcast 26 Apr. 2005.

Index

Alexander, 3, 118, 172, 217, 220

Amistad: as DreamWorks release, 136, 137, 138, 165; as ethnic film, 84; *Schindler's List* as influence, 100, 137

anti-Semitism: *The Passion*, 18, 187, 192–93, 194, 201–2; Spielberg's encounters with, 83–84, 110

audiences: as allegory in *Gladiator*, 156–57, 169–72; baby boomers, 113–16; children, 22–23, 43–45; decline in late 1940s, 24, 26, 46; demographics, 29, 42, 44–45, 46, 177; international, 26, 78, 178–80, 216; regard for epics, 41–42, 45, 47–48. *See also* educative significance of epics; transformative experiences

baby boomer filmmakers: evolving interests, 112–16; fantasy epics as vehicle, 112–13, 163, 164; formative experiences, 22–23, 44–45, 108–11, 126; nostalgia for childhood, 60, 113–16; roadshow epics as influence, 44–45, 47–48, 116, 126, 215–16; views of World War II, 117–19, 120, 122, 123–25

Ben-Hur: awards, 14, 106; earnings, 26, 45; educative significance, 43, 44, 47–48; as formative childhood experience, 22, 47–48; influence on contemporary

films, 7, 146, 163, 168; as political allegory, 31, 32–34, 40; in roadshow epic cycle, 5, 11, 26, 28, 188

biblical epics: avoided by Hollywood, 189–90; influence on science fiction/fantasy epics, 6, 162, 163–64, 189; *The Passion* as compared to, 18, 207–8; in roadshow era, 27–28, 32, 34–35, 188–89, 208

Braveheart: empire as theme, 218; influence of roadshow epics, 22, 72; as maverick epic, 71–72, 100; *The Passion* compared to, 196; *The Patriot* compared to, 160; running time, 15; shared production, 166; success, 14, 178, 179, 196, 216

Bruckheimer, Jerry: as baby boomer filmmaker, 111; as blockbuster filmmaker, 6, 106, 136, 160; formative childhood experiences, 22; *Gladiator* as influence on, 172; stylistic preferences as contrasted with epics, 136

Cameron, James: as baby boomer filmmaker, 107, 110–11, 112, 118, 215–16; as maverick filmmaker, 2–3, 6, 116, 215, 216; roadshow epics as influence, 1–2, 12–13, 15, 215–16. *See also Titanic*

CGI. *See* computer-generated imagery (CGI)

commemoration as theme: as feature of 1990s epics, 17, 206–7; *Saving Private Ryan*, 117, 122–25, 206, 207; *Schindler's List*, 78, 88, 97–98, 206–7

computer-generated imagery (CGI): *Antz*, 138; *Gladiator*, 14–15, 167, 168; *The Prince of Egypt*, 147–48; as providing epic quality, 163; *Star Wars*, 168

conservatism, American: baby boomers' challenge to, 113–14; Christian evangelicals, 65, 188, 193, 194–96, 197–98; culture wars, 65, 67, 194–96, 197

Costner, Kevin: as baby boomer, 110–11, 116; revival of epic western, 16, 55, 59–62, 65–67; Spielberg compared to, 78, 81, 87

cultural significance of epics: authenticity as expression of, 78, 121, 147–48, 206–7; baby boomers' perspectives, 48, 113–16, 126, 215–16; educative importance, 12, 41–45, 47–48, 119, 148; exploited by DreamWorks, 17–18, 131–32, 137–38, 144, 151–52; as feature of cycle, 10–14; filmmakers' prestige as reflecting, 11–15, 98, 100, 148, 197–98; *Gladiator* as defence, 169–72; as reflection of contemporary concerns, 18–19, 97–99, 119–20, 197–98, 217–20; roadshow era, 25–26, 33–34, 38–39, 40–41, 44

culture wars. *See* conservatism, American

cycles. *See* historical epic cycles; historical epics of 1990s; roadshow epics

Dances with Wolves: as allegory, 16, 62–63, 65–67, 148; *Braveheart* compared to, 71–72; DVD release, 178; empire as theme, 217; impact on epic cycle, 6, 16–17, 54–55, 69–71, 72; marketing, 55, 68–69; nostalgia as theme, 62–64, 65, 116; overseas popularity, 179; production, 59–62; Spielberg's films compared to, 77–78, 81; TV miniseries compared to, 58, 66; video sales/rentals, 177; in western film cycle, 54, 56–57, 59, 68, 70. *See also* Costner, Kevin

DeMille, Cecil B.: as educator, 42–43, 44; as member of Studio Generation, 111–12; religious/political agenda, 12, 34–35, 40–42, 141, 144; as reviving historical epics, 5, 25, 27, 55; role in film history, 4, 22–23; Spielberg compared to, 47, 48, 85, 92; stylistic preferences, 167. *See also Ten Commandments, The*

DreamWorks SKG: as allegory, 144–46, 148, 149; animated releases, 149–50; creative vision, 131, 135, 137, 139, 150–51; early releases, 136–38; epics as brand identity, 17–18, 131–32, 137–38, 144, 151–52; establishment, 133–35; founders' reputations, 17, 135–36, 149; origins, 145–46; production of *Gladiator*, 165–67, 172; as rival to Disney, 132, 137, 143–44; success, 133, 138, 150

DVD market. *See* economic viability of epics

economic viability of epics: decline in 1970s/1980s, 28–29, 45–46, 57–58; DVD market, 18, 176–77, 178, 180, 216–17; industry recognition, 157–58, 159–62, 172, 181, 216–17; maverick projects, 6, 62, 71–72, 100–101, 106–7; overseas market, 18, 26, 78, 178–80, 216; perceived as risky investments, 5–6, 28–29, 57, 61, 157–58; roadshow era, 4–5, 25–29

educative significance of epics: cultural importance as reflection of, 12, 41–45, 47–48, 119, 148; DreamWorks SKG's exploitation of, 131–32, 143, 144; filmmakers as historians/educators, 42–44, 47, 92, 171–72; roadshow era, 12, 41–45, 47–48; *Saving Private Ryan*, 117, 119, 124–25; *Schindler's List*, 47–48, 78, 87, 91–92, 98–100

empire as theme, 163, 169–72, 181, 217–20

Empire of the Sun, 80–82

fantasy epics, 6, 46, 112–13, 162–64, 189

film industry: as allegory in *Dances with Wolves*, 55, 65–67; as allegory in *Gladiator*, 156–57, 169–72; as allegory in *Schindler's List*, 98–99, 100; critics of, 65, 67, 82, 169–70, 194–96; DreamWorks SKG's penetration of, 133–35; economic strategies of 1950s, 24–27, 29–30; epics returning to favour, 157–58, 159–62, 172, 181, 216–17; exploitation of DVD market, 175–76, 177; exploitation of television market, 26, 173–74; formula for genre production, 55, 69–70, 159; impact of Paramount Decrees, 24–25, 29–30, 40; overproduction, 28–29, 45; reluctance to fund epics, 5–6, 28–29, 57, 61, 157–58; shared production, 165–66

filmmakers, epic: childhood viewing experiences, 22–23, 44–45, 59–60; cultural prestige, 11–15, 98, 100, 148, 197–98; driven by personal agendas, 30–31, 32–36, 71–72, 85–87, 191–92; generational turnover of 1960s/1970s, 111–12; *Gladiator* as allegorical defence of, 169–72; as historians/educators, 42–44, 47, 92, 171–72; as independents, 29–30, 35, 72; overview, 2–3, 6, 17, 217; political consciousness of, 36–38, 40–41; roadshow epics as influence, 44–45, 47–48, 116, 126, 215–16; World War II as influence, 37–40. *See also* baby boomer filmmakers

Forrest Gump, 14, 114, 115, 216

generational address as theme: baby boomer perspectives, 114–16, 117–19, 120, 122, 125; *The Prince of Egypt*, 143, 144; *Saving Private Ryan*, 116–18, 119, 120–22, 123–25

Gibson, Mel: career, 160, 196–98; as cultural warrior, 194, 197; as maverick filmmaker, 6, 71–72, 100, 111; religious convictions, 190–93, 199; roadshow epics as influence, 22, 72

Gladiator: as allegory, 156–57, 169–72; DVD sales, 176; hyped as risky investment, 181; influence on epic cycle, 172–73; overseas popularity, 179; production, 165–67, 172; as reconstructed roadshow epic, 7, 14–15, 158, 167–68, 218; *Saving Private Ryan* as influence, 126; studio willingness to fund, 6, 159, 162, 172

greatest generation. *See* World War II

Heaven's Gate: *Dances with Wolves* and, 61, 181; as revisionist epic, 46; as test of epic genre viability, 5–6, 46, 57, 157

historical epic cycles: in American cinema, 3–7; content dramatising production as feature, 10–12, 14–15, 144–45; definition, 7, 9–13; fantasy films compared to, 6, 46, 112–13, 162–64, 189; formula for genre production, 55, 69–70, 159; identifying, 7–8, 54, 55, 69–70; method of study, 16–19; as overlapping trends, 9–10, 12, 56; political allegory as feature, 13, 18–19, 30–31, 217, 220; religious appeal, 179–80, 188. *See also* cultural significance of epics; educative significance of epics; historical epics of 1990s; roadshow epics

historical epics of 1990s: independent production as model, 72; as mainstream productions, 157–58, 159–62, 172, 181, 216–17; as maverick projects, 6, 62, 71–72, 100–101, 106–7; roadshow epics compared to, 14–15. *See also* transformative experiences

Hollywood majors. *See* film industry

Holocaust: Bosnian war compared to, 86–87, 97–98; public discourse on, 47–48, 78–79, 87, 92, 97–98; roadshow epics, 40; *Saving Private Ryan*, 117, 120–21; *Schindler's List*, 17, 78, 88–92, 94–98, 206–7; Spielberg's preoccupation with, 83, 84, 86–87, 100, 120–21; television as raising awareness of, 58, 79. *See also* anti-Semitism

How the West Was Won: as influence on Costner, 22, 56, 59–60, 66–67, 68; as western epic, 28, 56, 144–45

Katzenberg, Jeffrey: as baby boomer, 110–11; founding of DreamWorks, 17–18, 131, 132, 135, 145–46; motivations for making *The Prince of Egypt*, 141, 143–44, 148, 149; relations with Disney, 135, 136, 145–46; on *Schindler's List*, 99

Kingdom of Heaven, 3, 7, 172–73, 217, 219–20

Lawrence of Arabia: *Dances with Wolves* compared to, 69; as DVD release, 178; influence on modern epic filmmakers, 22, 78, 80–81, 139, 149; in roadshow epic cycle, 2, 11, 28

Lean, David: as influence on Katzenberg, 139, 149; as influence on Spielberg, 78, 80–81; as influence on *The Patriot*, 160; as member of Studio Generation, 112

marketplace, film. *See* economic viability of epics; film industry

mass culture, 169–72. *See also* conservatism, American

maverick epics. *See* economic viability of epics; historical epics of 1990s

movie industry. *See* film industry

overseas market, 26, 78, 178–80, 216

Passion of the Christ, The, 18; accusations of anti-Semitism, 18, 187, 192–93, 194, 201–2; American religious appeal, 179–80, 188; audiences, 187–88, 190, 193–94, 197–98; biblical epics compared to, 188–90, 207–8; culture wars as backdrop, 194–96, 197; as emotional experience, 198, 202–6, 208; narrative, 199–201, 202, 205; as personal project, 190–92, 196–97. *See also* Gibson, Mel

Patriot, The, 125, 160–61, 196–97

Pearl Harbor: 1990s epic cycle as context, 6, 15, 125, 160, 161; as baby boomer epic, 22, 111; revenues, 161, 176–77, 179

political expression in epics: audiences' understanding of, 38–39, 40, 41–42,

218; *Ben-Hur*, 31, 32–34, 40; *Dances with Wolves*, 67–68, 71; as feature of cycle, 13, 18–19, 30–31, 217, 220; imperial ambition as allegory, 169–72, 181, 217–20; origins, 36–38, 40–41; *The Passion*, 194–96, 197; *Schindler's List*, 86–87, 97–99; *The Ten Commandments*, 12, 34, 35, 40, 141; *Tora! Tora! Tora!*, 35–36, 39

Prince of Egypt, The: as allegory, 144–46, 148, 149, 218; as brand identity, 132, 137–38, 144, 151; consultants for, 143, 193; *Gladiator* compared to, 170; narrative, 139–40, 142, 146–47; overview, 6–7; *The Passion* compared to, 190, 208; *The Ten Commandments* compared to, 6–7, 139–41, 142, 143, 146. *See also* Katzenberg, Jeffrey

producer's game (Rick Altman's), 55, 69–70, 159

Quo Vadis?: *Gladiator* compared to, 163, 168; *The Passion* compared to, 188; in roadshow epic cycle, 5, 27, 28, 34

roadshow epics: biblical films, 27–28, 32, 34–35, 188–89, 208; decline, 28–29, 35, 45–46, 215; DVD releases, 178; economic strategies, 24–27, 29–30; educative significance, 12, 41–45, 47–48; fantasy epics shaped by, 6, 46, 112–13, 162–64, 189; *Gladiator* compared to, 7, 14–15, 158, 167–68, 218; independent production as model, 29–30, 35; influence on baby boomer filmmakers, 44–45, 47–48, 116, 126, 215–16; linked to widescreen, 26, 27; origins of politicisation, 36–38, 40–41; overview, 5, 23; *The Prince of Egypt* compared to, 139–41, 142, 143, 146, 149; roadshowing, 10–11, 25–26, 46, 58; *Titanic* compared to, 1–2, 12–13, 15, 216; World War II as influence, 37–40

Robe, The: as formative childhood experience, 22; in roadshow epic cycle, 5, 26, 27–28, 39, 188

Saving Private Ryan: as brand identity, 137–38; educative significance, 117, 119, 124–25; empire as theme, 217–18; as generational address, 116–18, 119, 120–22, 123–25; impact on epic cycle, 6, 106–7, 125–26, 160; overseas popularity, 179; *The Passion* compared to, 206, 207; *The Prince of Egypt* compared to, 144; as resonating with American society, 117–20; *Schindler's List* compared to, 100, 120–21, 122. *See also* Spielberg, Steven

Schindler's List: as commemoration, 78, 88, 97–98, 207; DreamWorks SKG's releases compared to, 137, 139; DVD release, 178; as emotional experience, 92, 93–97, 98, 206–7; empire as theme, 217–18; as historical account, 78, 88–89, 90–92; impact on epic cycle, 17, 77–78, 100–101; marketing, 47–48, 77, 101; overseas popularity, 78, 179; as resonating with American society, 78–79, 87, 92, 97–98; *Saving Private Ryan* compared to, 100, 120–21, 122; Spielberg's motivations for making, 83, 85–87, 97–99, 116. *See also* Spielberg, Steven

science fiction epics, 10, 46, 158, 164–65

Scott, Ridley. *See Gladiator*; *Kingdom of Heaven*

Spartacus: DVD release of, 178; fantasy epics as compared to, 163; *Gladiator* as compared to, 7, 158, 168; political agenda, 34, 41; in roadshow epic cycle, 2, 5, 28

Spielberg, Steven: career, 80–83, 84–85, 112–13; formative childhood experiences, 83–84, 108–10; founding of DreamWorks, 17–18, 131, 135–36, 145–46; as historian/educator, 47, 92; as maverick filmmaker, 6, 71–72, 100–101, 106–7; Moses story as linked to, 85–86, 139; motivations for making *Saving Private Ryan*, 117–18, 119, 120–22, 124–25; motivations for making *Schindler's List*, 83, 85–87, 97–99, 116; nostalgia for childhood, 81–82,

112–13, 115, 116; roadshow epics as influence, 22, 47–48, 77–78, 99–100

technology, exhibition: historical epic genre linked to, 9, 11–12, 27, 28, 163; widescreen, 10–11, 22–23, 26, 27, 145. *See also* computer-generated imagery (CGI)

television: cinematic style of epics contrasted with, 9, 66; criticisms, 170, 195; film industry exploitation of, 26, 173–74; historical epics screened on, 5, 58–59, 70, 215; impact on baby boomers, 110, 111, 113–14, 115, 116; as raising awareness of Holocaust, 58, 79; TV Generation filmmakers, 112; westerns screened on, 56

Ten Commandments, The: content as dramatising film production, 11–12, 144; educative significance, 41–43, 44, 99–100; as example of DeMille's filmmaking style, 4; influence on modern epic filmmakers, 23, 85–86; *The Prince of Egypt* compared to, 7, 132, 139–43, 146; religious/political agenda, 12, 34, 35, 40, 141; as roadshow release, 2, 5, 26, 28, 188; *Schindler's List* compared to, 99–100; Spielberg as influenced by, 85–86. *See also* DeMille, Cecil B.

Titanic: Cameron's motivations for making, 1–2, 215–16; DVD sales, 176, 178; empire as theme, 218; impact on epic cycle, 100, 106–7, 160, 161–62, 216–17; overseas popularity, 179; *The Passion* compared to, 207; roadshow releases compared to, 1–2, 12–13, 15, 216; as shared production, 166. *See also* Cameron, James

Tora! Tora! Tora!, 35–36, 39, 43–44, 45, 46

transformative experiences: as feature of 1990s epics, 17, 100, 206–8; *The Passion* , 198, 202–6, 208; *Saving Private Ryan*, 121–22, 123, 206, 207; *Schindler's List*, 92, 93–97, 98, 206–7

viewers. *See* audiences

virtue as theme, 79, 92–95, 96–97, 120–
    21, 206–7

western films. *See Dances with Wolves*;
    Heaven's Gate
widescreen, 10–11, 22–23, 26, 27, 145
World War II: baby boomers'
    perspectives, 117–19, 120, 122,
    123–25; films about, 46, 58–59, 125,
    161–62; influence on roadshow epics,
    37–40; Spielberg's interest in, 80–81,
    109; veterans of, 40, 119–20, 121, 123,
    206. *See also* greatest generation
Wyler, William: Costner compared to,

55; political/educational agenda of,
    31–34, 39–40, 144; Scott compared to,
    167, 168; Spielberg compared to, 22,
    44, 47–48, 92; as member of Studio
    Generation, 112; success of, 14, 30,
    44, 106

Zanuck, Darryl F.: Costner compared
    to, 55; as independent producer, 29;
    political agenda, 35–36, 37–38, 40;
    Spielberg compared to, 47, 48; World
    War II experiences as influence,
    38–39, 40